Financial and Behavioral Health for Helping Professionals

Jeffrey Anvari-Clark

Financial and Behavioral Health for Helping Professionals

Springer

Jeffrey Anvari-Clark
Department of Social Work
University of North Dakota
Grand Forks, ND, USA

ISBN 978-3-032-02631-6 ISBN 978-3-032-02632-3 (eBook)
https://doi.org/10.1007/978-3-032-02632-3

This work was supported by the University of North Dakota.

This Springer imprint is published by the registered company Springer Nature Switzerland AG
The registered company address is: Gewerbestrasse 11, 6330 Cham, Switzerland

Preface

The emergence of financial health as a distinct field of study represents an evolution in how we understand human well-being. While decades of research have explored connections between money and mental health, debt and depression, financial stress and physical illness, or relationship conflicts over financial matters, these insights have remained scattered across disciplines. *Financial and Behavioral Health for Helping Professionals* addresses this fragmentation by presenting a framework that positions financial concerns as an integral domain of behavioral health—one that interacts dynamically with mental, physical, coping, and social dimensions of well-being.

This book emerged from a recognition that helping professionals across multiple fields increasingly encounter clients whose presenting concerns involve complex interactions between financial circumstances and other aspects of health. A client's anxiety may be inseparable from mounting medical debt; a couple's relationship strain may center on fundamentally different approaches to money management; an individual's substance use may both contribute to and result from financial precarity. Yet most professional training programs provide little guidance on how to understand, assess, or address these interconnections.

The financial domain of behavioral health encompasses three key components: financial precarity (the material and psychological impact of negative financial conditions), financial efficacy (one's ability and confidence to manage financial challenges), and financial well-being (a sense of current money management stress and expected future financial confidence). These elements interact continuously with other behavioral health domains, creating complex patterns that require nuanced understanding and integrated intervention approaches.

Several trends make this comprehensive resource particularly timely. Rising healthcare costs in the United States, increasing income volatility, and growing wealth disparities have intensified the financial pressures many individuals face. The COVID-19 pandemic highlighted the intricate connections between economic security and health outcomes. Meanwhile, emerging research on financial therapy, trauma-informed financial interventions, and the health impacts of financial stress has created a substantial knowledge base that has yet to be synthesized into practical guidance for helping professionals.

Traditional approaches that treat financial concerns as external "social determinants" often overlook the personal, relational, and behavioral dimensions of how people experience and respond to financial challenges. This book demonstrates why financial health deserves recognition as a behavioral health domain in its own right—one that helping professionals can meaningfully address within their scope of practice.

Thus, the primary audience for this book consists of helping professionals in social work, counseling and therapy, healthcare, and financial planning, counseling, and coaching who encounter clients facing financial challenges. The book serves as both an educational resource for those new to this intersection and a reference for experienced practitioners seeking to deepen their understanding. Secondary audiences include professors and graduate students in these disciplines, as well as researchers and policymakers in public health and behavioral health. The book can serve as a supplementary text in higher education courses on behavioral health, clinical practice, or financial counseling, and as a reference for continuing education programs. Electronic supplementary materials accompanying this book online include a PowerPoint presentation covering the main concepts from all chapters, a SMART Goals worksheet for both self-practice and use with clients, and a comprehensive list of resources for additional measures, assessments, and related information to support implementation in various professional contexts.

The book is organized into 10 chapters. Chapters 1 and 2 establish the theoretical foundation, beginning with the conceptual model of financial health and exploring key theoretical frameworks including complexity theory, financial capability and asset building, financial interdependence, family theories, and scarcity theory. Chapters 3 through 6 examine how financial concerns manifest within each behavioral health domain—mental, physical, coping, and social health. Chapter 7 discusses the limits of financial education and provides essential orientation to the professional landscape by introducing the various disciplines and types of services available to address financial health and behavior concerns—from financial therapy and coaching to financial planning and case management. This chapter helps readers understand the scope of practice for different professionals and serves as a foundation for making appropriate referrals. Chapter 8 explores the importance of self-work and understanding biases and provides an overview for implementation, including ethical and billing considerations. Chapter 9 then offers guidance on behavior change approaches, goal-setting strategies, and adapting the goal-design framework to varying professional contexts. Finally, in Chap. 10 is a discussion of research, policy, and future directions for practice integration. Throughout, case examples illustrate concepts and provide frameworks for assessment and treatment.[1] The book distinguishes between various types of financial interventions—financial therapy, financial coaching, financial counseling, and financial planning—helping

[1] All vignettes, case examples, and client scenarios presented in this book are fictional, created for educational purposes. No case represents any specific individual or actual client relationship. Any resemblance to real persons, living or deceased, is purely coincidental. These fictional scenarios have been developed, using artificial intelligence, to represent realistic and clinically plausible situations that helping professionals may encounter. Each vignette has been reviewed for authenticity based on professional experience.

readers understand when different approaches are most appropriate and how to make effective referrals.

What distinguishes this book from existing resources is its truly integrated perspective. Rather than addressing mental health in isolation or treating financial concerns as merely external stressors, it demonstrates how the financial and other behavioral health domains continuously influence each other. This holistic approach reveals why interventions targeting financial concerns often yield unexpected benefits across multiple areas of health and well-being. The book also emphasizes cultural humility and recognition of diverse financial values and practices. It explores concepts like financial interdependence—how financial decisions are embedded in family and community relationships—and challenges individualistic assumptions that may not align with clients' lived experiences.

Financial and Behavioral Health for Helping Professionals aims to transform how helping professionals understand and address the financial dimensions of their clients' lives. By recognizing financial health as a legitimate behavioral health domain worthy of professional attention, we can better serve clients facing the complex, interconnected challenges that characterize modern life. The financial challenges our clients face are not just about money—they are about dignity, relationships, hope, and the fundamental human need for security and choice. Understanding these connections is essential for providing effective service and compassionate care.

Grand Forks, ND, USA Jeffrey Anvari-Clark

On the Use of AI

My use of large language model (LLM) artificial intelligence (AI) tools is aptly framed by the following passage:

> [The] dynamic relationship between generative AI and human authorship is best understood as a collaborative and integrative process. Generative AI assists in the production and refinement of text, while human authors provide essential context, critical analysis, and domain-specific knowledge necessary for meaningful scientific communication inside the scientific social system. (Watson et al., 2025, 9)

In the process of writing this book, I explored how AI might enhance scholarly productivity while maintaining my commitment to providing accurate, accessible insights into the financial domain of behavioral health. As an assistant professor teaching digital literacy to students and faculty alike, I have experimented extensively with AI tools across research, teaching, and writing tasks.

My approach to AI is pragmatic: Does it help? Is it ethical? For this book, I used tools like Anthropic's Claude and OpenAI's ChatGPT to assist with drafting, editing, and creating realistic case vignettes that did not appropriate real clients' experiences. These tools helped me make new connections within the literature and increased productivity, allowing me to focus on critical analysis and refinement.

The responsibility for all content remains mine. I carefully reviewed and modified any AI-generated content to ensure accuracy and alignment with my expertise and intention. No AI tool is listed as an author because AI cannot be held accountable for content. Instead, I treated AI outputs as draft material requiring verification and integration with my own drafts, research, and experience.

Beyond explicit AI tools, technology assistance is increasingly ubiquitous in writing—from word prediction in email to reference management software. By thoughtfully incorporating these technologies while maintaining scholarly standards, I have aimed to produce a more comprehensive, accessible resource for helping professionals and their clients.

In short, *Financial and Behavioral Health for Helping Professionals* is a product of my expertise, research, and scholarly judgment, enhanced but not replaced by technology.

Reference

Watson, S., Brezovec, E., & Romic, J. (2025). The role of generative AI in academic and scientific authorship: An autopoietic perspective. *AI & Society*. https://doi.org/10.1007/s00146-024-02174-w

Acknowledgments

I acknowledge, with much gratitude, the support of many people and institutions who have made this book possible. At the University of North Dakota, Dean Rebecca Bichel and Brittany Fischer at the Chester Fritz Library allocated funding for this project to support our mutual commitment to open access learning. Vice Provost Randi Tanglen and Associate Professor Liz Legerski helped me navigate this new arena of scholarship. Dean Maridee Shogren, the College of Nursing and Professional Disciplines, and the Department of Social Work provided support and encouragement for educating broadly on the importance of this topic. Cara Macksoud at Bank Roll'd (and Money Habitudes LLC) provided support for me to focus on writing during the summer of 2024 and numerous conversations on the topic. I am grateful for the contributions from AARP's Thought Leadership program, led by Julie Miller, via the Financial Interdependence Project who also helped support early thinking on the topic and making this book open access. Early collaborators Christine Callahan and Jin Huang helped mentor and prepare the proposal and were part of the early research presentations that caught the eye of Springer Nature. Academic mentors Jodi Frey and Fernando Wagner, along with my PhD dissertation committee members—Mathieu Despard, Judy L. Postmus, Theda Rose, Reginald Tucker-Seeley, and George Jay Unick—all have provided invaluable training, guidance, and prodding to think deeper about the relationships between financial and behavioral health. Much appreciation is due to clients and colleagues who have shared their experiences—know that accompaniment goes both ways. Thanks to Amanda Fackler, Joshua Caraballo, Emma Savage, and Nichole Dumlao for feedback, review, research, and general assistance. Thanks to the team at Springer Nature, especially Janet Kim, for your assistance to guide the process. Finally, thank you to my parents, wife, and children for your support and encouragement. I fully (and gratefully) acknowledge that my wife, Anahita Anvari-Clark, is the one who does the budgeting in our family. It's better for all of us that way.

Competing Interests The author declares the following as potential competing interests: Since 2023, I have provided occasional consulting services for Money Habitudes, LLC. However, I do not have a financial stake in the company. I also teach, with remuneration, continuing education and professional development classes on topics presented in this book. I coordinate the Financial Interdependence Project, in partnership with other affiliate members. My family personally uses You Need a Budget software.

Contents

About the Author

Jeffrey Anvari-Clark, PhD, MA, LMSW, is Assistant Professor in the Department of Social Work at the University of North Dakota. He established and is the primary coordinator of the Financial Interdependence Project. He holds an MA in Social Justice in Intercultural Relations from the School for International Training in Brattleboro, Vermont, and an MSW and PhD from the School of Social Work at the University of Maryland, Baltimore. His research focuses on financial social work, the financial domain of behavioral health, and financial interdependence. His work has appeared in various media outlets, including NPR, CNN, CBS Radio, The Conversation, and Fast Company, in addition to academic journals, such as *Journal of Financial Counseling and Planning, Journal of Teaching in Social Work, Encyclopedia, International Journal of Environmental Research and Public Health,* and *Journal of Family and Economic Issues*. He teaches continuing education and professional development seminars, in addition to undergraduate (BSSW) and graduate (MSW) courses on life span development, research, generalist practice, digital information literacy and AI, and financial social work. He has conducted financial education, advising, coaching, tax preparation, and eviction prevention case management, in addition to training-of-trainers and community development.

Chapter 1
The Financial Domain of Behavioral Health

On the surface, Brittany's life looked stable. She worked as a contractor at a nonprofit while her husband Bryan held a position at a small software company. Their ten-year-old twin daughters, Abby and Addison, were active in sports and thriving. However, Bryan's employer offered minimal benefits, including a high-deductible health insurance plan requiring the family to pay the first $5000 of annual healthcare costs.

When Abby broke her ankle playing soccer, the family's financial stability quickly unraveled. Orthopedist visits, prescription medications, and weekly physical therapy sessions created mounting expenses. Taking time off work to transport Abby to appointments—roughly three hours per visit including travel—reduced Brittany's billable hours and their household income. Meanwhile, medical bills accumulated on credit cards.

The financial strain manifested across multiple domains of Brittany's well-being. Mentally, she experienced persistent anxiety and insomnia, lying awake monitoring their growing debt on her phone. Physically, sleep deprivation affected her concentration and energy. Socially, financial stress created tension in her marriage and irritability with her children. Her coping mechanisms became increasingly maladaptive as she avoided opening bills and postponed financial decisions.

Despite having middle-class assets, Brittany felt overwhelmed by the complexity of their options. They could reduce expenses, seek family assistance, pursue additional income through overtime work, or explore emergency loans from Bryan's employer or their retirement accounts. After weeks of mounting anxiety, Brittany finally scheduled an appointment with a financial counselor. Simply taking this step—identifying a concrete next action—provided enough relief for her to sleep that night, illustrating how financial efficacy can begin to address financial precarity.

***

Supplementary Information The online version contains supplementary material available at https://doi.org/10.1007/978-3-032-02632-3_1.

J. Anvari-Clark, *Financial and Behavioral Health for Helping Professionals*,
https://doi.org/10.1007/978-3-032-02632-3_1

1.1 Introduction

Behavioral health encompasses interconnected domains that collectively determine an individual's overall well-being. Traditional domains include mental health (psychological states like stress, anxiety, and depression), physical health (biological functioning including blood pressure and chronic conditions), and coping health (both adaptive and maladaptive strategies for managing stress, from employing mindfulness practices to problem use of substances) (Mancini, 2021; McEwen & Wingfield, 2003). Recognition of behavioral health's complexity has also led to the exploration of additional domains. In particular, and included in the present framework, is social health, which encompasses relationship quality with family, friends, and community, providing emotional support and safety nets (Hutchison & Lee, 2015; Putnam, 2000).

Although beyond the scope of this book, it should also be acknowledged that environmental health considers how natural and physical surroundings—from neighborhood walkability to pollution and natural disaster exposure—impact behavioral well-being, and is leading to an increasing prevalence of "eco-anxiety" (Compton & Shim, 2015; Kurth & Pihkala, 2022). Furthermore, spiritual health involves a sense of meaning, purpose, and connection to something greater than oneself, which can have profound implications on financial health (Luger & Collins, 2022; Sarofim et al., 2020). Spiritual and financial health often connect through values-based financial decisions, in which religious or spiritual beliefs influence how people view money management and obligations. These beliefs can either enhance financial health by providing clear guidelines and community support or create tension when financial realities conflict with spiritual ideals.

Financial concerns increasingly demonstrate significant relationships with all these behavioral health domains, distinguishing it as an integral domain in its own right, rather than merely an external determinant (Anvari-Clark, 2022; Anvari-Clark & Rose, 2023). In this context, the *financial health* domain of behavioral health is defined as a person's capacity to wield material means in support of their overall well-being. As with any other form of health, people can have better and worse financial health. Rooted in conditions and behaviors, financial health is a dynamic state emerging from the evolving interactions between three interconnected components: *financial precarity* (material and psychological impacts of negative financial conditions; Anvari-Clark & Rose, 2023), *financial efficacy* (ability and confidence to manage financial challenges; Anvari-Clark & Rose, 2023; Hoge et al., 2020; Lown, 2011), and *financial well-being* (current money management stress and expected future financial security; Netemeyer et al., 2018).

These financial components create complex, often bidirectional relationships with other health domains. Financial problems can trigger or exacerbate mental health issues, while depression can impair financial decision-making. Medical expenses can create debt, while financial stress can worsen physical symptoms. These interconnections create cascading effects—for example, depression leading to work absenteeism, reducing income, increasing financial stress, and straining relationships, potentially triggering maladaptive coping behaviors.

Understanding behavioral health as an integrated system of mutually influencing domains is crucial for helping professionals, as addressing one domain in isolation may prove insufficient when others continue to undermine progress.

1.2 Conceptual Model

The behavioral health framework used here encompasses five interconnected domains: mental, physical, social, coping, and financial health. Since the 1980s, professionals have increasingly used the term "behavioral health" as they recognized relationships between mental and physical health—how anxiety elevates blood pressure or how exercise improves mood—leading to expanded conceptualizations of health (North & Pfefferbaum, 2022). These domains gradually expanded to include others as inter-influencing conditions were observed and defined. For instance, Mancini (2021) presents five domains of behavioral health—mental health, physical health, social determinants of health, substance use, and trauma—in the context of integrated behavioral health care practice.

Core Behavioral Health Domains Research into mental and physical health demonstrates the most established interconnections. Mental health encompasses emotional and psychological states that directly influence physical functioning, while physical conditions often relate with mental health outcomes. These bidirectional relationships form the foundation of behavioral health practice.

Coping health includes all stress management strategies, both adaptive (prayer, meditation, exercise, social connection) and maladaptive (substance use, gambling, compulsive behaviors). Often viewed as mental health components, addictive behaviors can be understood as problematic coping mechanisms that may be behavioral rather than substance-based and influenced by social environments. Additionally, social health reflects relationship quality and social connections that influence well-being. Loneliness significantly impacts physical and mental health while increasing substance use disorder risk (Aubut et al., 2020). Social influences shape behaviors through modeling and support—whether encouraging healthy activities like group running or enabling problematic behaviors—varying by context and individual vulnerabilities.

It should be noted that while coping health and social health represent less traditional inclusions in behavioral health frameworks, growing research demonstrates their central importance to overall well-being (Choi et al., 2015; Heaney & Israel, 2008; Pellmar et al., 2002). Coping health extends beyond individual mental health symptoms to encompass the full spectrum of stress management strategies that influence multiple health domains, with emerging evidence showing how coping abilities intersect with social health factors and physical health outcomes (Park & Iacocca, 2014; Piuzzi & Ring, 2021). Social health similarly transcends simple social support to represent relationship quality and social connections as fundamental determinants of behavioral health, with social isolation increasingly recognized as a critical factor in behavioral health frameworks (Choi et al., 2015). The inclusion of substance use and behavioral addictions within coping health reflects substantial research demonstrating these behaviors as problematic coping mechanisms rather than standalone disorders, with scholars increasingly exploring addiction as maladaptive responses to stress and emotional dysregulation (Blashill et al., 2011; Glanz & Schwartz, 2008; Sarin & Nolen-Hoeksema, 2010; Wang et al., 2018).

Financial Health as a Behavioral Health Domain Financial health represents the newest addition to this integrated framework. Extensive research documents connections between financial circumstances and all other behavioral health domains. For instance: debt correlating with depression and suicide (Richardson et al., 2013), medical expenses creating financial toxicity that impairs healing (Tucker-Seeley & Yabroff, 2016), financial stress triggering problematic gambling or spending (Klontz et al., 2015), and strong social support buffering the negative effects of financial stress (Åslund et al., 2014).

Many financial-behavioral health connections involve specific money disorders addressed through financial therapy. Others require different interventions—securing resources, changing environmental conditions, or addressing systemic barriers. Understanding these conditions and their behavioral health implications enables helping professionals to recognize when financial concerns contribute to presenting problems and how to address them effectively.

The interconnected nature of these five domains means that financial concerns rarely exist in isolation. As Brittany's vignette demonstrated, medical expenses (physical health) created debt and sleep disruption (mental health), work productivity issues (financial consequences), relationship tension (social health), and avoidance behaviors (maladaptive coping). Effective intervention requires understanding these complex interactions rather than addressing domains separately.

1.3 Financial Precarity

Financial precarity represents "a state in which both material and psychological well-being are impacted by negative financial conditions and perceptions" (Anvari-Clark & Rose, 2023). This definition acknowledges that financial challenges involve more than numbers—they carry emotional weight tied to personal history, relationships, and circumstances. Traditional debt reduction strategies focus on financial optimization (pay the highest interest rate first) or psychological momentum (pay the smallest balance first) but may miss deeper emotional factors. The debt that "feels ickiest"—whether from poor decisions, failed relationships, or unfair billing—may warrant priority attention despite lower balances or interest rates, as addressing these emotional burdens can catalyze healing and empowerment.

Most financial precarity assessments examine either objective measures (ability to cover \$400–\$2000 emergencies) or subjective experiences (perceived financial stress) separately (Gaffney et al., 2020; Meuris & Leana, 2017). However, financial precarity best integrates both dimensions, recognizing that material circumstances and psychological responses interact in complex, often bidirectional ways. Brittany's situation illustrates this integration: objective factors (medical bills, reduced income) combined with subjective experiences (sleep disruption, anxiety, avoidance) to create a state affecting multiple behavioral health domains.

Relationship with Behavioral Health Financial precarity demonstrates particularly complex relationships with all behavioral health domains, often involving bidirectional causation and feedback loops. Mental health provides perhaps the clearest example: Richardson et al. (2013) found debt significantly associated with suicide attempts, depression, and overall mental health deterioration, while mental health issues can impair executive functioning needed for timely bill payment, damaging credit scores. Physical health shows similar patterns, with financial strain correlating with hypertension and chronic illness (Sweet et al., 2013), while medical conditions increase expenses and reduce work capacity.

Social health suffers when financial stress creates relationship tension and limits social participation (Stack & Meredith, 2018), yet strong social networks can buffer financial stress effects (Åslund et al., 2014). Coping health demonstrates how financial precarity can trigger problematic behaviors like gambling or substance use, while adaptive coping strategies help manage financial stress (Canale et al., 2015).

External factors—generally conceptualized as social determinants or drivers of health—often compound these relationships. When therapy costs exacerbate financial strain, anxiety increases, creating destructive cycles. Without recognizing this complexity, professionals may address familiar domains while unknown financial factors undermine progress. During COVID-19, Despard and Roll (2024) demonstrated how liquid assets buffered financial distress following job loss, highlighting three intertwined elements: available cash, income loss, and experienced stress.

Component Influences on Financial Precarity Understanding financial precarity requires examining both its objective and subjective dimensions. Objective influences include measurable financial conditions: income sufficiency and volatility, liquid assets for emergencies, medical debt burden, ability to cover financial shocks, credit record quality, money left over after expenses, and employment stability. Subjective influences encompass psychological responses to financial circumstances: perception of having too much debt, impact of income drops, financial anxiety, financial stress and strain, financial hopelessness, sense of financial subsistence, and financial overwhelm. While these influences are distinct, they often interact and reinforce each other—for instance, employment instability (objective) can trigger financial anxiety (subjective), which may lead to avoidance behaviors that worsen credit records (objective). Several subjective influences, particularly financial hopelessness, subsistence, and overwhelm, demonstrate strong correlations ($r = 0.67$–0.72) while retaining distinct characteristics that warrant separate examination (Anvari-Clark & Rose, 2023).

1.3.1 *Objective Influences*

Income Sufficiency and Volatility Insufficient income forces difficult choices about which bills to pay, creating instability where even minor expenses can trigger missed payments, late fees, and credit damage. Income volatility, particularly common among freelancers, gig workers, and small business owners, makes budgeting nearly impossible when monthly income fluctuates unpredictably (Morduch & Schneider, 2017). This inconsistency, especially when combined with expense volatility (such as rising gas prices during income drops), creates chronic uncertainty and stress as individuals never know if they'll have enough to make ends meet.

Liquid Assets for Emergencies Emergency funds equivalent to 3 months of expenses provide crucial buffers against financial shocks like job loss or unexpected expenses, helping mitigate financial distress (Despard & Roll, 2024). Without adequate reserves—and with needs varying by circumstances (farmers and freelancers often needing more than salaried employees)—minor setbacks escalate into crises requiring high-interest debt or sacrificing essential needs. Psychologically, living paycheck-to-paycheck without safety nets creates chronic insecurity that impairs future planning, worsens decision-making, and limits risk-taking necessary for economic advancement.

Medical Debt Healthcare expenses can rapidly deplete savings and force impossible choices between medical care and basic necessities like rent or food. The debt-health cycle is particularly harmful: inability to pay medical bills leads to delayed treatment, worsening health conditions, and higher future medical costs. Medical debt affects approximately 6% of U.S. adults, with over $1000 owed (Rae et al., 2022). In the U.S. healthcare system, this burden falls disproportionately on those with minimal employer benefits, high-deductible plans, or no insurance coverage.

Ability to Cover Financial Shocks Large, unexpected expenses—typically measured as $400 or $2000 (Gaffney et al., 2020; Lusardi et al., 2011)—can trigger financial trajectory deterioration when individuals lack coverage capacity. Without resources, people resort to high-interest borrowing, skip essential expenses like meals or medical care, or make other sacrifices in critical life areas. These short-term solutions create compounding problems as interest accumulates, health issues worsen from neglect, and other essential needs go unmet, establishing chronic precarity patterns.

Credit Record Credit scores function as financial "report cards" reflecting debt management and payment history. Poor credit restricts access to affordable borrowing and increasingly affects housing applications and employment opportunities, as landlords and employers use credit reports for screening. Poor credit has been repeatedly linked with poor health (Prawitz et al., 2006). Higher borrowing costs associated with poor credit make financial improvement more difficult, while credit-based screening can limit advancement opportunities, creating barriers increasingly difficult to overcome without significant intervention and support.

Money Left Over Having surplus money after expenses enhances financial security, though this requires intentional planning regardless of income level—lifestyle inflation often eliminates surplus as earnings increase. Surplus enables savings, investment, and handling unexpected expenses without distress, fostering control and reducing strain. Research on scarcity suggests surplus also enables longer-term thinking and better financial management focus (Hamilton et al., 2024). Conversely, living paycheck-to-paycheck perpetuates worry cycles with no room for error, leading to credit reliance and debt accumulation.

Employment Stability Job insecurity or lack of sufficiently paying employment eliminates the ability to rely upon steady income and critical benefits like health insurance, retirement savings plans, and paid leave. Without these financial safeguards, individuals become vulnerable to economic shocks while struggling to maintain stability and plan for the future. Employment instability creates ripple effects: without steady income, people may rely on expensive credit options, miss wealth-building opportunities like homeownership or education investment, and face compound challenges when lack of health insurance leads to medical debt.

1.3.2 Subjective Influences

Perception of Too Much Debt How individuals feel about debt often matters more than objective amounts, making this primarily subjective despite measurable debt-to-income ratios (Asebedo & Wilmarth, 2017). Perception depends on repayment ability, debt size relative to comfort levels, circumstances of debt acquisition, and emotional responses. People feel differently about medical debt from accidents, education loans for unfinished degrees, and mortgages for dream homes. Family financial socialization significantly influences these perceptions—growing up with debt-stressed parents creates different attitudes than learning strategic credit use (Gudmunson & Danes, 2011). These feelings determine whether debt feels overwhelming or manageable, affecting all behavioral health aspects.

Income Drop Impact Sudden or sustained income reductions create severe psychological impacts beyond objective financial effects. While income drops have measurable consequences, subjective perception plays the much more crucial role (Anvari-Clark & Rose, 2023). Psychologically, negative events create more impact than positive ones (Baumeister et al., 2001). Income drops increase stress, anxiety, and insecurity as individuals struggle with both budget restructuring and mentally accepting new realities. This requires significant expectation shifts and financial identity reevaluation, creating instability that complicates future planning until adaptation occurs through increased income or reduced expenses.

Financial Anxiety Persistent worry about finances, even without immediate problems, characterizes this chronic emotional state that can dominate thoughts and impair daily functioning (Archuleta et al., 2013). Financial anxiety affects concentration, decision-making, and mental well-being, making work tasks and leisure activities difficult while decreasing quality of life. This chronic preoccupation creates emotional exhaustion and relationship strain through irritability and withdrawal, potentially leading to poor financial decisions through avoidance or impulsivity, ultimately trapping individuals in cycles of perceived precarity.

Financial Stress and Strain Financial stress differs from anxiety by responding to actual difficulties rather than hypothetical worries, though both often co-occur (Sinclair & Cheung, 2016). Managing finances under persistent economic pressure creates chronic strain affecting all behavioral health forms. Recent research suggests financial stress acts as a key mediator through which income drops and employment reduction impact mental and physical health, while also motivating behavioral change efforts (Heo et al., 2024).

Financial Hopelessness Belief that financial situations cannot improve creates self-perpetuating cycles where perceived lack of control prevents proactive improvement efforts. Often captured by statements like "Because of my financial situation, I feel like I will never have the things I want in life" (Consumer Financial Protection Bureau [CFPB], 2017), this mindset leads to paralysis preventing exploration of potential opportunities or resources. Financial hopelessness distorts reality perception, causing hyper-focus on current difficulties while overlooking improvement avenues or existing strengths, leading to poor decision-making and failure to utilize available support systems.

Sense of Financial Subsistence The perception that income barely meets basic needs, leaving no savings or emergency handling capacity, creates pervasive insecurity captured by "I am just getting by financially" (CFPB, 2017). This sense creates chronic stress about unexpected expenses like car repairs or medical bills, leading to hypervigilance and fear of financial disaster. Financial subsistence perceptions (whether accurate or not) limit future planning and growth investment, creating feelings of being "stuck" with no improvement path and contributing to financial hopelessness cycles.

Financial Overwhelm Feeling inundated by financial obligations and money management complexity characterizes this subjective experience. At extremes, feeling that "finances control my life" (CFPB, 2017) leads to psychological paralysis, where individuals feel unable to make financial decisions or take action. Financial overwhelm triggers avoidance behaviors as people attempt escaping emotional distress associated with confronting financial reality, leading to procrastination on bill payment, budgeting, or seeking financial advice, ultimately worsening circumstances and reinforcing overwhelm feelings.

1.4 Financial Efficacy

Financial efficacy represents one's ability and confidence to manage financial tasks and challenges through problem-solving capabilities, access to resources, and supportive networks (Hoge et al., 2020; Lown, 2011; Sherraden, 2013). These conceptualizations stem from Bandura's (1977) seminal work on general self-efficacy, which established that individuals' beliefs about their capabilities to perform behaviors significantly influence their actions and outcomes. Financial efficacy encompasses what you *do* about a financial situation—the activities carried out reactively to address arising situations and proactively to prevent, handle, or minimize potentially harmful financial events. Financial efficacy also includes activities that create positive financial outcomes supporting overall well-being.

Similar to coping health, which includes both helpful and harmful ways of managing emotions and situations, people develop patterns for dealing with financial situations that have varying short- and long-term consequences. Maladaptive patterns like using high-cost payday loans or "robbing Peter to pay Paul" create destructive feedback loops amplifying financial precarity (Meuris & Leana, 2017). Conversely, adaptive behaviors like budgeting, building emergency savings, and seeking professional guidance create stabilizing feedback loops, enhancing financial security over time (Lynch et al., 2010; O'Neill et al., 2005, 2017).

While often conceptualized as what an individual believes they can do (hence the more common phrasing "financial *self*-efficacy"), financial efficacy frequently derives from connections with others, shifting the locus of perceived capability from "me" to "we." Financial interdependence—collective reliance within families or communities—shapes perceptions and influences resources available to address financial problems and achieve goals (Anvari-Clark & Miller, 2023; Warmath et al., 2021). This interdependence can provide support and resilience during financial challenges through collective resources and problem-solving abilities. However, obligations to others can also constrain efficacy by limiting available means, tools, and processes for addressing financial situations. Thus, the more broadly encompassing phrase "financial efficacy" is used throughout this book.

Relationship with Behavioral Health Financial efficacy demonstrates intricate relationships with all behavioral health domains, often involving bidirectional influences and context-dependent effects. Strong financial efficacy enhances overall well-being by reducing stress, enabling better healthcare choices, and strengthening social relationships. With mental health, confidence in handling financial challenges reduces anxiety and depression symptoms (Asebedo & Wilmarth, 2017), while effective financial problem-solving prevents cognitive overwhelm associated with financial stress. Higher financial efficacy enables better healthcare decisions and medical expense management, with those having greater financial efficacy more likely to have better health outcomes (Weida et al., 2020). Just as people develop emotional stress management patterns, they establish financial coping mechanisms that can be adaptive or maladaptive, with strong financial efficacy correlating with healthier coping strategies and individuals who regularly budget tending to engage in more positive health behaviors (O'Neill et al., 2017). Financial efficacy and social health are deeply intertwined through relationships and support networks, often developing through family financial socialization and community connections (Gudmunson & Danes, 2011). Understanding financial efficacy within behavioral health reshapes intervention approaches, requiring recognition of how various health domains affect financial confidence and decision-making, with success often emerging when helping people strengthen multiple life aspects simultaneously (Phojanakong et al., 2020).

Component Influences on Financial Efficacy Financial efficacy encompasses five key capabilities helping people effectively manage their financial lives. At its foundation is problem-solving ability—both resourcefulness to generate creative solutions and adaptability to adjust strategies as circumstances change. During times of financial crisis, emotional regulation plays a crucial role, as managing financial stress and anxiety enables clearer decision-making and more balanced responses to financial challenges. Beyond handling immediate challenges, financial efficacy includes capacity to set and achieve meaningful financial goals, building on past successes to develop genuine confidence in managing money matters. Finally, it involves thoughtful risk management, taking precautions to prevent or minimize financial difficulties while being prepared to handle setbacks. These interconnected elements determine how effectively someone can wield financial resources to support overall well-being.

Problem-Solving Problem-solving involves addressing financial challenges and finding solutions when facing difficulties. Individuals with high financial efficacy believe in effort-based problem-solving, confident they can overcome financial obstacles by investing necessary time and energy (Hoge et al., 2020). This belief manifests through resourcefulness and creativity—negotiating payment plans, seeking alternative income sources, or finding innovative expense reduction methods (Carson & Runco, 1999). Adaptability is equally crucial, allowing strategy adjustment when initial solutions fail or circumstances change unexpectedly (Hou et al., 2021). Effective financial problem-solving through practical steps reduces stress and anxiety, while repeated difficulties without action lead to helplessness and financial avoidance (Archuleta et al., 2021; Asebedo & Wilmarth, 2017).

Emotional Regulation To have emotional regulation helps individuals manage feelings like anxiety, shame, or fear around money matters. Rather than being overwhelmed by financial stress or avoiding financial issues entirely, people with strong emotional regulation acknowledge financial concerns while taking constructive action (Hoge et al., 2020; Lown, 2011). This ability develops through experience and involves specific strategies—pausing before making emotional financial decisions, discussing money worries with trusted others, or using stress management techniques when reviewing bills or budgets.

The impact of emotional regulation extends throughout behavioral health. When people manage emotional responses to financial challenges, they may be more likely to maintain healthy eating and sleeping patterns rather than letting financial stress disrupt these behaviors (Hamilton et al., 2024). They may maintain regular spiritual or mindfulness practices, helping them stay grounded during financial challenges (positive coping health), rather than letting money worries overwhelm their sense of purpose or values (Sinha et al., 2021). By keeping emotions balanced during financial difficulties, individuals make clearer decisions and take more effective actions to improve situations.

Goal Attainment Financial efficacy strongly associates with ability to set and achieve financial goals. Highly efficacious individuals establish clear financial objectives and develop realistic accomplishment plans (Hoge et al., 2020; Lown, 2011). This involves breaking larger goals into manageable steps, monitoring progress, and adjusting strategies when needed. Success in reaching financial goals builds upon itself—each achievement enhances confidence and skills for future challenges (O'Neill et al., 2000). Meeting financial objectives reduces future worry and instills security; progress supports positive mental health and encourages healthy coping behaviors (Li et al., 2022). Conversely, consistently falling short of financial goals strains relationships through repeated assistance requests, leads to unhealthy coping behaviors like stress spending, or results in postponing important preventive healthcare to save money (Franco et al., 2019; Sweet et al., 2013).

Confidence One's confidence represents a central financial efficacy element, encompassing belief in financial abilities and trust in financial judgment (Hoge et al., 2020). Unlike overconfidence or false bravado, genuine financial confidence develops through experience—successfully navigating past financial challenges, learning from setbacks, and building practical money management skills over time. This earned confidence allows individuals to remain calmer during financial difficulties and take action rather than avoiding financial issues. To put it simply, if you've done it before, you know you can do it again.

When people trust their financial capabilities, they are more likely to seek preventive healthcare rather than postponing medical care due to cost concerns (Kangovi et al., 2013). They maintain stronger social connections rather than isolating due to financial stress (Serido & Shim, 2017). Confident individuals engage more in positive financial behaviors like retirement planning or building emergency savings, creating foundations for long-term well-being (Palameta et al., 2016).

Risk Management Financial efficacy involves managing financial risks effectively through preventive measures and responsive actions. Proactive risk management includes building emergency savings, maintaining adequate insurance coverage, or developing multiple income streams for financial stability. However, it extends beyond financial preparation—taking steps to protect overall well-being, like maintaining regular medical check-ups to prevent costly future health issues or strengthening social support networks providing assistance during difficulties (Warmath et al., 2021).

Effective risk management involves responding thoughtfully to financial challenges when they arise. People often make worse decisions under financial duress (Mullainathan & Shafir, 2013); pre-established protocols or heuristics help in these cases. Rather than making panicked decisions that worsen situations, financially efficacious individuals assess options carefully and draw on available resources and support systems (Gist-Mackey & Guy, 2019). This balanced approach prevents cascading negative outcomes associated with financial shocks—from deteriorating physical health due to stress, to strained relationships from financial pressure, to problematic coping behaviors like excessive drinking or gambling (Richardson et al., 2013).

1.5 Financial Well-Being

Financial well-being represents the third component of the financial domain of behavioral health, conceptualized as a dual sense of current money management stress and expected future financial security, enabling freedom to make value-aligned financial choices (CFPB, 2017; Netemeyer et al., 2018). This multifaceted concept has been measured with various objective and subjective elements over time. Objective measures focus on indicators such as income, expenditures, debt levels, and net worth (Xiao, 2016), while subjective measures capture individuals' perceptions and feelings about their financial situations, including sense of stress, security, choice, and optimism (CFPB, 2017; Netemeyer et al., 2018).

The Consumer Financial Protection Bureau (CFPB) identifies components of financial well-being as including: "having control over day-to-day and month-to-month finances, capacity to absorb financial shocks, being on track to meet financial goals, and having the financial freedom to make choices that allow one to enjoy life" (CFPB, 2017). These elements highlight the temporal dimension encompassing both present management and future security. Building on this framework, Netemeyer et al. (2018) conceptualized perceived financial well-being as consisting of two primary dimensions: current money management stress (feelings of anxiety, worry, and dissatisfaction with present financial situation) and expected future financial security (perceptions of ability to achieve financial goals and maintain future stability).

Financial well-being exists in dynamic relationship with financial precarity and financial efficacy within the broader financial domain. If viewing the relationship sequentially, financial precarity indicates current state, financial efficacy represents what a person can do in response to that state, and financial well-being reflects the resultant outcome. Netemeyer et al. (2018) found financial efficacy to be a significant contributor to expected future financial security, highlighting its importance in shaping financial well-being perceptions. Interestingly, external circumstances can reshape these perceptions—Tinghög et al. (2024) found that the COVID-19 pandemic positively impacted financial well-being among Swedish participants, suggesting that health crisis worries might have overshadowed current money management stresses or that reduced spending opportunities created more household budget slack.

Relationship with Behavioral Health Research increasingly demonstrates powerful connections between financial well-being and other behavioral health aspects, with Netemeyer et al. (2018) finding that current money management stress and expected future financial security collectively explained as much variance in overall well-being as job satisfaction, relationship satisfaction, and physical health status combined. Current money management stress demonstrates strong negative relationships with mental health outcomes, particularly for low-income individuals, while expected future financial security correlates positively with psychological well-being, life satisfaction, and optimism (Serido & Shim, 2017; Wilkinson, 2016). Financial well-being interacts with physical health through multiple pathways including healthcare utilization decisions, physiological stress responses, and health behavior changes, with research demonstrating associations between subjective financial stress and cardiovascular disease outcomes (Sweet et al., 2013). Financial stress can trigger various coping responses that may further compromise well-being, with low financial well-being associated with increased substance use, problem gambling, and compulsive buying behaviors (Grant et al., 2010; Klontz et al., 2012). Financial circumstances shape and are shaped by relationships, as conflict in intimate relationships can be shaped by changes in financial well-being, illustrating how financial and social domains interact (Dew, 2007; Jenkins et al., 2023). Understanding these interconnections provides foundation for recognizing how financial well-being contributes to overall health and quality of life.

Component Influences Drawing from the work by Netemeyer et al. (2018), financial well-being encompasses two distinct but related dimensions with different antecedents and pathways to overall well-being. Current money management stress reflects anxiety about present finances, while expected future financial security focuses on confidence in future financial outcomes. These components interact dynamically—high current stress often undermines future security perceptions, while positive financial behaviors and planning may buffer stress despite present challenges.

1.5.1 Current Money Management Stress

Current money management stress represents the present-oriented dimension of financial well-being, reflecting immediate feelings of anxiety, worry, and dissatisfaction with one's financial situation (Netemeyer et al., 2018). Three key factors significantly contribute to this stress: late or minimum payments on financial obligations, lack of self-control in financial behaviors, and materialistic attitudes toward possessions and consumption.

Late and Minimum Payments The pattern of making late payments on bills or only minimum payments on credit cards strongly associates with increased current money management stress (Netemeyer et al., 2018). Regular late payments trigger cascading financial problems including late fees, interest rate increases, and negative credit reporting, with individuals experiencing both objective financial penalties and subjective feelings of stress (Xiao & Kim, 2022). Making only minimum payments extends debt repayment periods and significantly increases total interest paid—for example, a $3000 credit card balance at 18% APR could take over 24 years to repay (at 2.5% of balance as minimum payment) and cost more than $8000 in interest, creating persistent stress and worry.

Lack of Self-Control Deficits in self-control significantly impact financial well-being through effects on spending and saving behaviors. Lack of self-control encompasses impulsivity and insufficient restraint elements (Maloney et al., 2012), with individuals scoring low in restraint demonstrating difficulty working toward long-term financial goals and resisting impulsive spending. High impulsivity correlates with problematic financial behaviors such as late payment fees and overdraft charges (Fernandes et al., 2014). This inability to delay gratification creates cycles where immediate desires consistently override long-term financial stability and can manifest in financial avoidance behaviors like neglecting to check account balances or open bills (Canale et al., 2015).

Materialism Materialistic values and attitudes represent a significant contributor to current money management stress. Materialism—the importance ascribed to acquiring and possessing material goods (Richins, 2004)—links consistently to excessive credit card debt, over-borrowing, and compulsive spending behaviors that directly increase stress by creating financial obligations exceeding available resources (Richins, 2011). Materialistic individuals report lower satisfaction with their financial situation regardless of actual income or assets, contributing directly to current money management stress. The relationship appears bidirectional, with materialistic values creating internal conflict when clashing with other important values like family connection or community involvement (Burroughs & Rindfleisch, 2002).

1.5.2 Expected Future Financial Security

Expected future financial security represents the future-oriented dimension focusing on individuals' perceptions about their ability to achieve financial goals and maintain stability in the future (Netemeyer et al., 2018). This dimension encompasses perceptions of having a financially secure future, being on track to meet financial goals, and having confidence in ability to handle future financial needs. Four key components particularly influence developing expected future financial security: perceived financial self-efficacy, positive financial behaviors, willingness to take investment risks, and planning for money long-term.

Perceived Financial Self-Efficacy This component represents an individual's confidence in their personal ability to effectively manage financial matters and make sound financial decisions, reflecting domain-specific beliefs about capacity to handle financial challenges (Netemeyer et al., 2018). Stronger beliefs in financial abilities predict more positive future financial outcomes, as confidence in financial decision-making serves as incentive for maintaining financial discipline (Hoge et al., 2020). Individuals with high financial self-efficacy feel less overwhelmed by financial challenges and more capable of navigating complex financial decisions, helping them remain motivated to address challenges rather than avoiding them (Lown, 2011). Perceived financial self-efficacy demonstrates strong positive relationships with expected future financial security and can be cultivated through appropriate interventions and experiences (Dare et al., 2023).

Positive Financial Behaviors These represent concrete actions individuals take to manage finances effectively, particularly those oriented toward future financial well-being, including establishing emergency savings, calculating retirement needs, opening savings accounts, purchasing bonds, and investing in mutual funds or stocks (Netemeyer et al., 2018). When individuals engage in such behaviors, they create tangible evidence of progress toward future financial security, subsequently enhancing their subjective perceptions of that security. The relationship between positive financial behaviors and expected future financial security has been consistently demonstrated, with behaviors like saving and investing showing strong associations with confidence in financial future (Xiao et al., 2014). These behaviors often become self-reinforcing habits that continuously contribute to building future financial security (O'Neill et al., 2005).

Willingness to Take Investment Risks Risk tolerance represents an individual's comfort with accepting uncertainty in financial decision-making in exchange for potential higher returns (Grable, 2016). This component plays a crucial role in expected future financial security because it significantly influences investment choices and long-term wealth accumulation. Those unwilling to accept prudent investment risks often make overly conservative financial choices that may fail to generate sufficient returns to meet long-term financial goals, while excessive risk-taking can lead to portfolio volatility undermining financial stability (Netemeyer et al., 2018). Research demonstrates that individuals with increased risk tolerance who make informed investment decisions typically experience greater confidence in their future financial security, stemming from both actual financial benefits of appropriate risk-taking and psychological comfort from actively engaging with financial choices (Cho & Lee, 2006; Warmath et al., 2021).

Planning for Money Long-Term This involves setting financial goals, developing achievement strategies, establishing spending priorities, and preferring deliberative approaches to financial decisions over spontaneous ones (Lynch et al., 2010). This component fundamentally shapes expected future financial security by creating structured frameworks for translating current actions into future financial outcomes. Having adequate insurance and carrying out active plans to reach financial goals helps instill greater confidence in ability to have choices and feel secure in the future.

1.6 Conclusion

The financial domain of behavioral health represents a critical addition to our understanding of human well-being, encompassing three interconnected components that collectively determine an individual's capacity to wield material means in support of their overall health. Financial precarity captures both the objective realities and subjective experiences of financial vulnerability, from income volatility and medical debt to financial anxiety and overwhelm. Financial efficacy represents the problem-solving capabilities, confidence, and emotional regulation that enable individuals to navigate financial challenges and achieve financial goals. Financial well-being reflects the dual experience of managing current financial stress while building confidence in future financial security, ultimately enabling value-aligned choices that support life satisfaction.

Understanding these financial components within the broader behavioral health framework reveals complex, bidirectional relationships that extend across all health domains. Financial stress can trigger mental health symptoms, physical health problems, maladaptive coping behaviors, and social relationship strain—while challenges in any of these domains can simultaneously impact financial functioning. For helping professionals across disciplines, recognizing these interconnections is essential for developing effective interventions that address the full spectrum of factors influencing client well-being. Rather than treating financial concerns only as external determinants, practitioners must understand how financial health operates as an integral domain of behavioral health, requiring the same attention and clinical consideration as mental, physical, and social health concerns. This integrated perspective provides the foundation for more holistic, effective approaches to supporting individuals and families in achieving comprehensive health and well-being.

References

Anvari-Clark, J. (2022). *Understanding financial behavioral health and race (racism), and their association with investment risk willingness* (doctoral dissertation). University of Maryland, Baltimore, Maryland. Retrieved from https://www.proquest.com/dissertations-theses/understanding-financial-behavioral-health-race/docview/2688127973/se-2.

Anvari-Clark, J., & Miller, J. (2023). Financial interdependence: A social perspective. *Encyclopedia*, 3(3), 996–1008. https://doi.org/10.3390/encyclopedia3030072.

Anvari-Clark, J., & Rose, T. (2023). Financial behavioral health and investment risk willingness: Implications for the racial wealth gap. *International Journal of Environmental Research and Public Health, 20*(10), 5835. https://doi.org/10.3390/ijerph20105835

Archuleta, K. L., Dale, A., & Spann, S. M. (2013). College students and financial distress: Exploring debt, financial satisfaction, and financial anxiety. *Journal of Financial Counseling and Planning, 24*(2), 50–62. https://eric.ed.gov/?id=EJ1043230

Archuleta, K. L., Glenn, C., Lawson, D. R., Clady, J. P., & Solomon, S. (2021). I know I should, but do I do it? Connecting covert and overt financial behaviors. *Journal of Financial Counseling and Planning, 32*(3), 15.

Asebedo, S. D., & Wilmarth, M. J. (2017). Does how we feel about financial strain matter for mental health? *Journal of Financial Therapy, 8*(1), 62–80. https://doi.org/10.4148/1944-9771.1130

Åslund, C., Larm, P., Starrin, B., & Nilsson, K. W. (2014). The buffering effect of tangible social support on financial stress: Influence on psychological Well-being and psychosomatic symptoms in a large sample of the adult general population. *International Journal for Equity in Health, 13*(1), 85. https://doi.org/10.1186/s12939-014-0085-3

Aubut, V., Wagner, V., Cousineau, M.-M., & Bertrand, K. (2020). Problematic substance use, help-seeking, and service utilization trajectories among seniors: An exploratory qualitative study. *Journal of Psychoactive Drugs*. https://doi.org/10.1080/02791072.2020.1824045

Bandura, A. (1977). Self-efficacy: Toward a unifying theory of behavioral change. *Psychological Review, 84*(2), 191–215. https://doi.org/10.1037/0033-295X.84.2.191

Baumeister, R. F., Bratslavsky, E., Finkenauer, C., & Vohs, K. D. (2001). Bad is stronger than good. *Review of General Psychology, 5*(4), 323–370. https://doi.org/10.1037/1089-2680.5.4.323

Blashill, A. J., Perry, N., & Safren, S. A. (2011). Mental health: A focus on stress, coping, and mental illness as it relates to treatment retention, adherence, and other health outcomes. *Current HIV/AIDS Reports, 8*(4), 215–222. https://doi.org/10.1007/s11904-011-0089-1

Burroughs, J. E., & Rindfleisch, A. (2002). Materialism and Well-being: A conflicting values perspective. *Journal of Consumer Research, 29*(3), 348–370. https://doi.org/10.1086/344429

Canale, A., Archuleta, K. L., & Klontz, B. T. (2015). Money disorders. In B. T. Klontz, S. L. Britt, & K. L. Archuleta (Eds.), *Financial therapy: Theory, research, and practice* (pp. 35–68). Springer.

Carson, D. K., & Runco, M. A. (1999). Creative problem solving and problem finding in young adults: Interconnections with stress, hassles, and coping abilities. *The Journal of Creative Behavior, 33*(3), 167–188. https://doi.org/10.1002/j.2162-6057.1999.tb01195.x

Cho, J., & Lee, J. (2006). An integrated model of risk and risk-reducing strategies. *Journal of Business Research, 59*(1), 112–120. https://doi.org/10.1016/j.jbusres.2005.03.006

Choi, H., Irwin, M. R., & Cho, H. J. (2015). Impact of social isolation on behavioral health in elderly: Systematic review. *World Journal of Psychiatry, 5*(4), 432–438. https://doi.org/10.5498/wjp.v5.i4.432

Compton, M. T., & Shim, R. S. (Eds.). (2015). *The social determinants of mental health*. American Psychiatric Publishing.

Consumer Financial Protection Bureau. (2017). *CFPB financial well-being scale: Scale development technical report.* https://www.consumerfinance.gov/data-research/research-reports/financial-well-being-scale/.

Dare, S. E., van Dijk, W. W., van Dijk, E., van Dillen, L. F., Gallucci, M., & Simonse, O. (2023). How executive functioning and financial self-efficacy predict subjective financial well-being via positive financial behaviors. *Journal of Family and Economic Issues, 44*(2), 232–248. https://doi.org/10.1007/s10834-022-09845-0

Despard, M., & Roll, S. (2024). Job loss and financial distress during COVID-19: The protective role of emergency savings. *Journal of Financial Counseling & Planning, 35*(2), 157–172. https://doi.org/10.1891/JFCP-2022-0048

Dew, J. (2007). Two sides of the same coin? The differing roles of assets and consumer debt in marriage. *Journal of Family and Economic Issues, 28*(1), 89–104. https://doi.org/10.1007/s10834-006-9051-6

Fernandes, D., Lynch, J. G., & Netemeyer, R. G. (2014). Financial literacy, financial education, and downstream financial behaviors. *Management Science, 60*(8), 1861–1883. https://doi.org/10.1287/mnsc.2013.1849

Franco, S., Olfson, M., Wall, M. M., Wang, S., Hoertel, N., & Blanco, C. (2019). Shared and specific associations of substance use disorders on adverse outcomes: A national prospective study. *Drug and Alcohol Dependence, 201*, 212–219. https://doi.org/10.1016/j.drugalcdep.2019.03.003

Gaffney, A. W., Himmelstein, D. U., McCormick, D., & Woolhandler, S. (2020). Health and social precarity among Americans receiving unemployment benefits during the COVID-19 outbreak. *Journal of General Internal Medicine, 35*(11), 3416–3419. https://doi.org/10.1007/s11606-020-06207-0

Gist-Mackey, A. N., & Guy, A. (2019). "You get in a hole, it's like quicksand": A grounded theory analysis of social support amid materially bounded decision-making processes. *Journal of Applied Communication Research, 47*(3), 237–259. https://doi.org/10.1080/00909882.2019.1617430

Glanz, K., & Schwartz, M. D. (2008). Stress, coping, and health behavior. In K. Glanz, B. K. Rimer, & K. Viswanath (Eds.), *Health behavior and health education: Theory, research, and practice* (4th ed.). Jossey-Bass.

Grable, J. E. (2016). Financial risk tolerance. In J. J. Xiao (Ed.), *Handbook of consumer finance research* (2nd ed., pp. 19–32). Springer International Publishing. http://link.springer.com/10.1007/978-3-319-28887-1. Accessed 19 February 2022

Grant, J. E., Schreiber, L., Odlaug, B. L., & Kim, S. W. (2010). Pathological gambling and bankruptcy. *Comprehensive Psychiatry, 51*(2), 115–120. https://doi.org/10.1016/j.comppsych.2009.04.002

Gudmunson, C. G., & Danes, S. M. (2011). Family financial socialization: Theory and critical review. *Journal of Family and Economic Issues, 32*(4), 644–667. https://doi.org/10.1007/s10834-011-9275-y

Hamilton, L., Choplin, V., & Paputseanos, T. (2024). From scarcity to security: Participant well-being in the first 2 years of a basic income pilot. *Analyses of Social Issues and Public Policy, 24*(1), 44–72. https://doi.org/10.1111/asap.12370

Heaney, C. A., & Israel, B. A. (2008). Social networks and social support. In K. Glanz, B. K. Rimer, & K. Viswanath (Eds.), *Health behavior and health education: Theory, research, and practice* (4th ed.). Jossey-Bass.

Heo, W., Yao, R., & Cho, S. H. (2024). Perceived mental and physical health during the pandemic: The role of financial stress. *Journal of Financial Counseling & Planning, 35*(2), 215–233. https://doi.org/10.1891/JFCP-2022-0108

Hoge, G. L., Stylianou, A. M., Hetling, A., & Postmus, J. L. (2020). Developing and validating the scale of economic self-efficacy. *Journal of Interpersonal Violence, 35*(15–16), 3011–3033. https://doi.org/10.1177/0886260517706761

Hou, W. K., Liang, L., Hougen, C., & Bonanno, G. A. (2021). Regulatory flexibility of sustaining daily routines and mental health in adaptation to financial strain: A vignette approach. *International Journal of Environmental Research and Public Health, 18*(6), 3103. https://doi.org/10.3390/ijerph18063103

Hutchison, E. D., & Lee, S. M. (2015). Communities. In E. D. Hutchison (Ed.), *Dimensions of human behavior: Person and environment* (5th ed., pp. 447–478). SAGE.

Jenkins, A. I. C., Le, Y., Surachman, A., Almeida, D. M., & Fredman, S. J. (2023). Associations among financial Well-being, daily relationship tension, and daily affect in two adult cohorts separated by the great recession. *Journal of Social and Personal Relationships, 40*(4), 1103–1125. https://doi.org/10.1177/02654075221105611

Kangovi, S., Barg, F. K., Carter, T., Long, J. A., Shannon, R., & Grande, D. (2013). Understanding why patients of low socioeconomic status prefer hospitals over ambulatory care. *Health Affairs, 32*(7), 1196–1203. https://doi.org/10.1377/hlthaff.2012.0825

Klontz, B., Britt, S. L., Archuleta, K. L., & Klontz, T. (2012). Disordered money behaviors: Development of the Klontz money behavior inventory. *Journal of Financial Therapy, 3*(1), 17–42. https://doi.org/10.4148/jft.v3i1.1485

Klontz, B. T., Britt, S. L., & Archuleta, K. L. (Eds.). (2015). *Financial therapy: Theory, research, and practice*. Springer.

Kurth, C., & Pihkala, P. (2022). Eco-anxiety: What it is and why it matters. *Frontiers in Psychology, 13*(981814), 1–13. https://doi.org/10.3389/fpsyg.2022.981814

Li, X., Curran, M., Serido, J., LeBaron-Black, A. B., Shim, S., & Zhou, N. (2022). Financial behaviors, financial satisfaction, and goal attainment among college-educated young adults: A mediating analysis with latent change scores. *Applied Developmental Science, 26*(3), 603–617. https://doi.org/10.1080/10888691.2021.1976182

Lown, J. M. (2011). 2011 outstanding AFCPE® conference paper: Development and validation of a financial self-efficacy scale. *Journal of Financial Counseling and Planning, 22*(2), 11.

Luger, C., & Collins, T. (2022). *The seven circles: Indigenous teachings for living well*. HarperCollins. https://harperone.com/9780063119208/the-seven-circles. Accessed 19 January 2023

Lusardi, A., Schneider, D. J., & Tufano, P. (2011, May). *Financially fragile households: Evidence and implications. Working Paper*. National Bureau of Economic Research. https://doi.org/10.3386/w17072

Lynch, J. G., Netemeyer, R. G., Spiller, S. A., & Zammit, A. (2010). A generalizable scale of propensity to plan: The long and the short of planning for time and for money. *Journal of Consumer Research, 37*(1), 108–128. https://doi.org/10.1086/649907

Maloney, P. W., Grawitch, M. J., & Barber, L. K. (2012). The multi-factor structure of the brief self-control scale: Discriminant validity of restraint and impulsivity. *Journal of Research in Personality, 46*(1), 111–115. https://doi.org/10.1016/j.jrp.2011.10.001

Mancini, M. A. (2021). *Integrated behavioral health practice*. Springer International Publishing. https://doi.org/10.1007/978-3-030-59659-0

McEwen, B. S., & Wingfield, J. C. (2003). The concept of allostasis in biology and biomedicine. *Hormones and Behavior, 43*(1), 2–15. https://doi.org/10.1016/S0018-506X(02)00024-7

Meuris, J., & Leana, C. R. (2017). The price of financial precarity: Personal finance as a barrier to work performance. *Academy of Management Proceedings, 2017*(1), 12992. https://doi.org/10.5465/AMBPP.2017.323

Morduch, J., & Schneider, R. (2017). *The financial diaries*. Princeton University Press.

Mullainathan, S., & Shafir, E. (2013). *Scarcity: Why having too little means so much*. Times Books, Henry Holt.

Netemeyer, R. G., Warmath, D., Fernandes, D., & Lynch, J. G. (2018). How am I doing? Perceived financial Well-being, its potential antecedents, and its relation to overall Well-being. *Journal of Consumer Research, 45*(1), 68–89. https://doi.org/10.1093/jcr/ucx109

North, C. S., & Pfefferbaum, B. (2022). The need to clarify professional terminology in psychiatry. *Annals of Clinical Psychiatry, 34*(3), 149–151. https://doi.org/10.12788/acp.0079

O'Neill, B., Xiao, J. J., Bristow, B., Brennan, P., & Kerbel, C. M. (2000). *Successful financial goal attainment: Perceived resources and obstacles*, 11.

O'Neill, B., Xiao, J. J., Sorhaindo, B., & Garman, E. T. (2005). Financially distressed consumers: Their financial practices, financial Well-being, and health. *Financial Counseling and Planning, 16*(1), 73–87. http://afcpe.org/journal-articles.php?volume=103&article=9

O'Neill, B., Xiao, J. J., & Ensle, K. (2017). Positive health and financial practices: Does budgeting make a difference? *Journal of Family and Consumer Sciences, 109*(2), 27–36. https://doi.org/10.14307/JFCS109.2.27

Palameta, B., Nguyen, C., Hui, T. S., & Gyarmati, D. (2016). *The link between financial confidence and financial outcomes among working-aged Canadians*. Social Research and Demonstration Corporation. https://srdc.org/wp-content/uploads/2022/07/fcac-full-report-on-financial-confidence-en.pdf. Accessed 26 May 2025

Park, C. L., & Iacocca, M. O. (2014). A stress and coping perspective on health behaviors: Theoretical and methodological considerations. *Anxiety, Stress, & Coping, 27*(2), 123–137. https://doi.org/10.1080/10615806.2013.860969

Pellmar, T. C., Brandt, E. N., & Baird, M. A. (2002). Health and behavior: The interplay of biological, behavioral, and social influences: Summary of an Institute of Medicine report. *American Journal of Health Promotion, 16*(4), 206–219. https://doi.org/10.4278/0890-1171-16.4.206

Phojanakong, P., Welles, S., Dugan, J., Booshehri, L., Brown Weida, E., & Chilton, M. (2020). Trauma-informed financial empowerment programming improves food security among families with young children. *Journal of Nutrition Education and Behavior, 52*(5), 465–473. https://doi.org/10.1016/j.jneb.2020.02.008

Piuzzi, N. S., & Ring, D. (2021). American Academy of orthopaedic surgeons appropriate use criteria: Early screening for psychosocial risk and protective factors. *JAAOS - Journal of the American Academy of Orthopaedic Surgeons, 29*(15), e760. https://doi.org/10.5435/JAAOS-D-20-00810

Prawitz, A. D., Garman, E. T., Sorhaindo, B., O'Neill, B., Kim, J., & Drentea, P. (2006). InCharge financial distress/financial well-being scale: Development, administration, and score interpretation. *Journal of Financial Counseling and Planning, 17*(1), 34–50. https://doi.org/10.1037/t60365-000

Putnam, R. D. (2000). *Bowling alone: The collapse and revival of American community*. Simon & Schuster.

Rae, M., Claxton, G., Amin, K., Wager, E., Ortaliza, J., & Cox, C. (2022, March 10). *The burden of medical debt in the United States*. Peterson-KFF Health System Tracker. https://www.healthsystemtracker.org/brief/the-burden-of-medical-debt-in-the-united-states/. Accessed 18 January 2024.

Richardson, T., Elliott, P., & Roberts, R. (2013). The relationship between personal unsecured debt and mental and physical health: A systematic review and meta-analysis. *Clinical Psychology Review, 33*(8), 1148–1162. https://doi.org/10.1016/j.cpr.2013.08.009

Richins, M. L. (2004). The material values scale: Measurement properties and development of a short form. *Journal of Consumer Research, 31*(1), 209–219. https://doi.org/10.1086/383436

Richins, M. L. (2011). Materialism, transformation expectations, and spending: Implications for credit use. *Journal of Public Policy & Marketing, 30*(2), 141–156. https://doi.org/10.1509/jppm.30.2.141

Sarin, S., & Nolen-Hoeksema, S. (2010). The dangers of dwelling: An examination of the relationship between rumination and consumptive coping in survivors of childhood sexual abuse. *Cognition & Emotion, 24*(1), 71–85. https://doi.org/10.1080/02699930802563668

Sarofim, S., Minton, E., Hunting, A., Bartholomew, D. E., Zehra, S., Montford, W., et al. (2020). Religion's influence on the financial Well-being of consumers: A conceptual framework and research agenda. *Journal of Consumer Affairs, 54*(3), 1028–1061. https://doi.org/10.1111/joca.12315

Serido, J., & Shim, S. (2017). *Approaching 30: Adult financial capability, stability, and well-being (No. Wave 4)*. Take Charge America Institute for Consumer Financial Education and Research. https://www.aplushappiness.org/reports

Sherraden, M. (2013). Building blocks of financial capability. In J. Birkenmaier, M. Sherraden, & J. Curley (Eds.), *Financial capability and asset development: Research, education, policy, and practice* (pp. 3–43). Oxford University Press.

Sinclair, R. R., & Cheung, J. H. (2016). Money matters: Recommendations for financial stress research in occupational health psychology. *Stress and Health: Journal of the International Society for the Investigation of Stress, 32*(3), 181–193. https://doi.org/10.1002/smi.2688

Sinha, N. K., Kumar, P., & Priyadarshi, P. (2021). Relating mindfulness to financial well-being through materialism: Evidence from India. *International Journal of Bank Marketing*. https://doi.org/10.1108/IJBM-07-2020-0375

Stack, R. J., & Meredith, A. (2018). The impact of financial hardship on single parents: An exploration of the journey from social distress to seeking help. *Journal of Family and Economic Issues, 39*(2), 233–242. https://doi.org/10.1007/s10834-017-9551-6

Sweet, E., Nandi, A., Adam, E. K., & McDade, T. W. (2013). The high price of debt: Household financial debt and its impact on mental and physical health. *Social Science & Medicine, 91*, 94–100. https://doi.org/10.1016/j.socscimed.2013.05.009

Tinghög, G., Asutay, E., Barrafrem, K., & Västfjäll, D. (2024). The effect of COVID-19 on subjective financial well-being. *Journal of Financial Counseling & Planning, 35*(2), 234–243. https://doi.org/10.1891/JFCP-2022-0112

Tucker-Seeley, R. D., & Yabroff, K. R. (2016). Minimizing the "financial toxicity" associated with cancer care: Advancing the research agenda. *Journal of the National Cancer Institute, 108*(5). https://doi.org/10.1093/jnci/djv410

Wang, K., Burton, C. L., & Pachankis, J. E. (2018). Depression and substance use: Towards the development of an emotion regulation model of stigma coping. *Substance Use & Misuse, 53*(5), 859–866. https://doi.org/10.1080/10826084.2017.1391011

Warmath, D., Chen, P.-J., Grable, J., & Kwak, E. J. (2021). Soft landings: Extending the cushion hypothesis to financial Well-being in collectivistic cultures. *Journal of Consumer Affairs, 55*(4), 1563–1590. https://doi.org/10.1111/joca.12408

Weida, E. B., Phojanakong, P., Patel, F., & Chilton, M. (2020). Financial health as a measurable social determinant of health. *PLoS One, 15*(5), 1–14. https://doi.org/10.1371/journal.pone.0233359

Wilkinson, L. R. (2016). Financial strain and mental health among older adults during the great recession. *The Journals of Gerontology Series B: Psychological Sciences and Social Sciences, 71*(4), 745–754. https://doi.org/10.1093/geronb/gbw001

Xiao, J. J. (2016). Consumer financial capability and wellbeing. In J. J. Xiao (Ed.), *Handbook of consumer finance research* (2nd ed.). Springer International Publishing. http://link.springer.com/10.1007/978-3-319-28887-1. Accessed 19 February 2022

Xiao, J. J., & Kim, K. T. (2022). The able worry more? Debt delinquency, financial capability, and financial stress. *Journal of Family and Economic Issues, 43*(1), 138–152. https://doi.org/10.1007/s10834-021-09767-3

Xiao, J. J., Chen, C., & Chen, F. (2014). Consumer financial capability and financial satisfaction. *Social Indicators Research, 118*(1), 415–432. https://doi.org/10.1007/s11205-013-0414-8

Chapter 2
Theories and Frameworks

2.1 Introduction

Understanding the financial domain of behavioral health requires drawing from multiple theoretical traditions that illuminate how money, relationships, and well-being intersect in complex ways. While each helping profession brings its own theoretical lens, the multifaceted nature of the relationships among the domains demands an integrated approach that spans disciplinary boundaries.

The theories and frameworks explored in this chapter operate at different levels of analysis, from individual cognitive processes to family dynamics to broader social systems. Complexity theory provides the overarching framework for understanding how these levels interact, revealing why financial concerns can trigger cascading effects across multiple domains of health. Financial capability and asset-building theory grounds us in the practical realities of how structural factors enable or constrain individual financial actions. Financial interdependence theory challenges Western assumptions about individual financial responsibility by highlighting the social nature of financial decisions.

Life course and family stress theories help explain how financial experiences unfold over time and across generations, while understanding the role of scarcity illuminates the psychological mechanisms through which financial strain affects decision-making. Financial socialization theory reveals how past experiences shape present financial behaviors, often in unconscious ways. Finally, the evolution toward "drivers of health" language helps practitioners understand their role in addressing financial concerns.

Rather than competing explanations, these frameworks complement each other, each contributing essential insights for helping professionals seeking to understand and address the complex relationships between financial circumstances and

Supplementary Information The online version contains supplementary material available at https://doi.org/10.1007/978-3-032-02632-3_2.

J. Anvari-Clark, *Financial and Behavioral Health for Helping Professionals*, https://doi.org/10.1007/978-3-032-02632-3_2

behavioral health outcomes. Together, they provide the theoretical foundation for effective practice across the financial domain of behavioral health.

2.2 Complexity Theory

Complexity theory studies how interacting components create patterns, behaviors, and systems greater than, and even different from, the sum of their parts (Theise, 2023; Turner & Baker, 2019). In behavioral health, this manifests when financial stress triggers cascading effects across multiple domains—such as affecting mental well-being through anxiety, physical health through elevated blood pressure, coping behaviors through increased substance use, and social relationships through strained family dynamics. These effects cannot be predicted by examining any single domain in isolation.

Unlike traditional scientific approaches that analyze components separately, complexity theory illustrates how elements self-organize to generate emergent properties (Theise, 2023; Turner & Baker, 2019). For instance, financial efficacy emerges from interactions between knowledge, confidence, and successful money management experiences, then influences future financial decisions in ways difficult to predict from studying these elements separately.

Fundamentals of Complexity Theory Complex systems are composed of many interacting parts that self-organize to create new, unpredictable patterns and behaviors. In behavioral health, this self-organization appears when seemingly independent domains—mental, physical, social, coping, and financial—interact to produce overall well-being outcomes that transcend any single domain. These emergent properties cannot be reduced to or predicted by studying individual components in isolation (Theise, 2023).

Financial precarity demonstrates this complexity. Job loss or debt can trigger anxiety (mental health), elevated blood pressure (physical health), increased alcohol use (coping health), and relationship tension (social health) (Richardson et al., 2013; Sweet et al., 2013). Mental health and finances relate bidirectionally—debt-related depression may lead to unopened bills and late fees increasing financial stress and amplifying the original issues (Richardson et al., 2013). These effects create compounding feedback loops, worsening symptoms, and potentially leading to more expenses that further compound financial stress (Mukherjee & Nobles-Knight, 2013).

Complex systems exhibit "quenched disorder"—low-level randomness allowing adaptation while maintaining stability (Theise, 2023). In the financial health domain, this manifests as unpredictable yet bounded responses to financial challenges. While outcomes cannot be precisely predicted, patterns emerge—some households build resilience through social support networks while others develop problematic coping mechanisms (Anvari-Clark & Miller, 2023; Klontz et al., 2015; Stack, 1974).

At overall behavioral health levels, multi-domain interactions produce emergent well-being patterns transcending individual domain effects. Outcomes reflect complex interplay of all factors rather than simple summation of financial, mental, physical, coping, and social health impacts. This explains why interventions targeting financial concerns in combination with other treatments often yield unexpected benefits across multiple health domains, such as trauma healing with financial efficacy training producing improvements in food security (Phojanakong et al., 2020).

Feedback Networks Feedback networks are a key aspect of complexity theory. They operate through interconnected loops that either amplify (positive feedback) or stabilize (negative feedback) system changes. The financial domain participates through bidirectional relationships with other health domains.

Consider financial stress feedback cycles: Initial financial precarity increases anxiety (mental health), raising blood pressure (physical health), potentially leading to medical expenses creating additional financial strain. Without intervention, this positive feedback loop can spiral, destabilizing the person's entire behavioral health system (Mukherjee & Nobles-Knight, 2013).

Negative feedback loops maintain system stability. Financial efficacy enables better money management under stress (Dare et al., 2023). Strong social support networks provide resources buffering financial shocks (Åslund et al., 2014). Effective coping strategies help regulate emotional responses to financial challenges (Netemeyer et al., 2018). These stabilizing loops can be intentionally strengthened as interventions countering destructive positive feedback cycles. If financial stress drives increased substance use, strengthening financial efficacy through coaching while building social support networks can break amplifying cycles of financial and health problems.

Understanding feedback networks reveals why isolated interventions often fail while integrated approaches succeed. Simply advising someone to budget money proves less effective than connecting them with trauma-informed financial empowerment groups (Phojanakong et al., 2020). Effective interventions must address positive feedback loops that amplify problems while strengthening negative feedback loops promoting stability. Combining financial coaching with stress management and social support creates mutually reinforcing benefits across domains (Archuleta et al., 2015).

These interconnected patterns demonstrate how the financial domain functions as an integral part of the behavioral health system rather than an isolated component. Changes in any domain can cascade through networks, producing outcomes affecting overall well-being in complex and often unexpected ways.

2.3 Financial Capability and Asset Building

Financial capability and asset building (FCAB) originated with Michael Sherraden's landmark *Assets and the Poor* (1991) in response to the Great Risk Shift—the transfer of retirement responsibility from government and employer pensions to individual contribution plans like IRAs and 401(k) accounts (Hacker, 2019). Asset building was recognized as providing more than retirement savings: assets serve as safety nets against crises, cushions for entrepreneurial risks, downpayments for homeownership, and pathways to educational opportunities enabling economic mobility.

The psychological impact of assets proved equally important. Simply having a college savings account, regardless of amount, improved college attendance likelihood, especially for first-generation students (Elliott & Beverly, 2011). Asset ownership opened new possibilities and goal-setting opportunities previously unimagined (Sherraden & McBride, 2010). However, recent systematic reviews find mixed evidence for asset-building initiatives, suggesting more modest outcomes than anticipated or requiring better evaluation research (Birkenmaier et al., 2022, 2023).

The financial capability concept emerged a decade later (Johnson & Sherraden, 2007), culminating in a comprehensive framework rooted in a capabilities approach (Sherraden, 2013). This framework integrated disparate components—access to asset-building products (opportunity to act) with ability to act—into a cohesive model accounting for structural, psychological, and social influences. The framework demonstrates how supportive macro social and economic environments, micro-level financial literacy and individual behaviors, and mezzo-level product availability enable opportunities to act in one's financial best interests, resulting in reduced precarity and increased financial well-being. Without supportive influences or with marginalizing forces present, precarity increases and well-being becomes harder to achieve.

Drawing from social work's person-in-environment perspective, the framework incorporates personal agency within contextual realities. Financial actions depend on family values and culture, financial knowledge, available guidance, product availability, and crisis prevention/response abilities (Sherraden, 2013). These variables create highly contextualized processes of developing financial capability that, depending on experiences of economic marginalization or privilege, can lead to vastly different outcomes.

Those facing systemic barriers may require navigating complex bureaucracies, relying on alternative financial services, or leveraging social capital through informal support networks (Anvari-Clark & Miller, 2023; Morduch & Schneider, 2017). Conversely, those with greater socioeconomic advantages access formal education, professional advice, and wider arrays of financial products and services (Sherraden, 2013).

While individual agency plays a role, FCAB approaches emphasize institutional and structural factors shaping abilities to manage financial resources, build assets, and achieve financial well-being (Huang et al., 2015). Interventions must address individual-level factors and broader social, economic, and policy contexts creating disparities in access and opportunity. This comprehensive, equity-oriented approach recognizes complex interplay between personal and environmental factors.

Relationship to Financial Domain of Behavioral Health FCAB and the financial capability framework significantly overlap with the financial domain of behavioral health, particularly as financial efficacy drives ability to act, with outcomes relating to lowered precarity and improved financial well-being. This decision-making ability, typically framed as financial literacy within the capability framework, derives from lifelong financial socialization, financial education, and financial guidance.

Helping professionals in social, health, and financial sectors can play significant roles in this area while understanding other framework components encompassing external opportunities and influences—social determinants or drivers of financial health. Within broader social work and public health disciplines, financial topics tend to be relegated to macro or social drivers domains (Anvari-Clark, 2024), though this is changing. This book provides a deeper focus on more neglected personal-level aspects of the financial capability framework, addressing professional inattention to financial issues rather than framework limitations.

The financial capability framework's emphasis on both ability and opportunity to act aligns with complexity theory's recognition that individual outcomes emerge from interactions between personal agency and structural contexts. Understanding these interactions helps practitioners recognize when financial difficulties stem from capability deficits versus structural barriers, informing more targeted interventions that address root causes rather than symptoms alone.

2.4 Financial Interdependence

Financial interdependence illustrates how financial decisions and behaviors emerge from complex interactions within social relationships. Rather than operating in isolation, individuals' financial choices both shape and are shaped by connections to others, creating patterns transcending simple individual decision-making (Rusbult & Van Lange, 2008; Theise, 2023). This challenges the dominant narrative of financial independence as an achievable goal; in reality, financial responsibility and capability develop within fundamentally interdependent social contexts.

In financially interdependent relationships, decisions are made and resources are pooled, shared, or exchanged based on mutual obligation, trust, and reciprocity (Anvari-Clark & Miller, 2023). This takes many forms: joint banking between romantic partners, remittances to family members, informal lending within social networks, or financial support during crises (Anvari-Clark & Miller, 2023; Morduch & Schneider, 2017; Stack, 1974). For example, funeral arrangements often require community members to contribute funds, help with feasts, and provide emotional support through formal burial societies or informal family assistance (Collins et al., 2009). Notably, obligations to help can take precedence over personal needs, so individuals in precarious states may experience further hardship.

These interconnected relationships manifest across multiple scales. At the couple level, Pearson and McCoy (2024) found that people in committed relationships better weathered COVID-19 financial strain through mutual emotional and financial support, demonstrating how local interactions create resilience. In families, adult children support aging parents through direct assistance or in-kind support like shared housing, showing how financial responsibilities adapt to changing circumstances (Park, 2018).

At community levels, financial interdependence emerges through self-organizing structures, particularly in collectivistic cultures or communities with limited formal financial institution access (Danes et al., 2016; Morduch & Schneider, 2017). Rotating Savings and Credit Associations (ROSCAs) arise naturally from local and cultural interactions rather than top-down planning (Quiñones & Grier-Reed, 2023). People may simultaneously maintain individual bank accounts while participating in informal savings groups, creating overlapping financial support systems (Castro-Cosío, 2024).

Feedback Loops and System Dynamics These financial relationships operate through feedback loops that either amplify or stabilize behaviors. Positive feedback can lead to problematic escalation—excessive financial enabling or overwhelming remittance obligations. Negative feedback maintains stability through reciprocity and mutual support, preventing resource concentration or depletion in any system part (Canale et al., 2015; Stack, 1974). Healthy financial interdependence requires a balance of responsibility—sufficient structure for stability but enough flexibility for adaptation.

Behavioral Health Implications Financial interdependence's behavioral health implications are particularly evident in its relationship to social health. Financial involvement in relationships exists on a spectrum from isolation to enmeshment, with either extreme being potentially detrimental. Moderate, balanced financial interdependence—characterized by clear communication, appropriate boundaries, and reciprocity—tends to foster both financial and social well-being (Gudmunson & Danes, 2011).

This perspective helps explain how financial precarity operates within social networks. Individuals facing hardship may rely on network support through borrowing or in-kind assistance, potentially mitigating immediate impacts (Morduch & Schneider, 2017). However, obligations to support others despite limited resources can create ongoing strain (Park, 2018). Many money disorders stem from imbalanced relationship boundaries, including financial enabling, enmeshment, or infidelity (Canale et al., 2015).

Financial efficacy emerges from these complex social interactions. Strong, supportive financial relationships enhance efficacy through shared knowledge and resources (Danes et al., 2016). The "cushioning" concept suggests network support enables greater risk-taking in pursuing financial goals (Illiashenko, 2019; Warmath et al., 2021). However, cultural expectations or family obligations can constrain financial agency when people perceive lack of control over decisions due to family influence or cultural expectations.

"Black Tax" and remittance concepts frequently intersect with this dynamic. Financial responsibilities tied to social support obligations can impact personal finance management ability (Mangoma & Wilson-Prangley, 2019). This generally involves pressure to support extended family or contribute to communal resources and may divert funds from personal savings or investments, complicating financial planning and potentially perpetuating economic disadvantage cycles and associated stress.

Financial well-being is deeply intertwined with social dimensions of financial life. The Financial Well-Being Scale explicitly asks respondents about hardship entailed in giving gifts for social occasions (Consumer Financial Protection Bureau, 2017). Financially interdependent relationships can provide belonging, support, and resilience, contributing to overall well-being despite financial challenges (Quiñones & Grier-Reed, 2023). However, financial well-being can be hindered by interdependence if individuals feel burdened by others' financial needs or experience relationship conflict and strain (Jenkins et al., 2023).

Practice Implications For helping professionals trained in individualistic approaches, recognizing inherent financial interdependence patterns can transform practice. Consider how practitioners' own financial lives involve multiple interconnecting systems—retirement plans pooling resources across participants, insurance distributing risk across networks, or mortgages connecting them to complex financial markets. Simple practices like contributing to a niece's college savings or helping an adult child through crisis exemplify present (if unrecognized) financial interdependence.

Understanding such connections helps practitioners by revealing how financial behaviors emerge from interactions between individual choices and social contexts. Rather than viewing financial decisions as purely personal, practitioners can better understand how clients' financial lives are shaped by and shape relationships with family, community, and institutions (Park, 2018).

This systems-level understanding enables more effective interventions working with, rather than against, existing financial interdependence patterns. When practitioners recognize financial interdependence as a natural feature of complex social systems rather than cultural peculiarity, they can better help clients navigate financial challenges by supporting beneficial financial networks while establishing healthy boundaries, or helping them understand how financial decisions ripple through social relationships (Danes et al., 2016; Stack, 1974).

2.5 Family Theories

Several theories from family science provide insight into relationships between the financial domain and other behavioral health areas. Life course theory and stress and resilience theory offer contextually informed understandings of how financial health is shaped over varying time spans.

Life Course Theory Life course theory examines how individuals' lives are shaped by the interplay of various factors across different life stages (Allen & Henderson, 2017; Elder et al., 2003). It analyzes how historical, social, and personal contexts influence life trajectories from birth to death through key elements: linked lives, agency, historical and social context, timing, generations, and cumulative advantage and disadvantage.

Linked Lives refers to interconnected and interdependent individual lives where one person's experiences and choices significantly impact others (Elder et al., 2003). In financial interdependence contexts, linked lives are evident in how financial decisions, resources, and obligations are shared and negotiated within families and social networks (Anvari-Clark & Miller, 2023). Parents' financial choices profoundly affect children's economic opportunities and outcomes, while adult children may provide financial support to aging parents or family members in need. Individual financial well-being is closely tied to loved ones' and communities' financial well-being, highlighting the importance of considering social relationships and networks in understanding and addressing financial challenges and commensurate mental health challenges (Umberson, 2017).

Agency refers to individuals' ability to make choices and take actions shaping life trajectories within the constraints and opportunities provided by social and historical contexts (Elder et al., 2003). Financial efficacy—belief in one's ability to manage financial challenges and achieve financial goals—represents key agency manifestation in the financial domain (Ferraro & Shippee, 2009). Individuals with higher financial efficacy levels engage more in positive financial behaviors like saving, investing, and seeking professional advice, contributing to greater financial well-being over time (Shippee et al., 2012). However, financial domain agency can be constrained by factors like lack of access to financial resources and education, discrimination, and structural inequalities, limiting individuals' ability to make effective financial choices and achieve desired outcomes (Huang et al., 2015).

Timing refers to how life events and transitions impact individuals' outcomes depending on when they occur in the life course and how they interact with factors like age, development, and social roles (Elder et al., 2003). In the financial domain, timing has significant implications for building financial efficacy, accumulating wealth, and achieving financial well-being over time (Wilkinson et al., 2019). Early career investments in education and skill development provide strong foundations for future earnings and financial stability, while delayed labor market entry or caregiving-related interruptions can limit long-term financial prospects (Shippee et al., 2012). Similarly, timing of major financial decisions—purchasing homes, starting businesses, or saving for retirement—can have lasting impacts on financial trajectories depending on market conditions, interest rates, and personal circumstances (Wilkinson et al., 2019).

Cumulative Advantage and Disadvantage refer to how early life experiences and conditions compound over time, leading to widening disparities in health, wealth, and well-being between individuals and groups (Shippee et al., 2012). In the financial domain, early access to financial resources, education, and opportunities provides foundations for long-term stability and growth, while early experiences of financial hardship, discrimination, and exclusion create lasting barriers to financial well-being (Willson et al., 2007). Institutional and systemic factors—racial and gender wealth gaps, predatory lending practices, and unequal financial service access—exacerbate these disparities over the life course, significantly impacting mental and physical health, social relationships, and overall quality of life (Wilkinson et al., 2019).

Stress and Resilience Theory Stress and resilience theory provides frameworks for understanding how individuals and families adapt to and cope with stressful life events and circumstances (Allen & Henderson, 2017). The theory emphasizes both stressor nature and severity, as well as resources and protective factors individuals and families can draw upon to maintain well-being facing adversity.

The **ABC-X model** of family stress posits that stressor event (A) impact on family functioning is mediated by family resources (B) and their event perception (C), resulting in family stress or crisis level (X) (Rosino, 2016). For example, in job loss or housing instability cases (A), crisis severity (X) experienced by a young couple depends on financial resources, social support, and coping skills (B), as well as their situation appraisal and belief in their ability to overcome challenges (C); many of the components of their financial efficacy.

Stressor Events are challenging or disruptive experiences that strain individuals and families—financial hardship, illness, or relationship conflicts (Allen & Henderson, 2017). In financial health contexts, stressor events include job loss, medical debt, or legal fees from substance use disorders. These stressors significantly impact multiple behavioral health domains, including: mental health (stress, anxiety, depression), social health (strained relationships, isolation), and physical health (chronic illness, lack of healthcare access) (Heo et al., 2024).

Family Resilience refers to families' ability to bounce back from adversity and maintain healthy functioning facing stressful life events (Allen & Henderson, 2017). Resilient families are characterized by cohesion, flexibility, open communication, and shared purpose. In job loss and housing instability cases, resilient couples may draw strength from strong marital bonds, maintain positive outlooks, and actively seek support and resources to navigate crises.

The **Double ABC-X model** extends the original by considering cumulative impact of multiple stressors over time, known as pile-up stressors (McCubbin & Patterson, 1983). Pile-up stressors can be particularly relevant for minority families experiencing chronic and interconnected stressors related to marginalized status—ongoing financial strain, discrimination, and lack of resource access. For example, families dealing with substance use disorder consequences and legal fees who also belong to minority groups may face additional pile-up stressors like job insecurity, housing discrimination, and inadequate healthcare access, compounding initial stressor event impacts on mental and physical health (Asebedo & Wilmarth, 2017).

These family theories demonstrate how financial experiences are embedded in larger social and temporal contexts, providing practitioners with frameworks for understanding how financial challenges both emerge from and contribute to broader patterns of advantage, disadvantage, and resilience across the life course.

2.6 Financial Socialization

Family financial socialization theory posits that individuals form financial knowledge, attitudes, and behaviors through interactions within social environments, including peers, religious institutions, schools, media, romantic partners, and personal experiences, with family units during early formative years playing the most crucial role (Curran et al., 2018; Gudmunson & Danes, 2011; LeBaron & Kelley, 2021). This process involves transmission of financial norms and practices from parents to children, where parental guidance and modeling play crucial roles in developing financial literacy and responsible behaviors—or passing on problematic beliefs and behaviors (LeBaron & Kelley, 2021).

Research indicates financial socialization encompasses active participation in financial practices and discussions within families rather than only passive information absorption (LeBaron & Kelley, 2021). Overt financial education provided by parents is positively associated with healthier financial management behaviors in emerging adults (LeBaron et al., 2019). The family financial socialization model suggests that financial behaviors learned in childhood significantly influence adult financial well-being, highlighting long-term impacts of early socialization experiences (Acharya & Poudel, 2023).

Theoretical Perspectives and Life Course Timing Several theoretical perspectives illuminate financial socialization's significance, including life course theory, financial interdependence, and the financial capability framework. The concept of timing—impact of event and stage sequences along the life course—is particularly relevant. Early modeling and explicit education on financial processes and products help set foundations for later well-being through activities like taking children to banks to open first accounts, modeling and teaching money planning and allocation according to values, learning from choice outcomes, and managing first credit cards and bill payments to build healthy credit profiles. With these skills and tools obtained during adolescence and early adulthood, individuals develop strong foundations for financial efficacy, leading to abilities to effectively prevent, mitigate, or navigate financial shocks and life's vagaries generally.

Cultural Dimensions and Financial Interdependence Financial socialization is deeply rooted in culture, where many expressions of financial interdependence are modeled and perpetuated. These include watching parents make regular contributions according to religious teachings, observing how parents share money with friends or extended family during crises, seeing provision for elders' financial needs, or attending savings group meetings or having group leaders visit homes. Such observations and experiences teach children lessons in reciprocity and responsibility for community well-being, appropriate help-seeking behaviors, and when problematic money behaviors may be formed or perpetuated.

Financial Capability Framework Integration Within the financial capability framework, financial socialization is a primary contributor to ability to act in one's financial best interest (referred to as financial literacy). Alongside financial education and financial guidance components, financial socialization is where early assumptions, biases, and patterns for literacy development are formed. It may play an outsized and moderating role on other components—Pahlevan Sharif and Naghavi (2020) found that parental financial socialization (through both modeling and explicit teaching) accounted for over 50% of variance in financial information seeking behavior from educational resources or advisors.

Furthermore, financial socialization contributes significantly to overall financial well-being (Acharya & Poudel, 2023). Children may be taught that sharing personal money topics with others outside family is inappropriate, creating distrust or unwillingness to seek financial professional guidance. Or they may find that financial education delivered in schools or community agencies promulgates financial independence narratives at odds with their interdependence obligations. Thus, financial socialization may profoundly shape situations and abilities to effect behavior improvements.

2.7 Scarcity

Mullainathan and Shafir (2013a, 2013b) advance scarcity as a mindset arising when individuals lack sufficient resources—sleep, time, or money—leading to heightened focus on immediate needs at the expense of long-term goals. This scarcity mindset significantly affects cognitive functioning and financial decision-making through decreased mental bandwidth and tunneling effects.

Mental bandwidth pertains to cognitive resources available to make and carry out decisions. Experiencing unexpected medical debt and worrying about payment reduces ability to control impulses and make beneficial decisions, negatively impacting already precarious financial situations. **Tunneling** is focus on immediate issues with inability to thoughtfully consider secondary and tertiary consequences. For instance, someone facing pending eviction may focus all their attention on preventing homelessness by the deadline. They will be willing to consider high-interest payday loans or renting places requiring 80% of income because such options are available and secure housing past eviction dates, meeting urgent needs. However, these options simply postpone additional financial difficulties through increased debt or inability to meet new rent obligations. Because of tunneling effects and immediate focus, people become cognitively unable to consider subsequent implications and longer-term housing sustainability.

Combined, reduced mental bandwidth and tunneling effects from scarce resources hinder people, regardless of mental and demographic characteristics, from making financial decisions or carrying out behaviors improving overall well-being.

Research Evidence on Scarcity and Cognitive Performance Several studies explore relationships between financial scarcity and cognitive performance. In a large meta-analysis, de Almeida et al. (2024) found that scarcity negatively impacts cognitive performance. Severity and timing of scarcity affected this relationship, with more extreme scarcity levels and scarcity experienced in adulthood or throughout lifetimes having larger impacts on cognitive dysfunction compared to childhood scarcity. Additionally, as people experiencing scarcity seek government and social supports, administrative burdens required to access and maintain such supports may further erode mental bandwidth abilities (de Bruijn, 2021).

Psychological Impact and Consumer Behavior Financial scarcity's psychological impact extends beyond immediate decision-making. Hamilton et al. (2019) introduce a framework that sheds light on the ways in which financial scarcity shapes consumer behavior. The framework considers four distinct perspectives: resource scarcity, choice restriction, social comparison, and environmental uncertainty. Additionally, it takes into account the different temporal stages consumers go through when faced with financial constraints, namely, reacting, coping, and adapting. Although the framework acknowledges the clear negative consequences of financial constraints, it also highlights the resilience of consumers and their ability to develop coping mechanisms and adaptive strategies in response to these constraints, such as becoming more interdependent with others. This emphasizes that while financial scarcity can be detrimental, consumers are not necessarily helpless in the face of these challenges. Instead, they can actively work to mitigate the impact of financial constraints on their lives by employing various strategies and adjusting their behavior over time.

Finally, a study by Hamilton et al. (2024) offers insights into the potential benefits of basic income programs in addressing the negative effects of financial scarcity on mental health. The researchers conducted a pilot study on a guaranteed income program and found that participants reported significant improvements in their overall mental well-being. By providing a stable source of income, the program helped alleviate the stress and anxiety participants experienced due to financial insecurity. These findings underscore the promising role that interventions, such as annuities or basic income programs, can play in mitigating the detrimental impact of financial scarcity on individuals' well-being. By directly addressing the root cause of financial stress and anxiety, these interventions can create a more supportive environment that promotes mental health and resilience in the face of economic challenges.

Scarcity's Relationship with Financial Efficacy Beyond direct impacts on financial stress and anxiety, scarcity has notable intertwined relationships with financial efficacy affecting financial and behavioral health. Zhang et al. (2023) found that a sense of financial scarcity leads to increased anxiety, thereby reducing financial efficacy. Notably, this relationship was weakened when people had strong social support—evidence of interdependence and social health importance in mitigating financial and mental health challenges. The cushioning concept (where family is known to be "if-needed" safety nets) helps explain this dynamic. Knowing family will provide support gives peace of mind to maintain confidence, effectively problem-solve, and make good decisions.

Acute vs. Chronic Scarcity Not all scarcity is the same. Chen and Warmath (2022) distinguished between acute and chronic scarcity, similar to acute versus chronic stress distinctions. They found (correlationally) that people can wield efficacy, problem-solve better, and develop different coping strategies when experiencing acute scarcity compared to chronic scarcity conditions. They also found acute scarcity was associated with higher financial well-being levels and seeking professional help, leading to better outcomes across myriad behavioral health domains. Additionally, duration and intensity also matter. As resources become insufficient to repeatedly address financial scarcity, efficacy erodes. Someone can be creative, but if problem-solving tools are exhausted, no amount of budgeting will prevent poverty. With reduced bandwidth and increased tunneling, people become less adaptable, less able to manage risk, and less likely to find their own ways out of predicaments.

This understanding of scarcity theory provides insights into why traditional financial education often fails during times of financial stress: a participant simply cannot focus on learning new behaviors when their attention is completely focused on more pressing matters. Thus, interventions must account for cognitive limitations imposed by resource constraints while building supportive environments that expand mental bandwidth and decision-making capacity.

2.8 Determinants and Drivers of Health

The language used to describe factors affecting health outcomes continues to evolve, reflecting deeper understandings of human agency, social contexts, and systemic influences. Just as this book purposefully uses the broader term "financial efficacy" rather than "financial self-efficacy" to encompass both individual and collective capabilities in financial management, a similar evolution is occurring in the broader discourse of how to describe fundamental causes and protective and risk factors that influence health.

The World Health Organization defines the widely-used term "social determinants of health" as "the conditions in which people are born, grow, work, live, and age, and the wider set of forces and systems shaping the conditions of daily life" (n.d.). These include economic policies, social systems, development agendas, social norms, and political structures, and the privileges and inequities that they perpetuate. However, the word "determinants" can suggest an inevitability that hinders both individual and collective capacity for change.

In response, many institutions are now adopting the more dynamic term "drivers of health." This phrasing better captures the complex interplay between individual agency and systemic factors in shaping health outcomes (Lumpkin et al., 2021). "Drivers" acknowledges that while social conditions significantly influence health, these conditions themselves can be influenced and changed through individual and collective action.

Reframing Practice Opportunities A common misconception among clinicians involves viewing financial matters as exclusively macro-level determinants outside their scope of practice or influence. While financial systems and economic policies operate at institutional levels, this oversimplified view overlooks multiple levels at which finances affect behavioral health outcomes and can lead practitioners to miss crucial intervention opportunities. Behaviorally oriented financial concerns manifest across different social levels, such as at individual levels through current money management stress impacting mental health (Asebedo & Wilmarth, 2017), at family levels through strain on relationship dynamics (Stack & Meredith, 2018), and at community levels through obliged sharing of financial resources (Mangoma & Wilson-Prangley, 2019).

Clinicians have meaningful opportunities to address financial concerns within their scope of practice, and research demonstrates that doing so improves behavioral health outcomes. Practitioners can screen for financial strain during assessment, incorporate financial goals into treatment planning, and make appropriate referrals to financial professionals when needed. Studies show that when practitioners help clients navigate financial barriers to care or connect them with financial coaching services, both health and financial outcomes improve (White et al., 2022). This requires understanding how drivers, causes, factors, and outcomes relate and how effects help or hinder intervention efforts.

Fundamental vs. Proximal Causes Framework Understanding relationships between financial factors and health outcomes requires distinguishing between different types of causes. Link and Phelan's (1995) seminal work on fundamental causes of disease provides a crucial framework for understanding how different financial and other matters can operate as "drivers of health" or components of behavioral health themselves. This framework helps differentiate between proximal causes (immediate factors affecting health) and distal or fundamental causes (underlying social conditions giving rise to health disparities).

Consider a client experiencing financial anxiety who works in food services. The proximal cause of anxiety might be unpredictable scheduling and fluctuating hours that make budgeting difficult. However, the fundamental cause—or driver of health—is the widespread shift toward just-in-time scheduling practices that transfer business risks onto workers. While individual interventions like emergency savings strategies may help manage symptoms, the underlying driver continues creating vulnerability. This distinction helps practitioners understand why certain interventions may have limited effectiveness while avoiding attributing lack of progress to personal failure.

Key Pathways of Health Drivers The drivers of health framework illuminate several key pathways through which social conditions affect both financial and behavioral health outcomes:

Healthcare Access represents a fundamental driver with clear pathways to health outcomes (Compton & Shim, 2015). In the United States, limited insurance coverage and provider availability can lead to delayed preventive care and reliance on emergency services. Resulting financial outcomes often include medical debt, reduced work capacity affecting income, and depleted savings.

Housing Situations demonstrate how environmental conditions drive both health and financial outcomes. Poor neighborhood conditions and housing instability create higher living costs and maintenance expenses, while environmental hazards affect health. Research by Desmond and Kimbro (2015) shows how these factors combine to trigger cycles of financial hardship and depression.

Early Life Experiences shape lifelong trajectories through multiple pathways. Adverse childhood experiences (ACEs), including poverty and family instability, affect cognitive development and financial socialization. As Pearlin et al. (2005) note, these early experiences create cascading effects influencing both financial efficacy and health outcomes throughout life.

Discrimination operates as pervasive driver affecting multiple domains simultaneously. Systemic racism, gender bias, and other forms of prejudice create barriers to economic opportunities and wealth building, resulting in reduced access to financial services and intergenerational wealth gaps. Williams and Sternthal (2010) demonstrate how these patterns compound over time.

Practice Implications This framework enhances understanding of financial health behaviors in several ways. It reveals how broader social forces create and perpetuate financial precarity, explains disparate outcomes across populations, and suggests more effective intervention points by addressing both proximal and fundamental causes.

For practitioners, this understanding supports more holistic approaches to care. Rather than viewing financial concerns as outside their scope, they can integrate financial awareness into clinical practice while recognizing systemic constraints. Specific actions might include screening for financial strain, incorporating financial goals into treatment planning, and advocating for systemic changes addressing fundamental drivers of health inequities. This dual focus on individual and structural factors allows practitioners to provide meaningful support while acknowledging broader contexts shaping client outcomes.

2.9 Conclusion

The theoretical frameworks explored in this chapter provide helping professionals with conceptual tools for understanding the complex relationships between financial circumstances and behavioral health outcomes. Rather than competing explanations, these multidisciplinary perspectives complement each other, each contributing unique insights that together form a comprehensive foundation for effective practice across the financial domain of behavioral health.

Complexity theory serves as the overarching framework, revealing how financial health emerges from dynamic interactions between multiple domains rather than isolated factors. This perspective helps practitioners understand why financial stress can trigger cascading effects across mental, physical, social, and coping domains, and why interventions targeting single components may have limited effectiveness. The emergent properties of complex systems remind us that small changes in one area can have profound effects throughout the entire system, suggesting strategic intervention points that might otherwise be overlooked.

The financial capability and asset-building framework grounds us in practical realities, demonstrating how individual agency operates within structural constraints. This dual focus on ability and opportunity to act helps practitioners distinguish between situations where clients need skill development or behavior modification, versus those requiring advocacy for systemic change. By recognizing how institutional factors enable or constrain financial actions, practitioners can design more effective interventions that address root causes rather than symptoms alone.

Financial interdependence theory fundamentally challenges Western assumptions about individual financial responsibility, revealing how financial decisions emerge from complex social relationships and cultural obligations. This perspective is particularly valuable for practitioners working with diverse populations, as it helps them understand how financial behaviors that may appear problematic through an individualistic lens often reflect adaptive responses to interdependent social contexts. Recognizing these patterns enables more culturally responsive interventions that work with, rather than against, existing social support systems.

Life course and family stress theories illuminate how financial experiences unfold over time and across generations. The concepts of cumulative advantage and disadvantage help explain persistent disparities in financial outcomes, while understanding timing effects reveals critical intervention windows. Family stress theory provides frameworks for understanding how financial stressors affect family functioning and relationships, emphasizing the importance of addressing family dynamics in financial interventions.

Financial socialization theory traces how early family experiences shape lifelong money attitudes and behaviors, often in unconscious ways. This understanding helps practitioners recognize how past experiences influence present financial behaviors and identify opportunities for addressing harmful patterns while building on positive foundations. The cultural dimensions of financial socialization are particularly important for understanding how different populations transmit financial knowledge and values across generations.

Scarcity theory elucidates the psychological mechanisms through which financial strain affects cognitive functioning and decision-making. By understanding how resource constraints impair mental bandwidth and create tunneling effects, practitioners can design interventions that account for these cognitive limitations while building supportive environments that expand decision-making capacity. The distinction between acute and chronic scarcity provides important insights into why traditional financial education often fails during times of financial stress.

Finally, the evolution from "social determinants" to "drivers of health" language helps practitioners understand their role in addressing financial concerns by emphasizing the dynamic interplay between individual agency and systemic factors. This framework assists practitioners in distinguishing between proximal and fundamental causes while recognizing intervention opportunities at multiple levels. Rather than viewing financial matters as exclusively macro-level concerns outside their scope, practitioners can integrate financial awareness into clinical practice while advocating for broader systemic changes.

These theoretical foundations have important implications for practice across helping professions. They suggest that effective interventions must address both individual and structural factors, recognize the social nature of financial decisions, account for cognitive limitations imposed by financial stress, and work within existing cultural frameworks rather than imposing external values. Most importantly, they demonstrate that financial concerns are legitimate behavioral health issues deserving attention from all helping professionals, not just those in explicitly financial roles.

As the field continues to evolve, these theoretical frameworks provide the foundation for developing more sophisticated and effective approaches to addressing the financial domain of behavioral health. By understanding how financial circumstances influence well-being through multiple pathways, practitioners can better serve their clients while contributing to broader efforts to promote health equity and social justice.

References

Acharya, P., & Poudel, O. (2023). Interplay of financial socialization, financial behavior, and adult financial well-being. *Management Dynamics, 26*(1), 33–42. https://doi.org/10.3126/md.v26i1.59149

Allen, K. R., & Henderson, A. C. (2017). *Family theories: Foundations and applications*. Wiley-Blackwell.

American Psychiatric Association. (2022). *Diagnostic and statistical manual of mental disorders (5th, Text Revision ed.)*. American Psychiatric Association. https://dsm.psychiatryonline.org/doi/book/10.1176/appi.books.9780890425787

Anvari-Clark, J. (2024). Integrating financial and economic justice content into social work education. *Journal of Teaching in Social Work, 44*(3), 245–260. https://doi.org/10.1080/08841233.2024.2344464

Anvari-Clark, J., & Miller, J. (2023). Financial interdependence: A social perspective. *Encyclopedia, 3*(3), 996–1008. https://doi.org/10.3390/encyclopedia3030072

Anvari-Clark, J., & Rose, T. (2023). Financial behavioral health and investment risk willingness: Implications for the racial wealth gap. *International Journal of Environmental Research and Public Health, 20*(10), 5835. https://doi.org/10.3390/ijerph20105835

Archuleta, K. L., Burr, E. A., Bell Carlson, M., Ingram, J., Irwin Kruger, L., Grable, J., & Ford, M. (2015). Solution focused financial therapy: A brief report of a pilot study. *Journal of Financial Therapy, 6*(1). https://doi.org/10.4148/1944-9771.1081

Archuleta, K. L., Mielitz, K. S., Jayne, D., & Le, V. (2020). Financial goal setting, financial anxiety, and solution-focused financial therapy (SFFT): A quasi-experimental outcome study. *Contemporary Family Therapy, 42*(1), 68–76. https://doi.org/10.1007/s10591-019-09501-0

Archuleta, K. L., Glenn, C., Lawson, D. R., Clady, J. P., & Solomon, S. (2021). I know I should, but do I do it? Connecting covert and overt financial behaviors. *Journal of Financial Counseling and Planning, 32*(3), 15.

Asebedo, S. D., & Wilmarth, M. J. (2017). Does how we feel about financial strain matter for mental health? *Journal of Financial Therapy, 8*(1), 62–80. https://doi.org/10.4148/1944-9771.1130

Åslund, C., Larm, P., Starrin, B., & Nilsson, K. W. (2014). The buffering effect of tangible social support on financial stress: influence on psychological well-being and psychosomatic symptoms in a large sample of the adult general population. *International Journal for Equity in Health, 13*(1), 85. https://doi.org/10.1186/s12939-014-0085-3

Birkenmaier, J., Maynard, B., & Kim, Y. (2022). Interventions designed to improve financial capability: A systematic review. *Research on Social Work Practice, 32*(6), 651–677. https://doi.org/10.1177/10497315221080127

Birkenmaier, J., Kim, Y., & Maynard, B. (2023). Financial outcomes of interventions to improve financial capability through children's development accounts: A systematic review. *Journal of the Society for Social Work and Research, 14*(2), 523–552. https://doi.org/10.1086/716103

Bufe, S., Roll, S., Kondratjeva, O., Skees, S., & Grinstein-Weiss, M. (2022). Financial shocks and financial well-being: What builds resiliency in lower-income households? *Social Indicators Research, 161*(1), 379–407. https://doi.org/10.1007/s11205-021-02828-y

Consumer Financial Protection Bureau. (2017). *CFPB Financial well-being scale: Scale development technical report.* https://www.consumerfinance.gov/data-research/research-reports/financial-well-being-scale/

Canale, A., Archuleta, K. L., & Klontz, B. T. (2015). Money disorders. In B. T. Klontz, S. L. Britt, & K. L. Archuleta (Eds.), *Financial therapy: Theory, research, and practice* (pp. 35–68). Springer.

Castro-Cosío, A. (2024). 'Informal' financial practices in the South Bronx: Family, compadres, and acquaintances. *Journal of Family and Economic Issues, 45*, 327–342. https://doi.org/10.1007/s10834-023-09912-0

Chen, P.-J., & Warmath, D. (2022). Maintaining financial well-being: Differences in response to acute versus chronic scarcity. *Consumer Interests Annual, 68.*

Collins, D., Morduch, J., Rutherford, S., & Ruthven, O. (2009). *Portfolios of the poor: How the world's poor live on $2 a day*. Princeton University Press.

Compton, M. T., & Shim, R. S. (2015). The social determinants of mental health. *Focus, 13*(4), 419–425. https://doi.org/10.1176/appi.focus.20150017

Curran, M. A., Parrott, E., Ahn, S. Y., Serido, J., & Shim, S. (2018). Young adults' life outcomes and well-being: Perceived financial socialization from parents, the romantic partner, and young adults' own financial behaviors. *Journal of Family and Economic Issues, 39*(3), 445–456. https://doi.org/10.1007/s10834-018-9572-9

Danes, S. M., Meraz, A. A., & Landers, A. L. (2016). Cultural meanings of resource management for Mexican–Americans. *Journal of Family and Economic Issues, 37*(4), 607–623. https://doi.org/10.1007/s10834-015-9476-x

Dare, S. E., van Dijk, W. W., van Dijk, E., van Dillen, L. F., Gallucci, M., & Simonse, O. (2023). How executive functioning and financial self-efficacy predict subjective financial well-being via positive financial behaviors. *Journal of Family and Economic Issues, 44*(2), 232–248. https://doi.org/10.1007/s10834-022-09845-0

de Almeida, F., Scott, I. J., Soro, J. C., Fernandes, D., Amaral, A. R., Catarino, M. L., et al. (2024). Financial scarcity and cognitive performance: A meta-analysis. *Journal of Economic Psychology, 101*(2024), 102702. https://doi.org/10.1016/j.joep.2024.102702

de Bruijn, E.-J. (2021). *The financial and administrative burden of financially vulnerable households* (Disse, October 6). Wageningen University. Retrieved from https://research.wur.nl/en/publications/the-financial-and-administrative-burden-of-financially-vulnerable

Desmond, M., & Kimbro, R. T. (2015). Eviction's fallout: Housing, hardship, and health. *Social Forces, 94*(1), 295–324. https://doi.org/10.1093/sf/sov044

Elder, G. H., Johnson, M. K., & Crosnoe, R. (2003). The emergence and development of life course theory. In J. T. Mortimer & M. J. Shanahan (Eds.), *Handbook of the life course*. Kluwer Academic/Plenum Publishers.

Elliott, W., & Beverly, S. G. (2011). The role of savings and wealth in reducing 'wilt' between expectations and college attendance. *Journal of Children and Poverty, 17*(2), 165–185. https://doi.org/10.1080/10796126.2011.538375

Ellsworth, S. (1992). *Death in a promised land: The Tulsa Race Riot of 1921*. Louisiana State University Press. https://books.google.com/books/about/Death_in_a_Promised_Land.html?id=u9SlbjZHeHgC

Fergus, D., & Shanks, T. R. (2022). The long afterlife of slavery in asset stripping, historical memory, and family burden: Toward a third reconstruction. *Families in Society, 103*(1), 7–20. https://doi.org/10.1177/10443894211061283

Ferraro, K. F., & Shippee, T. P. (2009). Aging and cumulative inequality: How does inequality get under the skin? *The Gerontologist, 49*(3), 333–343. https://doi.org/10.1093/geront/gnp034

Green, D., & McDermott, F. (2010). Social work from inside and between complex systems: Perspectives on person-in-environment for today's social work. *British Journal of Social Work, 40*(8), 2414–2430. https://doi.org/10.1093/bjsw/bcq056

Gudmunson, C. G., & Danes, S. M. (2011). Family financial socialization: Theory and critical review. *Journal of Family and Economic Issues, 32*(4), 644–667. https://doi.org/10.1007/s10834-011-9275-y

Hacker, J. S. (2019). *The great risk shift: The new economic insecurity and the decline of the American dream* (2nd ed.). Oxford University Press.

Hamilton, R. W., Mittal, C., Shah, A., Thompson, D. V., & Griskevicius, V. (2019). How financial constraints influence consumer behavior: An integrative framework. *Journal of Consumer Psychology, 29*(2), 285–305. https://doi.org/10.1002/jcpy.1074

Hamilton, L., Choplin, V., & Paputseanos, T. (2024). From scarcity to security: Participant well-being in the first 2 years of a basic income pilot. *Analyses of Social Issues and Public Policy, 24*(1), 44–72. https://doi.org/10.1111/asap.12370

Heo, W., Yao, R., & Cho, S. H. (2024). Perceived mental and physical health during the pandemic: The role of financial stress. *Journal of Financial Counseling & Planning, 35*(2), 215–233. https://doi.org/10.1891/JFCP-2022-0108

Huang, J., Nam, Y., & Lee, E. J. (2015). Financial capability and economic hardship among low-income older asian immigrants in a supported employment program. *Journal of Family and Economic Issues, 36*(2), 239–250. https://doi.org/10.1007/s10834-014-9398-z

Illiashenko, P. (2019). "Tough Guy" vs. "Cushion" hypothesis: How does individualism affect risk-taking? *Journal of Behavioral and Experimental Finance, 24*, 100212. https://doi.org/10.1016/j.jbef.2019.04.005

Jenkins, A. I. C., Le, Y., Surachman, A., Almeida, D. M., & Fredman, S. J. (2023). Associations among financial well-being, daily relationship tension, and daily affect in two adult cohorts separated by the great recession. *Journal of Social and Personal Relationships, 40*(4), 1103–1125. https://doi.org/10.1177/02654075221105611

Johnson, E., & Sherraden, M. (2007). From financial literacy to financial capability among youth. *Journal of Sociology and Social Welfare, 34*(3), 119–145.

Klontz, B.T., & Britt, S. L. (2012). How clients' money scripts predict their financial behaviors. *Financial Planning Association, 25*(11), 33–43. Retreived November 16, 2023, from https://www.financialplanningassociation.org/article/journal/NOV12-how-clients-money-scripts-predict-their-financial-behaviors.

Klontz, B., Britt, S., Mentzer, J., & Klontz, T. (2011). Money beliefs and financial behaviors: Development of the Klontz Money Script Inventory. *Journal of Financial Therapy, 2*(1), 1–22. https://doi.org/10.4148/jft.v2i1.451

Klontz, B. T., Britt, S. L., & Archuleta, K. L. (Eds.). (2015). *Financial therapy: Theory, research, and practice*. Springer.

Klontz, B., Kahler, R., & Klontz, T. (2016). *Facilitating financial health: Tools for financial planners, coaches, and therapists* (2nd ed.). The National Underwriter Company. Retreived October 11, 2023 from https://www.nationalunderwriter.com/facilitating-financial-health-tools-for-financial-planners-coaches-and-therapists-2nd-edition-1.html.

LeBaron, A. B., & Kelley, H. H. (2021). Financial socialization: A decade in review. *Journal of Family and Economic Issues, 42*(1), 195–206. https://doi.org/10.1007/s10834-020-09736-2

LeBaron, A. B., Runyan, S. D., Jorgensen, B. L., Marks, L. D., Li, X., & Hill, E. J. (2019). Practice makes perfect: Experiential learning as a method for financial socialization. *Journal of Family Issues, 40*(4), 435–463. https://doi.org/10.1177/0192513X18812917

Link, B. G., & Phelan, J. (1995). Social conditions as fundamental causes of disease. *Journal of Health and Social Behavior, 80–94*. https://doi.org/10.2307/2626958

Lumpkin, J. R., Perla, R., Onie, R., & Seligson, R. (2021). What we need to be healthy—And how to talk about it. *Health Affairs Forefront*. https://doi.org/10.1377/forefront.20210429.335599

Mangoma, A., & Wilson-Prangley, A. (2019). Black Tax: Understanding the financial transfers of the emerging black middle class. *Development Southern Africa, 36*(4), 443–460. https://doi.org/10.1080/0376835X.2018.1516545

McCubbin, H. I., & Patterson, J. M. (1983). The family stress process: The double ABCX model of adjustment and adaptation. In H. I. M. Cubbin, M. B. Sussman, & J. M. Patterson (Eds.), *Social stress and the family* (1st ed., pp. 7–37). Routledge.

McKenzie, C. B. (2022). *Trauma after trauma – navigating financial anxiety in the postpartum period*. National Endowment for Financial Education. Retreived October 24, 2024 from https://www.nefe.org/news/2022/03/navigating-postpartum-financial-anxiety.

Morduch, J., & Schneider, R. (2017). *The financial diaries*. Princeton University Press.

Mukherjee, K., & Nobles-Knight, D. (2013). Assessment of trade-offs made by people due to financial stress from medical care in the USA. *Journal of Pharmaceutical Health Services Research, 4*(2), 95–99. https://doi.org/10.1111/jphs.12015

Mullainathan, S., & Shafir, E. (2013a). Freeing up intelligence. *Scientific American Mind, 25*(1), 58–63. https://doi.org/10.1038/scientificamericanmind0114-58

Mullainathan, S., & Shafir, E. (2013b). *Scarcity: Why having too little means so much*. Times Books, Henry Holt.

Netemeyer, R. G., Warmath, D., Fernandes, D., & Lynch, J. G. (2018). How am I doing? Perceived financial well-being, its potential antecedents, and its relation to overall well-being. *Journal of Consumer Research, 45*(1), 68–89. https://doi.org/10.1093/jcr/ucx109

Pahlevan Sharif, S., & Naghavi, N. (2020). Family financial socialization, financial information seeking behavior and financial literacy among youth. *Asia-Pacific Journal of Business Administration, 12*(2), 163–181. https://doi.org/10.1108/APJBA-09-2019-0196

Park, S. S. (2018). Life events and Black–White differences in adult children's financial assistance to mothers. *The Gerontologist, 58*(5), 883–893. https://doi.org/10.1093/geront/gnx069

Pearlin, L. I., Schieman, S., Fazio, E. M., & Meersman, S. C. (2005). Stress, health, and the life course: Some conceptual perspectives. *Journal of Health and Social Behavior, 46*(2), 205–219. https://doi.org/10.1177/002214650504600206

Pearson, B., & McCoy, M. A. (2024). Having a significant other reduced financial strain during the COVID-19 pandemic. *Journal of Financial Counseling & Planning, 35*(2), 202–214. https://doi.org/10.1891/JFCP-2022-0105

Phojanakong, P., Welles, S., Dugan, J., Booshehri, L., Brown Weida, E., & Chilton, M. (2020). Trauma-informed financial empowerment programming improves food security among families with young children. *Journal of Nutrition Education and Behavior, 52*(5), 465–473. https://doi.org/10.1016/j.jneb.2020.02.008

Quiñones, M., & Grier-Reed, T. (2023). The tanda: An informal financial practice at the intersection of culture and financial management for Mexican American families. *Journal of Family and Economic Issues.* https://doi.org/10.1007/s10834-023-09913-z

Richardson, T., Elliott, P., & Roberts, R. (2013). The relationship between personal unsecured debt and mental and physical health: A systematic review and meta-analysis. *Clinical Psychology Review, 33*(8), 1148–1162. https://doi.org/10.1016/j.cpr.2013.08.009

Rosino, M. (2016, March 21). ABC-X model of family stress and coping. In C. L. Shehan (Ed.), *The Wiley Blackwell encyclopedia of family studies*. John Wiley & Sons. https://doi.org/10.1002/9781119085621.wbefs313

Rusbult, C. E., & Van Lange, P. A. M. (2008). Why we need interdependence theory. *Social and Personality Psychology Compass, 2*(5), 2049–2070. https://doi.org/10.1111/j.1751-9004.2008.00147.x

Sherraden, M. (1991). *Assets and the poor: A new American welfare policy*. M.E. Sharpe.

Sherraden, M. (2013). Building blocks of financial capability. In J. Birkenmaier, M. Sherraden, & J. Curley (Eds.), *Financial capability and asset development: Research, education, policy, and practice* (pp. 3–43). Oxford University Press.

Sherraden, M. S., & McBride, A. M. (2010). *Striving to save: Creating policies for financial security of low-income families*. The University of Michigan Press.

Shippee, T. P., Wilkinson, L. R., & Ferraro, K. F. (2012). Accumulated financial strain and women's health over three decades. *The Journals of Gerontology Series B: Psychological Sciences and Social Sciences, 67*(5), 585–594. https://doi.org/10.1093/geronb/gbs056

Stack, C. (1974). *All our kin*. Basic Books.

Stack, R. J., & Meredith, A. (2018). The impact of financial hardship on single parents: An exploration of the journey from social distress to seeking help. *Journal of Family and Economic Issues, 39*(2), 233–242. https://doi.org/10.1007/s10834-017-9551-6

Substance Abuse and Mental Health Services Administration. (2014a). *SAMHSA's concept of trauma and guidance for a trauma-informed approach* (No. HHS Publication No. (SMA) 14-4884). Substance Abuse and Mental Health Services Administration, U.S. Department of Health and Human Services. Retreived October 25, 2024 from https://store.samhsa.gov/sites/default/files/sma14-4884.pdf

Substance Abuse and Mental Health Services Administration. (2014b). *Trauma-informed care in behavioral health services* (No.) HHS Publication No. (SMA) 13-4801). Retreived September 30, 2024 from https://store.samhsa.gov/product/tip-57-trauma-informed-care-behavioral-health-services/sma14-4816

Sweet, E., Nandi, A., Adam, E. K., & McDade, T. W. (2013). The high price of debt: Household financial debt and its impact on mental and physical health. *Social Science & Medicine, 91*, 94–100. https://doi.org/10.1016/j.socscimed.2013.05.009

Theise, N. (2023). *Notes on complexity: A scientific theory of connection, consciousness, and being*. Spiegel & Grau. Retreived January 21, 2025.

Turner, J. R., & Baker, R. M. (2019). Complexity theory: An overview with potential applications for the social sciences. *Systems, 7*(1), 4. https://doi.org/10.3390/systems7010004

Umberson, D. (2017). Black deaths matter: Race, relationship loss, and effects on survivors. *Journal of Health and Social Behavior, 58*(4), 405–420. https://doi.org/10.1177/0022146517739317

Warmath, D., Chen, P.-J., Grable, J., & Kwak, E. J. (2021). Soft landings: Extending the cushion hypothesis to financial well-being in collectivistic cultures. *Journal of Consumer Affairs, 55*(4), 1563–1590. https://doi.org/10.1111/joca.12408

White, N., Packard, K., Kalkowski, J., Walters, R., Haddad, A. R., Flecky, K., et al. (2022). Improving health through action on economic stability: Results of the finances first randomized controlled trial of financial education and coaching in single mothers of low-income. *American Journal of Lifestyle Medicine, 15598276211069537*. https://doi.org/10.1177/15598276211069537

Wilkinson, L. R., Ferraro, K. F., & Mustillo, S. A. (2019). Wealth in middle and later life: Examining the life course timing of women's health limitations. *The Gerontologist, 59*(5), 902–911. https://doi.org/10.1093/geront/gny048

Williams, D. R., & Sternthal, M. (2010). Understanding racial-ethnic disparities in health: Sociological contributions. *Journal of Health and Social Behavior, 51*(1_suppl), S15–S27. https://doi.org/10.1177/0022146510383838

Willson, A. E., Shuey, K. M., & Elder, G. H., Jr. (2007). Cumulative advantage processes as mechanisms of inequality in life course health. *American Journal of Sociology, 112*(6), 1886–1924. https://doi.org/10.1086/512712

World Health Organization. (n.d.). *Social determinants of health*. Retreived December 2, 2024 from https://www.who.int/health-topics/social-determinants-of-health

Xiao, J. J., & Kim, K. T. (2022). The able worry more? Debt delinquency, financial capability, and financial stress. *Journal of Family and Economic Issues, 43*(1), 138–152. https://doi.org/10.1007/s10834-021-09767-3

Zhang, R., Ma, Q., & Guan, D. (2023). The impact of financial scarcity on green consumption: Sequential mediating effects of anxiety and self-efficacy. *Psychology & Marketing, 40*(6), 1162–1178. https://doi.org/10.1002/mar.21801

Chapter 3
Mental Health

3.1 Introduction

The relationship between financial and mental health represents one of the most thoroughly documented and deepest connections that pertains to the financial domain of behavioral health. This bidirectional relationship creates complex feedback loops where financial difficulties can trigger or exacerbate mental health conditions, while mental health challenges simultaneously impair financial decision-making and behaviors (Asebedo & Wilmarth, 2017; Richardson et al., 2013). Understanding these interconnections is essential for helping professionals across disciplines, as financial concerns frequently underlie or complicate presenting mental health symptoms.

Research consistently demonstrates strong associations between financial precarity and poorer mental health outcomes across multiple conditions and populations (Richardson et al., 2013). However, the relationship extends beyond simple causation. Financial efficacy—one's ability and confidence to manage financial challenges—may serve as a crucial protective factor that can moderate the relationship between financial strain and mental health symptoms. This suggests that interventions targeting financial capability could yield benefits that extend far beyond financial outcomes to encompass meaningful improvements in psychological well-being.

The complexity of financial-mental health interactions reflects the broader behavioral health framework presented throughout this book. Financial stress can manifest in anxiety, depression, trauma responses, or exacerbate existing mental health conditions. Conversely, mental health symptoms like cognitive impairment, poor concentration, or impaired judgment can significantly compromise financial management abilities, creating cycles that amplify both financial and psychological distress.

Supplementary Information The online version contains supplementary material available at https://doi.org/10.1007/978-3-032-02632-3_3.

J. Anvari-Clark, *Financial and Behavioral Health for Helping Professionals*,
https://doi.org/10.1007/978-3-032-02632-3_3

This chapter examines the intersection of financial and mental health domains across major categories, exploring how financial factors influence mental health conditions and how mental health affects financial behaviors and outcomes. We address specific conditions including trauma, anxiety, depression, stress, suicide risk, psychotic or manic episodes, and neurodivergence followed by evidence-based interventions that can simultaneously improve both financial and mental well-being. Throughout, we emphasize that effective intervention requires addressing both the practical financial concerns and the psychological factors that maintain problematic patterns.

Vignette: Elena's Journey Through Financial and Mental Health Recovery *Elena, a 34-year-old single mother of two children aged 8 and 12, worked as a retail manager at a department store. Following her divorce three years earlier, she had struggled with mounting credit card debt that accumulated during the marriage, largely from unexpected medical expenses and legal fees. When the store where she worked reduced staff hours during an economic downturn, Elena's financial situation became increasingly precarious.*

Initially, Elena experienced intense anxiety about making ends meet. The physical symptoms were overwhelming—her heart would race when she checked her bank balance, and she developed persistent insomnia, lying awake calculating and recalculating her monthly expenses. During the day, she found herself snapping at her children over minor expenses like school supplies or requests for new clothes, then feeling overwhelmed with guilt about her reactions.

"I started avoiding everything related to money," Elena later recalled. "I wouldn't open bills, wouldn't check my bank account, wouldn't answer calls from numbers I didn't recognize because they might be creditors. It felt like if I didn't look at it, maybe it would just go away somehow."

As her avoidance behaviors intensified, Elena's anxiety spread beyond financial concerns. She began experiencing panic attacks during routine activities, found it increasingly difficult to concentrate at work, and withdrew from friends to avoid conversations about money or social activities that required spending. Her children noticed the changes, with her 12-year-old daughter asking if they were going to lose their house.

The situation reached a crisis point when Elena nearly fainted at work during a particularly stressful shift. A concerned supervisor encouraged her to use the company's Employee Assistance Program. During her first call with the EAP counselor, Elena broke down describing how the constant financial worry was affecting every aspect of her life.

"I feel like I'm drowning," she confided. "Every time I think about money, my heart races and I can barely breathe. I've started having nightmares about being homeless with the kids. Some days I can hardly focus at work because I'm so worried about what's going to happen to us."

The EAP counselor, recognizing the interconnected nature of Elena's financial and mental health challenges, referred her to a community mental health center that had recently implemented an integrated approach to addressing financial and psychological concerns. Her assigned therapist, Dr. Martinez, had received training in financial trauma and collaborated closely with the center's financial social worker.

During the initial assessment, Dr. Martinez identified symptoms consistent with adjustment disorder with mixed anxiety and depressed mood, triggered by Elena's financial stressors. However, rather than treating the anxiety in isolation, the treatment team developed an integrated approach that addressed both Elena's psychological symptoms and the underlying financial concerns that were maintaining her distress.

The financial social worker, James, helped Elena face her financial reality in a supportive, nonjudgmental environment. Together, they reviewed her statements and bills, created a realistic budget that prioritized essential expenses, and developed a manageable plan for addressing her debt. Meanwhile, Dr. Martinez taught Elena anxiety management techniques specifically tailored to financial triggers and helped her process the feelings of shame and failure that had become associated with her financial difficulties.

"The turning point came when I realized I wasn't broken or stupid," Elena reflected months later. "I was just overwhelmed by circumstances that would have been hard for anyone to handle. Having someone help me look at the actual numbers instead of the scary stories in my head made such a difference."

Six months into treatment, Elena had made significant progress in both domains. Her debt hadn't disappeared, but she had successfully negotiated payment plans with her creditors and had even managed to build a small emergency fund of $200. More importantly, her panic attacks had stopped, she was sleeping better, and she felt capable of having conversations with her children about money that were honest but not frightening.

"I still have debt, but now I have a plan and I'm not afraid to look at my bank account anymore," Elena explained during a follow-up session. "The anxiety is manageable now, and I've learned ways to cope when financial stress does come up. I even started talking to my kids about budgeting in a way that feels educational rather than scary."

Elena's case illustrates several key principles in addressing financial-mental health intersections. Her symptoms were real and significant, meeting criteria for a mental health diagnosis, yet they were inextricably linked to concrete financial stressors. Traditional anxiety treatment alone might have provided some symptom relief, but addressing the underlying financial concerns proved essential for sustainable recovery. The integrated approach—combining evidence-based anxiety interventions with practical financial problem-solving—created a cycle where improved financial efficacy reduced anxiety, which in turn enhanced her capacity to make sound financial decisions. This vignette demonstrates how financial precarity can trigger mental health symptoms, how mental health symptoms can worsen financial management, and how integrated interventions can break these destructive cycles. Elena's recovery required attention to both her psychological responses to financial stress and the practical financial skills needed to create genuine stability and security.

***

The intersection of financial circumstances and mental health manifests across a wide spectrum of psychological conditions and symptoms. While the specific presentations vary, several common patterns emerge: financial stressors can trigger acute mental health episodes, chronic financial precarity can contribute to the development of persistent mental health conditions, and existing mental health symptoms often impair the financial management abilities needed to achieve stability. Understanding these patterns within specific diagnostic categories helps practitioners recognize when financial factors may be contributing to mental health presentations and when mental health symptoms may be undermining financial recovery efforts. The following sections examine how financial concerns intersect with major categories of mental health conditions, providing frameworks for assessment and intervention that address both domains simultaneously.

3.2 Trauma

Trauma refers to experiences that overwhelm an individual's coping resources and create lasting impacts across multiple domains of functioning (Substance Abuse and Mental Health Services Administration [SAMHSA], 2014). Trauma responses can manifest through symptoms including intrusive thoughts, hypervigilance, avoidance behaviors, emotional numbing, and negative alterations in cognition and mood. These responses extend beyond immediate psychological symptoms to affect how individuals perceive safety, trust, and control in their environment.

Financial trauma specifically encompasses responses to financial stressors that create psychological harm and lasting effects on financial behaviors (McKenzie, 2022). It can result from acute events such as foreclosure, bankruptcy, sudden job loss, or catastrophic medical expenses, or from chronic conditions including persistent poverty, predatory lending practices, or ongoing financial instability. Symptoms often mirror other trauma responses but manifest specifically around financial activities—intrusive thoughts about financial catastrophe, hypervigilance regarding money matters, avoidance of financial tasks, and emotional numbing when confronting financial realities.

Trauma's Impact on Financial Functioning Regardless of the origin of the trauma, responses can directly compromise the cognitive and emotional capacities essential for effective financial management. Hypervigilance can create obsessive financial monitoring while making long-term planning difficult. Avoidance symptoms may lead to complete disengagement from financial responsibilities, creating cycles where avoided tasks accumulate into overwhelming crises.

Executive functioning deficits are also common (American Psychiatric Association [APA], 2022). Trauma can impair working memory needed for tracking multiple financial obligations, create attention problems that interfere with budgeting and planning, and compromise judgment and impulse control, leading to decisions that provide short-term emotional relief but create long-term instability. The shame and self-blame frequently associated with trauma can prevent individuals from seeking help with financial problems or accessing resources that could improve their situation.

Bidirectional Relationships Financial stressors significantly impact trauma recovery processes. Financial instability perpetuates the sense of danger that maintains trauma symptoms, keeping the nervous system activated in survival mode. Financial precarity can trigger trauma responses even when current stressors are unrelated to original trauma, as the sensitized stress response system reacts intensely to financial threats.

For people who have experienced trauma, financial dependence on others may recreate dynamics of powerlessness and vulnerability that echo original trauma experiences. This is particularly relevant for those who have faced interpersonal violence, where financial abuse often accompanied other forms of abuse (Abdul Latif Jameel Poverty Action Lab (J-PAL), 2022). Traditional mental health interventions may provide limited benefit when underlying financial traumas remain unaddressed, while financial counseling may be ineffective if trauma responses interfere with the necessary skill and behavior development.

Understanding trauma's impact on financial functioning and vice versa provides essential context, enabling more effective intervention planning that addresses underlying connections between psychological and financial well-being rather than treating these concerns in isolation. Practitioners should sequence interventions appropriately and recognize when collaborative care involving both mental health and financial professionals may be most beneficial. The principles of trauma-informed care—including safety, trustworthiness, choice, collaboration, and empowerment—apply to financial interventions with trauma survivors (SAMHSA, 2014). Creating psychological safety around financial discussions, building collaborative relationships that respect client autonomy, and empowering clients to make informed financial choices all support both trauma recovery and financial stability.

3.3 Anxiety

Anxiety disorders represent the most common class of mental health conditions, characterized by excessive fear, anxiety, and related behavioral disturbances (APA, 2022). The physiological arousal, cognitive symptoms (excessive worry, catastrophic thinking, concentration difficulties), and behavioral symptoms (avoidance, restlessness) of anxiety directly affect financial decision-making abilities and often manifest in financial contexts as procrastination, excessive account checking, or avoidance of financial planning—all examples of impaired occupational functioning.

Financial Anxiety as a Distinct Phenomenon Financial anxiety represents persistent worry about financial matters that often exceeds what objective circumstances warrant (Archuleta et al., 2013, 2020). Unlike financial stress that corresponds to actual difficulties, financial anxiety can persist even when circumstances improve. This anxiety focuses specifically on money-related concerns and can occur independently or as part of broader anxiety presentations.

Financial anxiety manifests cognitively through persistent worry about future financial security, catastrophic thinking about potential outcomes, and rumination about past financial decisions. Physiologically, it triggers the same stress responses as other anxiety disorders—increased heart rate, muscle tension, sleep disturbances—when confronting financial tasks. Behaviorally, it creates patterns that paradoxically worsen financial circumstances through avoidance of bill payment, account checking, or financial decisions, or alternatively through compulsive behaviors like excessive monitoring or constantly seeking reassurance.

The Anxiety-Financial Management Cycle Anxiety significantly impairs cognitive processes essential for financial management (Shapiro & Burchell, 2012). Worry and rumination consume working memory needed for budgeting and planning. Concentration difficulties interfere with sustained attention required for financial tasks like reading policies or researching options. Decision-making becomes compromised as anxious individuals exhibit intolerance of uncertainty, leading to financial paralysis or hasty decisions made to reduce discomfort. Safety-seeking behaviors manifest as excessive financial conservatism that impedes long-term growth. While maintaining emergency funds is prudent, anxiety-driven behaviors often involve excessive risk aversion that prevents appropriate investment opportunities or career advancement.

Financial Stressors and Anxiety Maintenance Financial stressors can trigger initial anxiety episodes and maintain symptoms over time. The uncertainty inherent in financial situations—variable income, investment performance, economic conditions—is particularly problematic for anxiety-prone individuals, as uncertainty serves as a primary anxiety trigger. Financial instability creates chronic stress that sensitizes the anxiety response system, making individuals more reactive to various stressors.

The cognitive patterns of anxiety—overestimating threat and underestimating coping abilities—become particularly problematic in financial contexts. Manageable financial challenges become overwhelming when viewed through anxious cognition, leading to avoidance behaviors that worsen original problems. Treatment approaches must account for these bidirectional relationships, addressing both psychological symptoms and practical financial concerns to achieve sustainable improvement.

3.4 Depression

Depression affects approximately 8.3% of U.S. adults annually (National Institute of Mental Health (NIMH), 2023). Major depressive disorder is characterized by persistent sadness, anhedonia (loss of interest or pleasure), and various cognitive, behavioral, and physical symptoms that significantly impair functioning (APA, 2022). The cognitive symptoms of depression—including difficulty concentrating, indecisiveness, and negative thought patterns—severely compromise financial decision-making abilities, while the behavioral symptoms of withdrawal and reduced activity often lead to financial neglect and avoidance.

Bidirectional Relationship Between Depression and Financial Health The relationship between depression and financial circumstances operates through multiple interconnected pathways, creating cycles that can either perpetuate or alleviate both conditions. Financial precarity creates chronic stress that alters neurobiological systems involved in mood regulation, while the shame and self-blame often associated with financial difficulties can trigger or worsen depressive episodes (Richardson et al., 2013). Conversely, depression impairs the executive functioning, motivation, and energy needed for effective financial management, often leading to behaviors that worsen financial situations.

Depression's cognitive symptoms—including concentration difficulties, indecisiveness, and pessimistic thinking patterns—significantly impair financial problem-solving abilities (Asebedo & Wilmarth, 2017). These can make routine financial tasks feel overwhelming, leading to procrastination on bill payments, tax filing, or benefit applications. Anhedonia reduces motivation to engage in financial planning or pursue income-generating activities, while hopelessness creates beliefs that financial improvement is impossible.

Depression's Impact on Financial Behaviors Depression manifests in specific financial behavior patterns that often exacerbate financial precarity. Avoidance behaviors become prominent as individuals postpone opening bills, checking account balances, or addressing mounting financial problems, such as debt (Richardson et al., 2013). This financial avoidance temporarily reduces associated anxiety but allows problems to compound through late fees, missed opportunities, and deteriorating credit.

The energy depletion characteristic of depression affects work performance and attendance, potentially leading to reduced income or job loss (Sweet et al., 2013). Social withdrawal limits access to financial support networks and professional opportunities, while the tendency toward negative self-evaluation undermines confidence in financial decision-making abilities. Some individuals conduct impulsive spending as a temporary mood-lifting (coping) strategy, creating additional financial strain despite providing momentary relief from depressive symptoms.

Depression as a Barrier to Financial Recovery Depression creates significant obstacles to financial improvement by undermining the sustained effort required for financial behavior change. The cognitive distortions common in depression—such as all-or-nothing thinking and catastrophizing—make financial setbacks feel insurmountable and permanent. Low self-efficacy beliefs lead individuals to doubt their ability to improve financial circumstances, reducing motivation to seek help or implement financial strategies. Treatment approaches must address both the psychological symptoms of depression and practical financial concerns simultaneously, creating synergistic momentum for recovery in both areas.

3.5 Stress

Stress represents the psychological and physiological response to perceived threats to well-being, differing from anxiety in that it typically corresponds directly to actual challenges rather than excessive worry about hypothetical situations (Sinclair & Cheung, 2016). This characterizes the difference between financial stress and financial anxiety, as well. Financial stress affects individuals across all income levels, though its manifestations and consequences vary significantly based on available resources and coping mechanisms. Unlike other stressors that may be temporary, financial stress often becomes chronic due to the ongoing nature of financial obligations and economic uncertainty.

Physiological and Cognitive Impact of Financial Stress Financial stress activates the body's stress response system, triggering the release of cortisol and adrenaline that prepare the body for "fight or flight" responses (Sweet et al., 2013). Chronic activation of this system due to persistent financial pressures leads to elevated blood pressure, compromised immune function, sleep disturbances, and digestive problems. The cognitive impacts are equally significant, as financial stress consumes mental bandwidth essential for effective decision-making and problem-solving.

Mullainathan and Shafir's (2013) research on scarcity demonstrates that financial stress creates a "cognitive tax" that reduces performance on cognitive tasks unrelated to the stressor itself. This bandwidth reduction impairs working memory, attention regulation, and executive functioning—precisely the cognitive resources needed for effective financial management. The resulting cognitive overload leads to decisions that may provide short-term relief but create longer-term difficulties, such as accepting high-interest loans or avoiding necessary financial planning.

The Stress-Financial Management Cycle Financial stress creates a self-perpetuating cycle where stress impairs the very capabilities needed to address financial challenges effectively. Stressed individuals exhibit reduced impulse control, leading to poor financial decisions made to reduce immediate discomfort rather than optimize long-term outcomes. The urgency created by financial stress promotes "tunneling"—intense focus on immediate problems while losing sight of broader financial patterns and solutions (Mullainathan & Shafir, 2013).

Workplace productivity suffers under financial stress, with research documenting increased absenteeism, presenteeism (reduced performance while present), and higher turnover rates among financially stressed employees (Meuris & Leana, 2017). These workplace impacts create additional financial vulnerability, as reduced job performance may limit advancement opportunities or job security precisely when financial stability is most needed.

3.6 Suicide

Suicide represents a leading cause of death (Mancini, 2021), with financial factors constituting significant risk elements that operate through multiple pathways to increase suicidal ideation and behavior. Financial crises—including job loss, bankruptcy, foreclosure, and overwhelming debt—are consistently associated with elevated suicide rates across diverse populations (Frankham et al., 2020; Richardson et al., 2013). The relationship between financial circumstances and suicide risk reflects the profound impact that financial security has on fundamental human needs for safety, dignity, and hope for the future.

Financial Factors as Suicide Risk Elements Economic events and personal financial crises create psychological conditions that substantially increase suicide risk. Personal bankruptcy, foreclosure proceedings, and insurmountable debt create intense feelings of shame, failure, and hopelessness—psychological states strongly associated with suicidal thoughts and behaviors (Richardson et al., 2013; Sareen et al., 2011).

The psychological impact of financial crises often exceeds their objective severity due to the meaning individuals attach to financial circumstances (Asebedo & Wilmarth, 2017). Financial failure is frequently interpreted as personal failure, triggering profound shame and self-blame that can overwhelm coping resources (Houle & Light, 2017). The loss of financial security threatens core aspects of identity, particularly for individuals whose self-worth is closely tied to their ability to provide for themselves or their families.

Acute Financial Events and Crisis Periods Certain financial events create particularly acute suicide risk due to their sudden onset and devastating psychological impact. Home foreclosure represents both practical housing loss and symbolic failure, with research showing elevated suicide rates in areas experiencing high foreclosure rates (Houle & Light, 2017). The public nature of foreclosure proceedings compounds shame and social exposure, while the displacement disrupts social support networks precisely when they are most needed.

Aggressive debt collection practices can create or exacerbate suicidal ideation through persistent harassment that makes financial problems feel inescapable. Kim and You (2019) identified late bill payments as early risk factors for suicidal behavior, suggesting that early intervention during financial difficulties might prevent escalation to crisis levels. The perceived permanence of financial problems—particularly when combined with poor credit, legal consequences, or professional licensing threats—can create hopelessness that overwhelms coping resources.

Cultural and Demographic Variations The relationship between financial factors and suicide varies significantly across cultural contexts and demographic groups, reflecting different social norms, support systems, and coping resources. Cultural factors influence how suicide is perceived (Nombora et al., 2023) and financial difficulties are interpreted and whether seeking help is seen as acceptable or shameful. Some cultures emphasize collective responsibility and mutual aid, potentially buffering individual financial stress, while others emphasize individual achievement and self-reliance, potentially intensifying shame associated with financial difficulties (Illiashenko, 2019).

3.7 Psychotic and Bipolar Disorders

Psychotic disorders and bipolar disorder represent severe mental health conditions that can impact financial functioning through alterations in perception, judgment, and impulse control (APA, 2022). The episodic nature of these conditions creates unique challenges for financial stability, as periods of symptom exacerbation can result in dramatic changes in financial behavior that have lasting consequences extending well beyond acute episodes.

Financial Behaviors During Manic and Psychotic Episodes Manic episodes in bipolar disorder frequently involve dramatic changes in financial behavior characterized by poor judgment, grandiosity, and reduced impulse control (APA, 2022). During mania, individuals often engage in excessive spending, risky financial ventures, or uncharacteristic financial generosity that deviates markedly from their baseline functioning. These behaviors reflect the disinhibition, inflated self-esteem, and decreased need for sleep that characterize manic states, creating conditions where financial safeguards and typical decision-making processes become compromised.

Psychotic episodes can involve financial delusions—false beliefs about extraordinary wealth, financial persecution, or elaborate financial conspiracies that drive behaviors potentially compromising financial security (APA, 2022). Command hallucinations may direct individuals to make specific financial decisions, while disorganized thinking impairs the logical reasoning necessary for sound financial judgment. The cognitive disorganization associated with psychotic states affects basic financial tasks including bill payment, account management, and financial planning.

Cognitive Impairment and Financial Management Both psychotic disorders and bipolar disorder involve cognitive impairments that persist even during periods of symptom remission, creating ongoing challenges for financial management. Executive functioning deficits affect planning, organization, and decision-making abilities essential for maintaining financial stability (APA, 2022). Abstract reasoning difficulties can impair understanding of complex financial products, insurance policies, or investment strategies, making individuals vulnerable to financial exploitation or poor financial decisions despite adequate intelligence in other domains.

Stigma and Financial Discrimination The stigma associated with serious mental illness creates additional barriers to financial well-being that extend beyond symptom-related impairments. Employment discrimination limits income-generating opportunities and career advancement, while health care discrimination affects access to affordable treatment of sufficient quality (Voldby et al., 2022). Financial institutions may discriminate against individuals with known psychiatric histories, limiting access to credit, mortgages, or loans needed for financial advancement (Wright et al., 2015). These systemic barriers create financial vulnerability that persists even during periods of psychiatric stability, highlighting how social factors compound the direct effects of psychiatric symptoms on financial health.

Medication Adherence and Financial Considerations The relationship between financial circumstances and medication adherence creates critical feedback loops that affect both psychiatric stability and financial functioning. When financial resources are limited, individuals often face difficult choices between psychiatric medications and other necessities, potentially leading to medication discontinuation and symptom recurrence (Anderson et al., 2021; Compton & Shim, 2015). The high cost of many psychiatric medications, particularly newer antipsychotics and mood stabilizers, creates ongoing financial strain that may compromise treatment adherence.

Conversely, untreated psychiatric symptoms impair the judgment and organizational skills needed for effective financial management, potentially worsening financial circumstances and further limiting medication access. Insurance coverage gaps, prior authorization requirements, and pharmacy benefit restrictions add additional layers of complexity that can disrupt medication continuity, particularly during symptomatic periods when individuals have reduced capacity to navigate these systems effectively.

3.8 ADHD and Neurodivergent Conditions

Attention-Deficit/Hyperactivity Disorder (ADHD) affects a large number of U.S. adults and youth and represents one of the most underrecognized factors impacting financial functioning in adulthood (APA, 2022). The core symptoms of

ADHD—inattention, hyperactivity, and impulsivity—directly compromise the executive functioning skills essential for effective financial management. Neurodivergent conditions more broadly, including autism spectrum disorder and learning disabilities, create unique challenges and strengths that significantly influence financial behaviors and outcomes, often in ways that traditional financial advice fails to accommodate.

Executive Functioning Deficits and Financial Impact ADHD is considered to fundamentally impair the executive functioning processes that underlie successful financial management (APA, 2022). Attention deficits make it difficult to sustain focus during financial tasks such as budgeting, bill review, or investment research, leading to incomplete or abandoned financial activities. Working memory limitations affect the ability to hold multiple financial variables in mind simultaneously—such as tracking various account balances, due dates, and spending categories—making comprehensive financial planning exceptionally challenging. Organization difficulties and forgetfulness manifest in financial contexts through misplaced bills, forgotten payment deadlines, and chaotic record-keeping systems that create ongoing financial stress and penalties. Time management impairments lead to chronic lateness in bill payments despite adequate funds, resulting in unnecessary late fees and credit score damage.

Impulsivity and Financial Decision-Making The impulsivity characteristic of ADHD creates significant challenges for financial decision-making and long-term financial planning (APA, 2022). Impulsive spending behaviors often override planned budgets, as the immediate gratification from purchases temporarily alleviates the emotional dysregulation common in ADHD. This impulsivity is frequently misunderstood as simple lack of willpower rather than being recognized as a neurobiological symptom requiring specific accommodations and strategies.

Decision-making difficulties extend beyond spending to investment choices, career decisions, and major financial commitments. The ADHD tendency toward hyperfocus can lead to obsessive research on financial topics followed by impulsive decisions based on incomplete information. Conversely, decision paralysis may occur when multiple financial options create cognitive overload, leading to procrastination on important financial choices until external pressure forces hasty decisions.

Neurodivergent Strengths and Financial Innovation While neurodivergent conditions create financial challenges, they also provide unique strengths that can enhance financial outcomes when properly leveraged. Many individuals with ADHD demonstrate high creativity and entrepreneurial thinking that can generate innovative income streams or business opportunities (Artamoshina et al., 2023). The ADHD trait of hyperfocus, when directed toward financial interests, can lead to positive outcomes in specific investment areas or financial strategies. However, these strengths are frequently overlooked in traditional financial education and planning approaches that assume neurotypical cognitive processing.

Accommodations and Adaptive Strategies Effective financial management for neurodivergent individuals requires accommodations that work with rather than against their neurological differences. Automation of routine financial tasks—such as bill payments, savings transfers, and investment contributions—can bypass executive functioning difficulties while ensuring financial obligations are met consistently. Visual organization systems, including color-coding and clear labeling, can help individuals with attention and processing differences track financial information more effectively.

Technology accommodations, such as smartphone apps with reminder notifications, simplified interfaces, and gamification elements, can make financial management more accessible and engaging for neurodivergent individuals. Breaking complex financial tasks into smaller, discrete steps helps manage attention limitations and executive functioning challenges while providing regular opportunities for positive reinforcement. Budgeting for impulsive spending can help ensure key necessities are met while also planning for a realistic need for flexibility. Understanding these neurological differences enables more effective financial interventions that build on individual strengths rather than attempting to force conformity to neurotypical financial management approaches.

3.9 Conclusion

Financial circumstances and mental health conditions create complex, bidirectional relationships that can either perpetuate cycles of distress or, with appropriate intervention, facilitate recovery across both domains. In this chapter, various mental health conditions were examined—from anxiety and depression to trauma, bipolar disorder, and neurodivergent conditions—each presenting unique patterns of interaction with financial functioning. These relationships extend beyond simple causation to encompass complex feedback loops where financial precarity can trigger or worsen mental health symptoms, while mental health challenges simultaneously impair the cognitive and emotional capacities needed for effective financial management.

Any interventions attempted by professionals should address both psychological and practical dimensions of financial-mental health challenges. The key insight from this integration is that sustainable improvement often requires simultaneous attention to both domains rather than treating them in isolation. Elena's vignette illustrates this principle clearly: addressing her anxiety symptoms alone would have provided limited relief without also tackling the underlying financial stressors, while financial assistance without attention to her psychological responses would have failed to build the lasting capacity needed for financial stability.

For helping professionals across disciplines, recognizing these interconnections is essential for effective practice. Mental health practitioners must understand how financial factors may be contributing to or maintaining the symptoms they observe, while financial professionals need awareness of how mental health conditions affect their clients' capacity to implement financial strategies. This integrated perspective enables more comprehensive assessment, more effective intervention planning, and better outcomes for individuals navigating the complex relationship between their financial circumstances and psychological well-being.

References

Abdul Latif Jameel Poverty Action Lab (J-PAL). (2022). *The impacts of economic interventions on intimate partner violence*. Retrieved September 14, 2023 from https://www.povertyactionlab.org/policy-insight/impacts-economic-interventions-intimate-partner-violence.

American Psychiatric Association. (2022). *Diagnostic and statistical manual of mental disorders* (5th ed.). American Psychiatric Association. https://dsm.psychiatryonline.org/doi/book/10.1176/appi.books.9780890425787

Anderson, K. E., McGinty, E. E., Presskreischer, R., & Barry, C. L. (2021). Reports of forgone medical care among US adults during the initial phase of the COVID-19 pandemic. *JAMA Network Open, 4*(1), e2034882. https://doi.org/10.1001/jamanetworkopen.2020.34882

Archuleta, K. L., Dale, A., & Spann, S. M. (2013). College students and financial distress: Exploring debt, financial satisfaction, and financial anxiety. *Journal of Financial Counseling and Planning, 24*(2), 50–62. https://eric.ed.gov/?id=EJ1043230

Archuleta, K. L., Mielitz, K. S., Jayne, D., & Le, V. (2020). Financial goal setting, financial anxiety, and solution-focused financial therapy (SFFT): A quasi-experimental outcome study. *Contemporary Family Therapy, 42*(1), 68–76. https://doi.org/10.1007/s10591-019-09501-0

Artamoshina, P., Shirokova, G., Osiyevskyy, O., & Bodolica, V. (2023). ADHD symptoms of CEOs and business model innovation in the SME context. *Technovation, 128*, 102845. https://doi.org/10.1016/j.technovation.2023.102845

Asebedo, S. D., & Wilmarth, M. J. (2017). Does how we feel about financial strain matter for mental health? *Journal of Financial Therapy, 8*(1), 62–80. https://doi.org/10.4148/1944-9771.1130

Compton, M. T., & Shim, R. S. (Eds.). (2015). *The social determinants of mental health*. American Psychiatric Publishing.

Frankham, C., Richardson, T., & Maguire, N. (2020). Do locus of control, self-esteem, hope and shame mediate the relationship between financial hardship and mental health? *Community Mental Health Journal, 56*(3), 404–415. https://doi.org/10.1007/s10597-019-00467-9

Houle, J. N., & Light, M. T. (2017). The harder they fall? Sex and race/ethnic specific suicide rates in the U.S. foreclosure crisis. *Social Science & Medicine, 180*(2017), 114–124. https://doi.org/10.1016/j.socscimed.2017.03.033

Illiashenko, P. (2019). "Tough guy" vs. "cushion" hypothesis: How does individualism affect risk-taking? *Journal of Behavioral and experimental Finance, 24*, 100212. https://doi.org/10.1016/j.jbef.2019.04.005

Kim, S., & You, M. (2019). An empirical analysis of delayed monthly bill payments as an early risk factor of increased suicidal behavior. *International Journal of Environmental Research and Public Health, 16*(16), 2929. https://doi.org/10.3390/ijerph16162929

Mancini, M. A. (2021). *Integrated behavioral health practice*. Springer International Publishing. https://doi.org/10.1007/978-3-030-59659-0.

McKenzie, C. B. (2022). *Trauma after trauma—Navigating financial anxiety in the postpartum period*. National Endowment for Financial Education. Retrieved October 24, 2024 from https://www.nefe.org/news/2022/03/navigating-postpartum-financial-anxiety.

Meuris, J., & Leana, C. R. (2017). The price of financial precarity: Personal finance as a barrier to work performance. *Academy of Management Proceedings, 2017*(1), 12992. https://doi.org/10.5465/AMBPP.2017.323

Mullainathan, S., & Shafir, E. (2013). *Scarcity: Why having too little means so much*. Times Books, Henry Holt.

National Institute of Mental Health (NIMH). (2023, July). *Major depression*. Retrieved June 4, 2025 from https://www.nimh.nih.gov/health/statistics/major-depression.

Nombora, O., Silva, B. F., & Venâncio, Â. (2023). Suicide and culture: A reflection on suicidal behaviour through cultural context. *European Psychiatry, 66*(Suppl 1), S1114. https://doi.org/10.1192/j.eurpsy.2023.2370

Richardson, T., Elliott, P., & Roberts, R. (2013). The relationship between personal unsecured debt and mental and physical health: A systematic review and meta-analysis. *Clinical Psychology Review, 33*(8), 1148–1162. https://doi.org/10.1016/j.cpr.2013.08.009

Sareen, J., Afifi, T. O., McMillan, K. A., & Asmundson, G. J. G. (2011). Relationship between household income and mental disorders: Findings from a population-based longitudinal study. *Archives of General Psychiatry, 68*(4), 419–427. https://doi.org/10.1001/archgenpsychiatry.2011.15

Shapiro, G. K., & Burchell, B. J. (2012). Measuring financial anxiety. *Journal of Neuroscience, Psychology, and Economics, 5*(2), 92–103. https://doi.org/10.1037/a0027647

Sinclair, R. R., & Cheung, J. H. (2016). Money matters: Recommendations for financial stress research in occupational health psychology. *Stress and Health: Journal of the International Society for the Investigation of Stress, 32*(3), 181–193. https://doi.org/10.1002/smi.2688

Substance Abuse and Mental Health Services Administration. (2014). *SAMHSA'S concept of trauma and guidance for a trauma-informed approach* (no. HHS publication no. (SMA) 14-4884). Substance Abuse and Mental Health Services Administration, U.S. Department of Health and Human Services. Retrieved October 25, 2024 from https://store.samhsa.gov/sites/default/files/sma14-4884.pdf.

Sweet, E., Nandi, A., Adam, E. K., & McDade, T. W. (2013). The high price of debt: Household financial debt and its impact on mental and physical health. *Social Science & Medicine, 91*, 94–100. https://doi.org/10.1016/j.socscimed.2013.05.009

Voldby, K. G., Hellström, L. C., Berg, M. E., & Eplov, L. F. (2022). Structural discrimination against people with mental illness; a scoping review. *SSM - Mental Health, 2*, 100117. https://doi.org/10.1016/j.ssmmh.2022.100117

Chapter 4
Physical Health

4.1 Introduction

Physical and financial health interact through multiple interconnected pathways that create some of the most immediate and consequential challenges individuals face. Unlike other domains where connections may unfold gradually over time, physical health crises often trigger sudden financial catastrophes that can permanently alter life trajectories within weeks or months. A cancer diagnosis can transform a financially stable family into one drowning in medical debt; chronic conditions like diabetes or heart disease create ongoing medication expenses that strain monthly budgets indefinitely; and preventable illnesses go untreated because families cannot afford routine primary care, ultimately requiring far more expensive emergency interventions. These dynamics reflect a fundamental reality of the American healthcare system: serious illness frequently becomes a financial emergency regardless of insurance coverage, employment status, or prior financial planning. At the same time, financial stress itself becomes embodied as physical symptoms—elevated blood pressure, compromised immune function, and chronic inflammation—demonstrating how economic insecurity literally gets under the skin to affect biological processes. This chapter examines how financial concerns affect access to healthcare while health conditions simultaneously generate expenses that can devastate household finances, creating feedback loops that either perpetuate cycles of poor health and financial instability or, with appropriate intervention, facilitate recovery across both domains. Understanding these relationships enables helping professionals to recognize when financial barriers may be preventing clients from accessing needed medical care and when health conditions may be driving the financial crises that bring individuals and families to their attention.

Supplementary Information The online version contains supplementary material available at https://doi.org/10.1007/978-3-032-02632-3_4.

J. Anvari-Clark, *Financial and Behavioral Health for Helping Professionals*,
https://doi.org/10.1007/978-3-032-02632-3_4

Vignette: Marcus's Navigation Through Cancer and Financial Crisis

Marcus Williams, a 52-year-old construction foreman, had always prided himself on his physical strength and work ethic. As the primary breadwinner for his family, including his wife Sarah and their teenage daughter Emma, he had maintained steady employment for over 20 years, building a modest but stable financial foundation. Their health insurance through his union provided decent coverage, though like many working families, they carried a high-deductible plan that required them to pay the first $6000 of medical expenses annually.

The diagnosis came suddenly. What Marcus initially dismissed as persistent fatigue and occasional shortness of breath during work turned out to be stage II lung cancer. The oncologist explained that while the prognosis was generally favorable with aggressive treatment, the next eight months would involve surgery, chemotherapy, and radiation therapy that would make continuing his physically demanding job impossible.

"The first shock was the cancer," Marcus later reflected. "The second shock was realizing what it was going to cost us, even with insurance." The medical bills began accumulating immediately. The surgical consultation alone cost $800 out-of-pocket, followed by pre-surgical testing that added another $1200. When the surgery finally occurred, their portion of the hospital bill reached $4500, effectively exhausting their emergency savings before treatment had even begun.

As chemotherapy commenced, new expenses emerged that Marcus had never anticipated. The anti-nausea medications cost $200 per month even with insurance coverage. Travel to the cancer center three times weekly for treatments meant gas expenses and parking fees that added up to nearly $300 monthly. Sarah had to reduce her work hours to accompany Marcus to appointments and care for him during his worst days, cutting their household income by approximately $1500 per month just when expenses were highest.

"I felt like I was fighting two battles," Marcus explained. "One against the cancer, and one against going broke. Some days I wasn't sure which one was harder." The financial stress began affecting his physical recovery. Marcus started skipping some of the prescribed supportive medications to save money, despite warnings from his oncology team about the importance of maintaining his treatment regimen. He insisted on returning to work earlier than medically advised, leading to complications that required additional treatment and time off.

The psychological toll compounded both his physical and financial challenges. Marcus began experiencing anxiety attacks when medical bills arrived in the mail, and Sarah found herself lying awake at night calculating and recalculating their remaining financial resources. Their daughter Emma became increasingly withdrawn, sensing the family's stress but not fully understanding its source.

Three months into treatment, the family faced a critical decision point. Marcus's oncologist recommended a newer chemotherapy protocol that might be more effective but would cost an additional $8000 out-of-pocket over the remaining treatment period. Simultaneously, they received notice that Marcus's position would not be held beyond his current medical leave, meaning he would need to find new employment while managing ongoing cancer care.

"That's when we realized we needed help that went beyond medical care," Sarah later recalled. The cancer center's patient navigator mentioned their financial counseling services, connecting the family with Maria Santos, a financial social worker who specialized in medical financial toxicity. Maria's approach differed markedly from traditional financial counseling by recognizing how the intersection of serious illness and financial stress created unique challenges requiring integrated solutions.

Through Maria's guidance, the family learned about pharmaceutical assistance programs that reduced Marcus's medication costs by 80%. She helped them navigate the insurance appeals process for the recommended treatment protocol, ultimately securing coverage that reduced their out-of-pocket responsibility to $2000. Most importantly, Maria connected them with a medical debt relief program and helped Sarah understand family medical leave benefits that could provide some income replacement during Marcus's treatment.

The financial interventions had immediate impacts on Marcus's health outcomes. With access to affordable medications and reduced financial stress about treatment costs, Marcus could focus his energy on recovery rather than financial survival. His adherence to the treatment protocol improved significantly, and his medical team noted better tolerance of chemotherapy when he wasn't simultaneously dealing with the physiological stress of financial crisis.

"Having someone who understood both the medical side and the money side made all the difference," Marcus reflected six months later, having completed treatment with good response and secured new employment with a company that offered better health benefits. "I learned that taking care of my health meant taking care of our finances too. You can't really separate them."

The family's experience illustrates several important principles about the relationship between physical and financial health. The financial toxicity of serious illness extends far beyond direct medical costs to encompass lost income, ancillary expenses, and the hidden costs of navigating complex profit-driven healthcare systems. Financial stress does not merely accompany serious illness—it actively interferes with healing by creating psychological distress, compromising treatment adherence, and forcing patients to make decisions between medical care and financial stability. Effective intervention requires understanding these relationships and providing support that addresses both the practical financial barriers to care and the psychological stress that financial challenges create.

Marcus's story also demonstrates how financial efficacy—the ability and confidence to navigate financial challenges—becomes particularly crucial during health crises. Learning to advocate for insurance coverage, access assistance programs, and make informed decisions about treatment costs represented new skills that enhanced not only the family's financial resilience but Marcus's sense of agency during a period when illness had threatened his identity as a provider and protector. The integrated approach to addressing both his health and financial needs created a foundation for recovery that extended well beyond cancer treatment.

***

The relationship between financial and physical health operates through multiple interconnected pathways that create complex feedback loops affecting both immediate health outcomes and long-term well-being. Unlike other behavioral health domains where the connections may be primarily psychological or social, the physical health domain involves tangible, measurable impacts that create urgent practical challenges requiring immediate attention. Financial resources directly determine access to healthcare services, medications, and treatments, while physical health conditions simultaneously generate expenses that can rapidly deplete savings and create lasting financial hardship. Understanding these relationships across various health conditions provides essential context for helping professionals who encounter clients navigating the often-devastating intersection of serious illness and financial crisis.

4.2 Primary Care

Primary care serves as the foundation of healthcare systems and the first point of contact for most health concerns, yet financial barriers frequently prevent individuals from accessing these essential services even when they recognize the need for care (Dorsey et al., 2020). The relationship between financial circumstances and primary care utilization demonstrates how seemingly small financial obstacles can create cascading effects that ultimately result in more serious health problems and greater financial burden over time.

The direct costs of primary care visits create immediate barriers for many individuals, particularly those without comprehensive health insurance coverage. Even with insurance, copayments, deductibles, limits, and coinsurance requirements can make routine medical care financially prohibitive for families managing limited budgets. Research consistently demonstrates that even modest cost-sharing requirements significantly reduce healthcare utilization, with low-income populations showing the greatest sensitivity to these financial barriers (Barcellos & Jacobson, 2015). When individuals delay or avoid primary care due to cost concerns, minor health issues often progress to more serious conditions requiring expensive emergency interventions that create far greater financial hardship than the original preventive care would have cost.

The indirect costs of healthcare access compound these direct financial barriers in ways that particularly affect lower-income working populations. Transportation expenses, childcare needs during medical appointments, and lost wages from taking time off work create additional financial burdens that can make healthcare feel economically irrational even when individuals recognize its importance (Kangovi et al., 2013). For hourly workers without paid sick leave, a routine medical appointment may cost more in lost wages than the medical service itself, creating powerful incentives to delay care until symptoms become severe enough to justify the economic sacrifice (Compton & Shim, 2015).

Financial efficacy plays a crucial role in primary care access through its influence on individuals' ability to navigate complex insurance systems and healthcare bureaucracies (Dhaliwal et al., 2017). Understanding insurance benefits, locating in-network providers, obtaining prior authorizations, and advocating for coverage requires substantial knowledge and persistence that may be compromised when cognitive resources are already taxed by financial stress. Individuals with limited financial efficacy may struggle to maximize their insurance benefits, potentially paying more out-of-pocket than necessary or avoiding care due to misunderstanding their coverage.

The timing of primary care access relative to other financial obligations creates additional complications that reflect the broader challenges of financial prioritization under resource constraints (Anderson et al., 2021). When families face competing demands for limited financial resources, preventive healthcare often receives lower priority than immediate necessities like housing, food, and utilities. This rational short-term decision-making can have devastating long-term consequences when undiagnosed or poorly managed conditions progress to crisis levels requiring emergency intervention.

4.3 Nutrition, Obesity, and Diabetes

Financial health directly influences dietary quality through multiple mechanisms that affect both food access and food choices (Gorman et al., 2017; Mukherjee & Nobles-Knight, 2013). Higher-quality foods including fresh produce, proteins, and whole grains typically cost more per calorie than processed foods high in refined sugars and unhealthy fats. This price differential creates situations where families with limited food budgets must choose between achieving adequate caloric intake and maintaining nutritional quality. Research demonstrates consistent relationships between household income and diet quality (Ploubidis et al., 2011), with lower-income families consuming diets higher in processed foods and lower in nutrients essential for metabolic health.

Food insecurity represents an extreme manifestation of financial barriers to adequate nutrition that affects approximately ten percent of U.S. households and demonstrates direct connections to obesity and diabetes risk. The relationship between food insecurity and obesity may seem paradoxical, but it reflects the reality that affordable calories often come from nutrient-poor sources that promote weight gain while failing to support metabolic health (Suvarna, 2020). The psychological stress of food insecurity also contributes to metabolic dysfunction through chronic elevation of stress hormones that affect glucose metabolism and fat storage.

The relationship between diabetes management and financial stress creates bidirectional effects where poor disease control increases healthcare costs while financial stress undermines self-care behaviors essential for metabolic health (Wallace et al., 2018). The cognitive demands of managing complex medication regimens, dietary restrictions, and glucose monitoring may be compromised when mental bandwidth is consumed by financial concerns. Additionally, the restrictive diets often recommended for diabetes management may seem financially impossible for families already struggling to afford adequate food, leading to poor adherence and worsening health outcomes.

4.4 Oncology Treatment

Cancer diagnosis and treatment represent perhaps the most dramatic intersection of physical and financial health, creating what healthcare providers increasingly recognize as "financial toxicity"—the harmful financial effects of cancer treatment that can compromise both economic security and health outcomes (Desai & Gyawali, 2020). The financial impact of cancer extends far beyond direct medical costs to encompass lost income, family disruption, and long-term economic consequences that can persist well beyond successful treatment completion.

The direct costs of cancer treatment can rapidly overwhelm even well-prepared families, as surgical procedures, chemotherapy, radiation therapy, and supportive care generate substantial medical bills that often exceed annual insurance coverages multiple times throughout treatment. Beyond direct medical costs, cancer creates numerous ancillary expenses including transportation to treatment centers (sometimes requiring daily trips for weeks of radiation therapy), lodging for out-of-town treatment, modified dietary needs, home care assistance, and family travel costs that accumulate substantially over extended treatment periods, particularly for patients in rural areas or those requiring specialized care at distant medical centers. The income impact compounds this expense burden by reducing household resources precisely when financial demands are highest, as cancer patients frequently cannot maintain employment during intensive treatment while family members may need to reduce work hours or leave employment to provide care.

This financial toxicity demonstrates direct relationships with cancer outcomes through multiple pathways (Murphy et al., 2019), as patients experiencing severe financial hardship may delay treatment initiation, modify treatment plans to reduce costs, or discontinue treatment prematurely, with research consistently showing that financial distress correlates with poorer cancer survival outcomes, reduced quality of life, and increased psychological distress (Zheng et al., 2020). The psychological burden often feels more distressing to patients than physical symptoms, creating anxiety and depression that can compromise immune function and healing capacity while generating guilt about treatment costs and fear of financial ruin that dominates patients' emotional experiences and interferes with the psychological resources needed for fighting serious illness.

The long-term financial consequences of cancer treatment can persist for years or decades beyond successful treatment completion, affecting retirement security, housing stability, and family financial well-being across generations. Medical debt accumulated during cancer treatment may take years to resolve, while career disruptions and reduced earning capacity can have lasting impacts on lifetime earnings and wealth accumulation. These extended consequences highlight how acute health crises can create permanent changes in financial trajectories that affect long-term security and wellbeing (Bisgaier & Rhodes, 2011).

4.5 Medical Debt

Medical debt represents a pervasive form of financial precarity that affects approximately one in five U.S. households and demonstrates particularly complex relationships with ongoing health outcomes (Rakshit et al., 2024; Vankar, 2022). Unlike other forms of consumer debt that typically result from discretionary spending choices, medical debt often stems from unavoidable healthcare needs that create moral and psychological burdens alongside financial obligations. The presence of existing medical debt influences future healthcare decisions in ways that can perpetuate cycles of poor health and financial instability.

The accumulation of medical debt reflects both the high costs of healthcare services and the limitations of insurance coverage in protecting families from financial hardship during health crises. High-deductible health plans, while offering lower premium costs, expose families to substantial financial risk when serious health problems arise. Surprise billing practices, out-of-network charges, and coverage denials can create unexpected financial obligations that quickly exhaust savings and force families into debt even when they believed they had adequate insurance protection.

The presence of medical debt creates powerful incentives to avoid future healthcare utilization, leading to patterns of delayed care that can worsen health conditions and ultimately generate additional medical expenses (Tucker-Seeley et al., 2015). Individuals with outstanding medical debt often postpone routine preventive care, skip recommended follow-up visits, and delay seeking treatment for new health concerns due to fear of accumulating additional financial obligations. This avoidance behavior creates false economies where short-term savings result in more expensive interventions becoming necessary later.

The collection practices associated with medical debt create additional stress and financial hardship that can interfere with health and healing. Aggressive collection efforts, including frequent phone calls, threatening letters, and legal actions, create chronic stress that can exacerbate existing health conditions and interfere with recovery. The garnishment of wages or bank accounts can worsen financial instability and reduce resources available for ongoing healthcare needs and basic living expenses.

4.6 Gender Affirming Care and Gender Identity Debt

Gender affirming care represents a critical healthcare need for transgender and gender diverse individuals that involves unique financial challenges stemming from limited insurance coverage, high treatment costs, and the extended timeline often required for comprehensive transition-related care (Puckett et al., 2018). The financial burden of accessing gender affirming care creates what some advocates term "gender identity debt"—the accumulated financial obligations associated with pursuing medically necessary treatment for gender dysphoria that reflects both direct medical costs and indirect expenses related to legal, social, and logistical aspects of gender transition.

The medical costs of gender affirming care can be substantial due to the comprehensive nature of treatment and the limited insurance coverage available for many transition-related services (Jarrett et al., 2021). Hormone therapy, while less expensive than surgical interventions, represents an ongoing monthly expense that may continue for years or decades. Surgical procedures including chest reconstruction, genital reconstruction, and facial feminization surgeries can cost tens of thousands of dollars and often require multiple staged procedures over extended periods. Mental health services required for transition support and surgical clearance letters add additional costs that may not be covered by insurance plans.

The indirect costs associated with gender transition compound the direct medical expenses in ways that create substantial financial burden beyond healthcare costs. Legal name and gender marker changes involve court fees, document updates, and often require attorney assistance that can cost thousands of dollars. Travel expenses to access specialized providers may be necessary for individuals living in areas with limited access to experienced gender affirming care providers. Time off work for medical procedures and recovery can reduce income during periods of high expenses.

The extended timeline typically required for comprehensive gender transition creates sustained financial pressure that can strain household budgets for years or decades. Unlike acute medical events that generate intensive but time-limited expenses, gender transition often involves ongoing costs spanning multiple years as individuals pursue various components of care sequentially. This extended financial commitment requires careful planning and sustained financial capacity that may be challenging to maintain over such prolonged periods.

Financial barriers to gender affirming care create significant health consequences that extend beyond the direct effects of delayed or denied treatment. Gender dysphoria symptoms may worsen when individuals cannot access appropriate care, leading to increased mental health symptoms including depression, anxiety, and suicidal ideation (American Psychiatric Association, 2022). The stress of financial barriers to essential care compounds the psychological burden of gender dysphoria and can interfere with other aspects of health and well-being.

4.7 Hypertension, Heart Disease, and High Blood Pressure

The chronic nature of cardiovascular conditions creates ongoing financial obligations for medication, monitoring, and lifestyle modifications that can strain household budgets indefinitely, while financial stress itself contributes to cardiovascular risk through direct physiological mechanisms including chronic elevation of stress hormones and inflammatory markers (Dhaliwal et al., 2017). Financial stress directly affects cardiovascular health through well-documented physiological pathways that demonstrate how economic circumstances become embodied as physical health outcomes. Chronic financial strain activates stress response systems that elevate blood pressure, increase inflammation, and promote atherosclerosis through sustained elevation of cortisol and other stress hormones (Kahn & Pearlin, 2006). Research consistently demonstrates associations between financial hardship and increased rates of hypertension, heart disease, and stroke that persist even after controlling for other socioeconomic factors and health behaviors (Israel et al., 2014; Lippert et al., 2022).

The medication requirements for managing cardiovascular disease create ongoing financial obligations that can significantly impact household budgets and treatment adherence, as many patients require multiple medications and other cardioprotective therapies that may cost hundreds of dollars monthly even with insurance coverage. The lifestyle modifications recommended for cardiovascular health often involve challenging expenses for financially constrained households (Israel et al., 2014), as heart-healthy diets typically cost more than processed alternatives high in sodium and saturated fats, while exercise programs, gym memberships, recreational activities, and stress reduction services like massage, meditation classes, or counseling represent additional expenses that compete with other financial priorities. The monitoring and management requirements create ongoing healthcare utilization needs through regular physician visits, laboratory testing, and diagnostic procedures that generate recurring expenses while potentially interfering with employment obligations and creating lost income, particularly for hourly workers without paid sick leave.

Acute cardiovascular events including heart attacks and strokes create sudden, catastrophic expenses that can overwhelm household financial resources through emergency hospital care, intensive care unit stays, surgical interventions, and extended rehabilitation that frequently exceed annual insurance coverage, while the recovery period often requires extended time away from work and may result in permanent work limitations that reduce lifetime earning capacity. This creates bidirectional feedback loops where poor cardiovascular health increases healthcare costs and may reduce earning capacity, worsening financial stress that further compromises cardiovascular health, while conversely, interventions that reduce financial stress and improve financial security may support cardiovascular health through both direct physiological mechanisms and improved capacity for self-care behaviors.

4.8 Asthma and Other Respiratory Conditions

Respiratory conditions including asthma, chronic obstructive pulmonary disease (COPD), and other chronic lung diseases demonstrate significant interactions with financial circumstances through both the direct costs of disease management and the environmental health factors that influence disease severity and progression. Understanding these relationships requires recognizing how financial resources affect both access to appropriate treatment and the environmental conditions that determine respiratory health outcomes.

The medication requirements for managing respiratory conditions create substantial ongoing expenses that can significantly impact household budgets and treatment adherence. Controller medications for asthma and COPD often cost hundreds of dollars monthly, particularly for newer formulations that may be more effective but carry higher price tags. Rescue medications, nebulizers, and other respiratory equipment add additional costs that accumulate over time (Nurmagambetov et al., 2018), leading to poorer symptom control and increased emergency department visits that generate even greater healthcare expenses.

The relationship between respiratory conditions and work capacity creates bidirectional effects where respiratory symptoms may limit earning potential while financial needs may force continued exposure to respiratory hazards (Nurmagambetov et al., 2018). Severe asthma or COPD can reduce productivity, necessitate workplace accommodations, or require frequent absence from work during exacerbations. These work limitations may result in reduced income, job instability, or difficulty advancing in careers that require sustained physical capacity or regular attendance.

The emergency care needs associated with respiratory conditions can create sudden, substantial healthcare expenses that strain household budgets and create lasting financial hardship. Asthma exacerbations that require emergency department visits, hospitalizations for pneumonia or COPD complications, and intensive care treatment for severe respiratory failure generate medical bills that frequently exceed typical insurance coverage. The unpredictable nature of respiratory emergencies makes it difficult to plan financially for these expenses, while the potential severity of respiratory crises makes delaying care for financial reasons particularly dangerous.

4.9 Conclusion

The relationship between physical and financial health represents one of the most concrete and urgent connections within the behavioral health framework. As Marcus's journey through cancer treatment illustrates, serious illness creates immediate financial crises that extend far beyond direct medical costs to encompass lost income, ancillary expenses, and the complex navigation of healthcare systems designed more for profit than patient welfare. The bidirectional nature of these relationships—where financial stress compromises healing while treatment generates financial precarity—creates destructive cycles that can persist long after successful treatment completion. Medical debt, medication costs, and the ongoing expenses of chronic disease management demonstrate how health conditions fundamentally alter financial trajectories, often creating permanent changes in economic security that affect individuals and families across generations.

For helping professionals across disciplines, providing informed and comprehensive care acknowledges the reality of how Americans experience health and illness within profit-driven healthcare systems. Healthcare providers must recognize how financial barriers prevent patients from accessing care and following treatment recommendations, while financial professionals need awareness of how health conditions create unique financial planning challenges requiring specialized approaches. The principle of financial efficacy becomes particularly crucial in healthcare contexts, as individuals—in partnership with the helping professional—must develop confidence and skills to advocate for insurance coverage, access assistance programs, and make informed decisions about treatment costs that balance health outcomes with financial sustainability. By integrating financial considerations into health interventions and health awareness into financial services, practitioners can address the fundamental truth that physical and financial health are inseparable components of overall wellbeing.

References

American Psychiatric Association. (2022). *Diagnostic and statistical manual of mental disorders* (5th, Text Revision ed.). American Psychiatric Association. https://dsm.psychiatryonline.org/doi/book/10.1176/appi.books.9780890425787

Anderson, K. E., McGinty, E. E., Presskreischer, R., & Barry, C. L. (2021). Reports of forgone medical care among US adults during the initial phase of the COVID-19 pandemic. *JAMA Network Open, 4*(1), e2034882. https://doi.org/10.1001/jamanetworkopen.2020.34882

Barcellos, S. H., & Jacobson, M. (2015). The effects of medicare on medical expenditure risk and financial strain. *American Economic Journal: Economic Policy, 7*(4), 41–70. https://doi.org/10.1257/pol.20140262

Bisgaier, J., & Rhodes, K. V. (2011). Cumulative adverse financial circumstances: Associations with patient health status and behaviors. *Health & Social Work, 36*(2), 129–137. https://doi.org/10.1093/hsw/36.2.129

Compton, M. T., & Shim, R. S. (Eds.). (2015). *The social determinants of mental health*. American Psychiatric Publishing.

Desai, A., & Gyawali, B. (2020). Financial toxicity of cancer treatment: Moving the discussion from acknowledgement of the problem to identifying solutions. *EClinicalMedicine, 20*(2020), 100269. https://doi.org/10.1016/j.eclinm.2020.100269

Dhaliwal, K. K., King-Shier, K., Manns, B. J., Hemmelgarn, B. R., Stone, J. A., & Campbell, D. J. T. (2017). Exploring the impact of financial barriers on secondary prevention of heart disease. *BMC Cardiovascular Disorders, 17*(1), 1–8. https://doi.org/10.1186/s12872-017-0495-4

Dorsey, J. D., Hill, P., Moran, N., Azzari, C. N., Reshadi, F., Shanks, I., & Williams, J. D. (2020). Leveraging the existing US healthcare structure for consumer financial well-being: Barriers, opportunities, and a framework toward future research. *Journal of Consumer Affairs, 54*(1), 70–99. https://doi.org/10.1111/joca.12274

Gorman, K. S., McCurdy, K., Kisler, T., & Metallinos-Katsaras, E. (2017). Maternal strategies to access food differ by food security status. *Journal of the Academy of Nutrition and Dietetics, 117*(1), 48–57. https://doi.org/10.1016/j.jand.2016.07.010

Israel, S., Caspi, A., Belsky, D. W., Harrington, H., Hogan, S., Houts, R., et al. (2014). Credit scores, cardiovascular disease risk, and human capital. *Proceedings of the National Academy of Sciences, 111*(48), 17087–17092. https://doi.org/10.1073/pnas.1409794111

Jarrett, B. A., Peitzmeier, S. M., Restar, A., Adamson, T., Howell, S., Baral, S., & Beckham, S. W. (2021). Gender-affirming care, mental health, and economic stability in the time of COVID-19: A multi-national, cross-sectional study of transgender and nonbinary people. *PLoS One, 16*(7), e0254215. https://doi.org/10.1371/journal.pone.0254215

Kahn, J. R., & Pearlin, L. I. (2006). Financial strain over the life course and health among older adults. *Journal of Health and Social Behavior, 47*(1), 17–31. https://doi.org/10.1177/002214650604700102

Kangovi, S., Barg, F. K., Carter, T., Long, J. A., Shannon, R., & Grande, D. (2013). Understanding why patients of low socioeconomic status prefer hospitals over ambulatory care. *Health Affairs, 32*(7), 1196–1203. https://doi.org/10.1377/hlthaff.2012.0825

Lippert, A. M., Houle, J. N., & Walsemann, K. M. (2022). Student debt and cardiovascular disease risk among U.S. adults in early mid-life. *American Journal of Preventive Medicine, 0*(0), 1–9. https://doi.org/10.1016/j.amepre.2022.02.002

Mukherjee, K., & Nobles-Knight, D. (2013). Assessment of trade-offs made by people due to financial stress from medical care in the USA. *Journal of Pharmaceutical Health Services Research, 4*(2), 95–99. https://doi.org/10.1111/jphs.12015

Murphy, P. B., Severance, S., Savage, S., Obeng-Gyasi, S., Timsina, L. R., & Zarzaur, B. L. (2019). Financial toxicity is associated with worse physical and emotional long-term outcomes after traumatic injury. *The Journal of Trauma and Acute Care Surgery, 87*(5), 1189–1196. https://doi.org/10.1097/TA.0000000000002409

Nurmagambetov, T., Kuwahara, R., & Garbe, P. (2018). The economic burden of asthma in the United States, 2008–2013. *Annals of the American Thoracic Society, 15*(3), 348–356. https://doi.org/10.1513/AnnalsATS.201703-259OC

Ploubidis, G. B., DeStavola, B. L., & Grundy, E. (2011). Health differentials in the older population of England: An empirical comparison of the materialist, lifestyle and psychosocial hypotheses. *BMC Public Health, 11*(1), 390. https://doi.org/10.1186/1471-2458-11-390

Puckett, J. A., Cleary, P., Rossman, K., Mustanski, B., & Newcomb, M. E. (2018). Barriers to gender-affirming care for transgender and gender nonconforming individuals. *Sexuality Research & Social Policy, 15*(1), 48–59. https://doi.org/10.1007/s13178-017-0295-8

Rakshit, S., Rae, M., Claxton, G., Amin, K., & Cox, C. (2024). *The burden of medical debt in the United States*. Peterson-KFF. Retrieved June 24, 2024, from https://www.healthsystemtracker.org/brief/the-burden-of-medical-debt-in-the-united-states/

Suvarna, B. (2020). Health risk behaviours and allostatic load: A systematic review. *Neuroscience and Biobehavioral Reviews, 108*, 694–711. https://doi.org/10.1016/j.neubiorev.2019.12.020

Tucker-Seeley, R. D., Mitchell, J. A., Shires, D. A., & Modlin, C. S. (2015). Financial hardship, unmet medical need, and health self-efficacy among African American men. *Health Education & Behavior, 42*(3), 285–292. https://doi.org/10.1177/1090198114557125

Vankar, P. (2022, November 9). Share of adults with medical debt U.S. 2021. *Statista*. Retrieved February 4, 2025, from https://www.statista.com/statistics/1079659/share-of-adults-medical-debt-us/

Wallace, K., Zhao, X., Misra, R., & Sambamoorthi, U. (2018). The humanistic and economic burden associated with anxiety and depression among adults with comorbid diabetes and hypertension. *Journal of Diabetes Research, 2018*. https://doi.org/10.1155/2018/4842520

Zheng, Z., Jemal, A., Tucker-Seeley, R., Banegas, M. P., Han, X., Rai, A., et al. (2020). Worry about daily financial needs and food insecurity among cancer survivors in the United States. *JNCCN Journal of the National Comprehensive Cancer Network, 18*(3), 315–327. https://doi.org/10.6004/jnccn.2019.7359

Chapter 5
Coping Health

5.1 Introduction

Coping health represents the spectrum of strategies individuals develop to manage stress, emotional discomfort, and life challenges, ranging from adaptive approaches that enhance resilience to maladaptive patterns, such as addictive behaviors, that provide temporary relief while creating long-term complications (Anvari-Clark, 2022). Related to the financial domain of behavioral health, coping mechanisms frequently involve money-related behaviors that serve psychological functions beyond their apparent financial purposes. Understanding these connections requires recognizing that financial behaviors often represent attempts to regulate emotions, manage anxiety, assert control, or meet unmet psychological needs rather than simply reflecting knowledge deficits or poor financial planning.

The conceptualization of substance use and problem behaviors as forms of coping health, while not yet universally adopted in clinical practice, reflects a growing body of research examining these behaviors through the lens of stress management and emotional regulation (Ito & Matsushima, 2017; Wang et al., 2018). This framework positions addictive behaviors as problematic coping mechanisms that individuals employ to manage underlying distress, anxiety, or trauma, rather than viewing them solely as discrete psychiatric disorders (Sarin & Nolen-Hoeksema, 2010). Research increasingly demonstrates how consumption behaviors, including substance use, emerge as responses to psychological distress and serve coping functions, even when they ultimately create additional problems (Blashill et al., 2011; Glanz & Schwartz, 2008).

The complexity of financial-coping relationships reflects broader themes within the behavioral health framework presented throughout this book. Financial efficacy becomes compromised when emotional dysregulation overwhelms rational decision-making processes, while financial precarity creates chronic stress that

Supplementary Information The online version contains supplementary material available at https://doi.org/10.1007/978-3-032-02632-3_5.

J. Anvari-Clark, *Financial and Behavioral Health for Helping Professionals*,
https://doi.org/10.1007/978-3-032-02632-3_5

taxes coping resources and increases vulnerability to maladaptive responses. Financial well-being requires not only practical financial skills but also emotional regulation abilities that enable individuals to make financial decisions aligned with long-term goals rather than immediate emotional needs.

This chapter examines how financial factors intersect with coping health across substance use disorders, behavioral addictions, and money disorders that serve psychological rather than economic functions. We explore specific patterns including the role of financial stress in triggering addictive behaviors, the psychological functions of money disorders like compulsive buying and gambling, and the ways that financial avoidance serves to regulate emotional discomfort despite creating practical complications. Thus, any interventions attempted need to recognize that sustainable behavior change requires addressing both the practical financial skills needed for stability and the underlying emotional needs that drive problematic financial coping patterns.

Vignette: Sarah's Journey Through Financial Stress and Coping

Sarah Martinez, a 29-year-old graphic designer, had always considered herself financially responsible. She graduated from college with moderate student loan debt, maintained steady employment, and lived within her means in a shared apartment. However, when the small advertising agency where she worked laid off half its staff during an economic downturn, Sarah's carefully constructed financial stability began to unravel in ways that surprised and frightened her.

Initially, Sarah responded to unemployment with practical steps—updating her resume, networking with former colleagues, and applying for jobs while carefully budgeting her savings to cover essential expenses. She felt confident that her skills and experience would lead to new employment within a few weeks. When those weeks stretched into months, however, Sarah found herself facing not only financial pressure but also psychological distress that manifested in unexpected ways.

"I started shopping online when I couldn't sleep," Sarah later recalled. "Not for anything big or expensive, just little things—a new phone case, some art supplies, a sweater I didn't really need. It felt like I was doing something positive, like I was taking care of myself when everything else felt out of control." These small purchases provided brief moments of excitement and anticipation that temporarily distracted from her mounting anxiety about unemployment and dwindling savings.

As her job search continued without success, Sarah's spending patterns escalated. The packages arriving at her door became bright spots in increasingly difficult days, providing momentary relief from the constant stress of rejection emails and unanswered applications. She began spending hours browsing online stores, researching products, and reading reviews—activities that filled time while avoiding the emotional discomfort of facing her deteriorating financial situation.

"I knew I couldn't afford it, but somehow I convinced myself that each purchase was justified," Sarah explained. "I needed the art supplies for freelance work I might get. The clothes were for job interviews. The home goods were investments in

my living space that would improve my mental health. I had an explanation for everything, even though deep down I knew I was lying to myself."

The situation reached a crisis point when Sarah realized she had accumulated over $3000 in credit card debt within four months, money she had spent on items that now seemed unnecessary and even shameful. The interest charges meant her minimum payments were barely touching the principal balance, while her savings had been completely exhausted. More troubling was her recognition that the shopping had become compulsive—she found herself making purchases even when consciously trying to stop, driven by anxiety and the temporary emotional relief that buying provided.

Sarah's response to discovering her debt load demonstrated another layer of problematic coping. Rather than immediately addressing the situation, she entered a period of financial avoidance that she described as "sticking my head in the sand." She stopped checking her bank balance, avoided opening credit card statements, and declined to answer calls from numbers she didn't recognize, fearing they might be creditors. This avoidance provided temporary relief from anxiety but allowed problems to compound through late fees and continued unconscious spending.

"I felt so ashamed and stupid," Sarah reflected. "Here I was, an educated adult who had always been responsible with money, and I had created this mess during the worst possible time. I didn't want to face how bad it had gotten because that would mean admitting that I had lost control." The shame reinforced her avoidance behaviors, creating a cycle where increasing financial problems generated more emotional distress that triggered further avoidance.

The turning point came when Sarah's unemployment benefits were exhausted, and she faced the possibility of asking family for financial help. The prospect of revealing her situation to her parents, who had always viewed her as the responsible one among their children, forced her to confront the reality of her circumstances. During a particularly difficult evening, she called her sister Maria, a social worker, and through tears explained what had been happening.

Maria's response surprised Sarah. Rather than judgment or lectures about financial responsibility, she provided emotional support while helping Sarah understand that her behavior represented a common response to chronic stress and loss of control. "You're not stupid or weak," Maria explained. "You're someone who found a way to cope with an incredibly stressful situation, even though that coping mechanism created other problems. The question now is how we help you find better ways to manage the stress while also addressing the practical financial issues."

With Maria's support, Sarah began working with a financial counselor who specialized in behavioral aspects of money management. The counselor, James, helped Sarah understand that her shopping behavior had served important psychological functions—providing a sense of control when job searching felt futile, offering momentary pleasure during a period of constant stress, and creating anticipation and excitement that temporarily lifted her mood. Rather than simply focusing on budgeting and debt reduction, James used motivational interviewing skills in his work with Sarah and helped her identify alternative ways of meeting these emotional needs while developing practical strategies for financial recovery.

The integrated approach proved essential for sustainable change. Sarah learned stress management techniques including deep breathing and progressive muscle relaxation that she could use when feeling urges to shop. She developed new routines for job searching that included breaks for physical exercise and creative activities that provided the sense of accomplishment and control she had been seeking through purchases. Most importantly, she began addressing the underlying feelings of inadequacy and loss of professional identity that unemployment had triggered.

Six months later, Sarah had secured new employment and developed a realistic plan for paying off her debt. More significantly, she had developed awareness of her emotional triggers and alternative coping strategies that didn't compromise her financial stability. "I learned that my relationship with money was really about my relationship with myself," she explained. "When I felt scared or out of control, I used shopping to try to fix those feelings. Now I have other ways to take care of myself that actually work better and don't create new problems."

Sarah's experience illustrates several important principles about the relationship between financial health and coping behaviors. Her shopping served legitimate psychological functions during a period of significant stress, providing temporary relief from anxiety and a sense of agency when other areas of life felt uncontrollable. The financial consequences were real and serious but addressing them required understanding both the practical debt management needs and the underlying emotional drivers that made shopping feel necessary. The avoidance that followed her recognition of the problem represented additional layers of maladaptive coping that had to be addressed separately from the original spending behaviors.

Most importantly, Sarah's recovery required developing alternative ways to meet the psychological needs that shopping had been addressing. Simply eliminating the behavior without replacing its functions would likely have led to either relapse or the emergence of other problematic coping mechanisms. The integration of practical financial skills with emotional awareness and alternative stress management strategies created a foundation for both financial recovery and enhanced coping capacity that served her beyond the immediate crisis.

***

The financial concerns and coping behaviors interact through diverse patterns that reflect individual differences in stress responses, psychological needs, and available resources. While the specific presentations vary considerably, several common themes emerge that help practitioners understand when financial behaviors may be serving coping functions rather than economic purposes. These patterns often develop gradually as individuals discover that certain financial behaviors provide temporary emotional relief, leading to increased reliance on these strategies even when they create or worsen underlying financial problems.

5.2 General Substance Use and Behavioral Addiction

The relationship between financial circumstances and substance use operates through multiple interconnected pathways that create bidirectional effects where financial stress can trigger or worsen substance use while addiction simultaneously creates financial instability through direct costs and impaired decision-making capacity (Britt et al., 2015; Canale et al., 2015; Richardson et al., 2013). Understanding these relationships requires recognizing both the immediate ways that financial stressors affect substance use patterns and the longer-term cycles that develop as addiction compromises financial stability and limits recovery resources.

Financial stress serves as a powerful trigger for substance use through several psychological and physiological mechanisms that reflect the broader impact of economic insecurity on mental health and coping capacity. Chronic financial strain activates stress response systems that increase vulnerability to addictive behaviors by altering brain chemistry, compromising impulse control, and creating psychological states that substances temporarily alleviate (Mulia et al., 2021). The uncertainty inherent in financial instability—not knowing whether expenses can be covered or how long resources will last—creates chronic anxiety that individuals may attempt to manage through use of alcohol, drugs, or other substances that provide temporary relief from this persistent emotional distress.

The cognitive burden of financial stress, as described by Mullainathan & Shafir (2013), depletes mental bandwidth essential for making sound decisions about substance use. When cognitive resources are consumed by financial worries and planning, individuals have reduced capacity for exercising the self-control needed to resist substance use urges or maintain recovery behaviors. This cognitive depletion helps explain why financially stressed individuals often relapse or develop new substance use problems even when they intellectually understand the risks and consequences involved.

The social consequences of financial stress compound these individual vulnerabilities by affecting relationships and support systems that typically protect against substance use problems. Financial strain can create isolation as individuals withdraw from social activities they cannot afford, reduce contact with supportive family and friends to avoid discussions of financial struggles, or generate conflict in relationships as stress and resource limitations create tension (Stack & Meredith, 2018). This social isolation removes important protective factors while increasing exposure to substance use as a way of managing loneliness and emotional distress.

Furthermore, substance use creates substantial financial consequences that extend far beyond the direct costs of purchasing alcohol or drugs. The immediate expenses can be significant, particularly for individuals with severe addictions who may spend hundreds or thousands of dollars monthly on substances, money that could otherwise address basic needs or reduce financial stress. The indirect costs often prove even more devastating, including lost income from reduced work performance, absenteeism, or job loss; increased healthcare expenses from substance-related health problems; legal fees and fines from substance-related legal issues; and damaged credit and financial obligations from impaired financial decision-making during periods of intoxication.

The recovery process itself involves unique financial challenges that can create barriers to sustained sobriety if not adequately addressed. Treatment costs, including residential programs, outpatient services, and ongoing counseling, can strain household budgets even when insurance provides coverage. Many individuals in early recovery face the financial consequences of past substance use—damaged credit, outstanding debts, lost employment, or housing instability—while simultaneously trying to establish new patterns of behavior and rebuild their lives. The stress associated with these financial challenges during recovery can trigger relapse if individuals lack adequate support and alternative coping strategies.

Behavioral addictions including gambling, gaming, shopping, and internet use demonstrate similar patterns of interaction with financial circumstances, though the specific mechanisms and consequences vary by behavior. These addictions often develop as coping mechanisms for underlying emotional distress, anxiety, or trauma, with the behavioral pattern providing temporary relief from negative emotional states while creating progressive tolerance that requires increased engagement to achieve the same emotional effects (American Psychiatric Association [APA], 2022). Unlike substance addictions, behavioral addictions may initially appear less harmful or even socially acceptable, allowing them to develop gradually without recognition of their addictive nature until significant consequences have accumulated. Furthermore, the financial impact of behavioral addictions can be substantial and often exceeds what individuals consciously recognize due to the gradual escalation of the behavior and cognitive distortions that maintain the addiction.

5.3 Money Disorders (Individual)

Money disorders represent a specialized category of financial behaviors that serve psychological functions rather than economic purposes, characterized by persistent patterns that cause significant distress or impairment despite negative financial consequences (Klontz et al., 2012). These disorders demonstrate how financial behaviors can become maladaptive coping mechanisms that address an individual's underlying emotional needs while creating substantial financial and relational difficulties. Understanding money disorders requires recognizing that the problematic financial behaviors often represent logical responses to psychological distress, even though they create practical problems that may worsen the original emotional difficulties. In this book, money disorders are contextualized as being either individual or relational. Individual disorders are distinguished by a person acting on their own to satisfy a personal emotional need, whereas relational disorders have a distinctly social component in which at least one other person is involved. Relational money disorders are addressed in the chapter on social health.

Compulsive Buying Disorder represents one of the most prevalent money disorders, characterized by persistent urges to purchase items that go beyond meeting practical needs and create significant distress or financial problems (Canale et al., 2015; McElroy et al., 1994). Despite not being included in the DSM-5-TR due to lack of peer-reviewed evidence (APA, 2022), the disorder affects approximately five to eight percent of the general population and demonstrates clear connections to emotional regulation difficulties, particularly around depression, anxiety, and low self-esteem (Canale et al., 2015; Mueller et al., 2010). Individuals with compulsive buying often describe the purchase process as providing a temporary "high" or sense of excitement that temporarily alleviates negative emotional states, followed by feelings of guilt, shame, and regret that may trigger additional purchasing episodes.

The psychological functions served by compulsive buying help explain why the behavior persists despite obvious negative consequences. Shopping provides a sense of control and agency during periods when other life areas feel chaotic or unmanageable, offers temporary mood enhancement during depression or anxiety, creates anticipation and excitement that interrupts negative thought patterns, and can serve as a form of self-nurturing or reward during difficult emotional periods (Mueller et al., 2010). The escalating nature of compulsive buying reflects tolerance patterns similar to those seen in substance addictions, where individuals require increasingly frequent or expensive purchases to achieve the same emotional relief (Canale et al., 2015). This escalation, combined with the temporary nature of the emotional benefits, creates cycles where mounting financial consequences generate additional stress and negative emotions that trigger further buying episodes. The resulting debt, relationship conflicts, and practical complications often worsen the underlying emotional distress that buying was meant to address.

Gambling Disorder involves persistent and recurrent problematic gambling behavior that leads to clinically significant impairment or distress, affecting approximately one to three percent of adults with higher rates among certain demographic groups (APA, 2022). The disorder demonstrates clear patterns of progression from recreational gambling to compulsive behavior driven by psychological needs rather than realistic expectations of financial gain. Understanding gambling disorder requires recognizing the multiple psychological functions that gambling serves and how these functions become entrenched even as financial consequences escalate.

The psychological appeal of gambling involves several mechanisms that make it particularly compelling for individuals experiencing stress, depression, or anxiety (Barrault et al., 2019). The intermittent reinforcement schedule inherent in gambling—unpredictable rewards that occasionally follow long periods without winning—creates powerful conditioning that maintains behavior even during extended losing periods. The excitement and anticipation associated with gambling can temporarily alleviate depression or provide escape from anxiety and worry. For some individuals, gambling provides a sense of control and skill that may be lacking in other life areas, even though gambling outcomes are ultimately determined by chance.

The concept of "chasing losses"—continuing to gamble in attempts to recover money already lost—demonstrates how gambling disorder involves cognitive distortions that maintain the behavior despite mounting financial consequences (Parente, 2021). These distortions include beliefs that losses are temporary setbacks that will be recovered through continued gambling, that past losses somehow increase the probability of future wins, or that gambling skills can overcome mathematical odds. These cognitive patterns help explain why individuals continue gambling even when they intellectually understand that continued play will likely worsen their financial situation.

The financial consequences of gambling disorder often prove devastating due to the rapid pace at which money can be lost and the tendency for gambling episodes to involve larger sums as the disorder progresses. Unlike other money disorders where financial damage accumulates gradually through repeated small purchases, gambling can result in catastrophic losses during single episodes that immediately threaten housing, relationships, and basic financial security. The aftermath of major gambling losses often involves additional problematic financial behaviors including borrowing from family or friends, obtaining cash advances on credit cards, or engaging in illegal activities to finance continued gambling.

Hoarding Disorder when it involves financial components, demonstrates how saving and spending behaviors can become maladaptive when they serve psychological rather than practical functions (Canale et al., 2015). Financial hoarding involves extreme reluctance to spend money even on necessary items. Conversely, some individuals with hoarding disorder accumulate material possessions through excessive purchasing that strains financial resources while serving emotional needs for security or control.

The psychological functions underlying hoarding behaviors often relate to early experiences of deprivation, loss, or trauma that create intense needs for security and control over one's environment (Canale et al., 2015). Money and possessions may represent safety and protection against future hardship, making it extremely difficult to spend money or discard items even when practical considerations suggest these actions would be beneficial. The cognitive aspects of hoarding disorder—including difficulty making decisions, problems with categorization and organization, and strong emotional attachments to objects—can severely impair financial management abilities even when individuals possess adequate knowledge and resources.

Financial Denial involves persistent avoidance of financial awareness or responsibility that serves as a maladaptive coping mechanism for financial anxiety or overwhelm (Canale et al., 2015). Unlike temporary avoidance of financial tasks during particularly stressful periods, financial denial represents an ongoing pattern that significantly impairs financial functioning while temporarily reducing anxiety associated with financial awareness. The behavior typically develops gradually as individuals discover that avoiding financial information provides immediate emotional relief, leading to increased reliance on avoidance despite accumulating practical consequences.

The manifestations of financial denial include avoiding opening bills or financial statements, refusing to check account balances or monitor spending, procrastinating on financial decisions or tasks, and declining to discuss money matters with family members or financial professionals. The resulting complications—missed payments, accumulating late fees, deteriorating credit, missed opportunities—often worsen the underlying financial situation and create additional anxiety that reinforces the avoidance pattern.

5.4 Conclusion

Financial health and coping behaviors have a complex relationship defined by psychological needs and practical constraints interacting to create patterns that can either support or undermine overall well-being. As Sarah's vignette illustrates, financial behaviors often serve important emotional functions that must be understood and addressed for sustainable change to occur. Her shopping provided temporary relief from anxiety and a sense of control during unemployment, serving legitimate psychological needs even while creating practical financial problems that ultimately worsened her stress.

The issues explored in this chapter—from substance use and behavioral addictions to money disorders including compulsive buying, gambling, hoarding, and financial denial—demonstrate how financial behaviors can become maladaptive coping mechanisms that address underlying emotional distress while creating significant practical consequences. These patterns develop because they provide immediate psychological relief, making them difficult to change through approaches that focus solely on financial education or practical skills without addressing the emotional needs they serve. Thus, when attempting interventions, professionals may find complementary strategies necessary for addressing both the practical financial skills needed for stability and the emotional regulation capacities required for sustained behavior change.

Several key principles emerge from this exploration of financial-coping relationships. Sustainable behavior change requires addressing both practical financial skills and underlying emotional drivers rather than treating these domains separately. Problematic financial coping behaviors often serve legitimate psychological functions that must be replaced rather than simply eliminated. Shame and self-criticism frequently maintain problematic patterns while preventing help-seeking and positive change. Integration across intervention modalities proves essential for addressing the complexity of most coping-related financial issues.

For helping professionals across disciplines, understanding the coping functions of financial behaviors enables more comprehensive assessment and treatment planning that addresses root causes rather than just symptoms. Mental health practitioners must recognize how financial stress affects their clients' psychological well-being while understanding how mental health symptoms can impair financial management capacity. Financial professionals need awareness of how emotional factors influence their clients' financial behaviors and when referrals to mental health professionals might enhance outcomes. Addiction counselors should understand how financial stress affects recovery while recognizing how financial problems may develop as consequences of addictive behaviors.

The financial domain of behavioral health provides a framework for understanding these complex relationships while supporting interventions that promote both financial stability and emotional well-being. By recognizing that financial behaviors often reflect attempts to meet psychological needs, practitioners can develop more effective approaches that address both practical financial concerns and underlying emotional drivers, creating conditions for sustainable recovery and enhanced overall well-being.

References

American Psychiatric Association. (2022). *Diagnostic and statistical manual of mental disorders* (5th, Text Revision ed.). American Psychiatric Association. https://dsm.psychiatryonline.org/doi/book/10.1176/appi.books.9780890425787

Anvari-Clark, J. (2022). *Understanding financial behavioral health and race (racism), and their association with investment risk willingness* (doctoral dissertation). University of Maryland, Baltimore, Maryland. Retrieved from https://www.proquest.com/dissertations-theses/understanding-financial-behavioral-health-race/docview/2688127973/se-2

Barrault, S., Mathieu, S., Brunault, P., & Varescon, I. (2019). Does gambling type moderate the links between problem gambling, emotion regulation, anxiety, depression and gambling motives. *International Gambling Studies, 19*(1), 54–68. https://doi.org/10.1080/14459795.2018.1501403

Blashill, A. J., Perry, N., & Safren, S. A. (2011). Mental health: A focus on stress, coping, and mental illness as it relates to treatment retention, adherence, and other health outcomes. *Current HIV/AIDS Reports, 8*(4), 215–222. https://doi.org/10.1007/s11904-011-0089-1

Britt, S. L., Klontz, B. T., & Archuleta, K. L. (2015). Financial therapy: Establishing an emerging field. In B. T. Klontz, S. L. Britt, & K. L. Archuleta (Eds.), *Financial therapy: Theory, research, and practice* (pp. 3–14). Springer. https://www.scopus.com/inward/record.uri?eid=2-s2.0-84955124051&doi=10.1007%2f978-3-319-08269-1_1&partnerID=40&md5=25dc4f757ae8205de468f111dc295a43

Canale, A., Archuleta, K. L., & Klontz, B. T. (2015). Money disorders. In B. T. Klontz, S. L. Britt, & K. L. Archuleta (Eds.), *Financial therapy: Theory, research, and practice* (pp. 35–68). Springer.

Glanz, K., & Schwartz, M. D. (2008). Stress, coping, and health behavior. In K. Glanz, B. K. Rimer, & K. Viswanath (Eds.), *Health behavior and health education: Theory, research, and practice* (4th ed.). Jossey-Bass.

Ito, M., & Matsushima, E. (2017). Presentation of coping strategies associated with physical and mental health during health check-ups. *Community Mental Health Journal, 53*(3), 297–305. https://doi.org/10.1007/s10597-016-0048-9

Klontz, B., Britt, S. L., Archuleta, K. L., & Klontz, T. (2012). Disordered money behaviors: Development of the Klontz money behavior inventory. *Journal of Financial Therapy, 3*(1), 17–42. https://doi.org/10.4148/jft.v3i1.1485

McElroy, S. L., Keck, P. E., Pope, H. G., Smith, J. M., & Strakowski, S. M. (1994). Compulsive buying: A report of 20 cases. *The Journal of Clinical Psychiatry, 55*(6), 242–248. https://pubmed.ncbi.nlm.nih.gov/8071278/

Mueller, A., Mitchell, J. E., Black, D. W., Crosby, R. D., Berg, K., & de Zwaan, M. (2010). Latent profile analysis and comorbidity in a sample of individuals with compulsive buying disorder. *Psychiatry Research, 178*(2), 348–353. https://doi.org/10.1016/j.psychres.2010.04.021

Mulia, N., Ye, Y., Karriker-Jaffe, K. J., Li, L., Kerr, W. C., & Greenfield, T. K. (2021). The great recession, behavioral health, and self-rated health: An examination of racial/ethnic differences in the US. *Addictive Behaviors, 118*(2021), 106873. https://doi.org/10.1016/j.addbeh.2021.106873

Mullainathan, S., & Shafir, E. (2013). *Scarcity: Why having too little means so much.* Times Books, Henry Holt.

Parente, A. S. (2021, March 1). *The basics of problem gambling virtual training*. Training presented at the Problem Gambling Basic Clinical Training, Online. Retrieved June 6, 2021, from https://www.mdproblemgambling.com/training/problem-gambling-basic-clinic-training/

Richardson, T., Elliott, P., & Roberts, R. (2013). The relationship between personal unsecured debt and mental and physical health: A systematic review and meta-analysis. *Clinical Psychology Review, 33*(8), 1148–1162. https://doi.org/10.1016/j.cpr.2013.08.009

Sarin, S., & Nolen-Hoeksema, S. (2010). The dangers of dwelling: An examination of the relationship between rumination and consumptive coping in survivors of childhood sexual abuse. *Cognition & Emotion, 24*(1), 71–85. https://doi.org/10.1080/02699930802563668

Stack, R. J., & Meredith, A. (2018). The impact of financial hardship on single parents: An exploration of the journey from social distress to seeking help. *Journal of Family and Economic Issues, 39*(2), 233–242. https://doi.org/10.1007/s10834-017-9551-6

Wang, K., Burton, C. L., & Pachankis, J. E. (2018). Depression and substance use: Towards the development of an emotion regulation model of stigma coping. *Substance Use & Misuse, 53*(5), 859–866. https://doi.org/10.1080/10826084.2017.1391011

Chapter 6
Social Health

6.1 Introduction

Social health encompasses the quality and nature of interpersonal relationships that provide meaning, support, and connection throughout life, fundamentally influencing both individual well-being and collective resilience (Hutchison & Lee, 2015; Putnam, 2000). Within the financial domain of behavioral health, social relationships serve as both contexts where financial decisions unfold and mechanisms through which financial stress or stability ripple across families and communities. Unlike other domains where financial impacts may be primarily individual, the social domain reveals how financial circumstances become shared experiences that either strengthen relationships through mutual support and shared goals or strain connections through conflict, power imbalances, and competing priorities.

The inclusion of social health as a distinct domain within behavioral health frameworks builds upon extensive research demonstrating how relationship quality and social connections fundamentally influence mental health, physical health, and coping behaviors (Heaney & Israel, 2008; Piuzzi & Ring, 2021). Although social factors are often framed as external (social) determinants of health, emerging evidence supports their recognition as a core feature of behavioral health, with social isolation and relationship dysfunction directly impacting behavioral health outcomes across multiple domains (Choi et al., 2015; Pellmar et al., 2002). This perspective acknowledges that social health encompasses not only the availability of social support but also the quality of interpersonal relationships and their influence on individual coping capacity and overall well-being (Heaney & Israel, 2008).

The complexity of financial-social interactions reflects fundamental human needs for both autonomy and connection that must be balanced within relationships where money serves multiple symbolic and practical functions. Financial resources enable social participation and relationship maintenance while also creating

Supplementary Information The online version contains supplementary material available at https://doi.org/10.1007/978-3-032-02632-3_6.

J. Anvari-Clark, *Financial and Behavioral Health for Helping Professionals*,
https://doi.org/10.1007/978-3-032-02632-3_6

opportunities for control, manipulation, and conflict when managed without attention to relationship dynamics and communication patterns. Research consistently demonstrates how financial stress affects relationship quality and stability while relationship problems influence financial decision-making and outcomes (Dew, 2007; Jenkins et al., 2023).

Financial interdependence represents a central concept for understanding how financial and social health intersect through patterns of collaborative decision-making, resource sharing, mutual obligation, and collective activities that characterize most significant relationships (Anvari-Clark & Miller, 2023). Unlike individualistic models that emphasize financial independence as an ideal, financial interdependence recognizes that most people navigate financial decisions within relationship contexts where others' needs, preferences, and circumstances influence available options and optimal choices. This interdependence can create resilience through shared resources and mutual support while also generating vulnerability when relationship dynamics become dysfunctional or exploitative. In this regard, a goal outcome is improving levels of personal financial responsibility, rather than "independence."

This chapter examines how financial factors intersect with social functioning across diverse relationship contexts, exploring some challenges created by these interactions. We investigate financial abuse as a systematic pattern that isolates and controls victims through economic manipulation, examine how financial disagreements reflect deeper relationship issues around power and communication, and explore relational money disorders that emerge from dysfunctional financial dynamics within families and partnerships. Any interventions then should recognize that sustainable improvement often requires addressing both practical financial skills and underlying relationship patterns that shape how financial decisions unfold within social contexts.

Vignette: The Chen Family's Financial and Relational Journey

The Chen family had immigrated to the United States 12 years earlier when their daughter Amy was six years old. Li Wei worked as an engineer while his wife Mei Lin managed the household and worked part-time at a community health center. Their careful saving and financial planning had enabled them to purchase a modest home and build what appeared to be a stable middle-class life. However, beneath this surface success lay complex financial and relational dynamics that would eventually require professional intervention to resolve.

The first signs of tension emerged when Amy began her senior year of high school and started discussing college plans. Li Wei had always assumed Amy would study engineering or computer science at a prestigious university, viewing this as both honoring family expectations and ensuring financial security. He had been saving diligently for her education and felt confident they could afford tuition at excellent schools. Amy, however, expressed interest in social work and wanted to attend a state university with a strong program, which would cost significantly less than Li Wei's preferred options.

"I couldn't understand why she would choose a profession that pays so little when we had the resources for her to do anything," Li Wei later explained. "In our culture, parents sacrifice everything for children's education and success. It felt like she was rejecting not just my financial planning but everything we had worked for." The disagreement escalated when Amy applied to her preferred school without Li Wei's knowledge, using her mother as a confidential reference and for emotional support.

Mei Lin found herself caught between her husband's expectations and her daughter's emerging autonomy. She secretly supported Amy's career interests but feared confronting Li Wei directly about their different perspectives. Instead, she began providing Amy with money for application fees and campus visits without Li Wei's knowledge, using her part-time income and small amounts from their household budget. "I thought I was helping keep peace while supporting Amy," Mei Lin reflected. "But I realize now I was teaching both of them that we couldn't be honest about our disagreements."

The deception was discovered when Li Wei reviewed their bank statements and noticed unusual expenses and cash withdrawals. When he confronted Mei Lin, she initially provided vague explanations before eventually revealing her support for Amy's college plans. Li Wei felt deeply betrayed not only by the financial secrecy but by what he perceived as undermining his authority and judgment as head of the household. "It wasn't really about the money," he later acknowledged. "It was about feeling like my family was making important decisions without me, and that my years of planning and saving didn't matter to them."

The conflict that followed revealed deeper patterns of communication and power dynamics that had been developing throughout their marriage. Li Wei had always managed major financial decisions unilaterally, consulting Mei Lin on household expenses but making investment, insurance, and planning choices independently. Mei Lin had accepted this arrangement early in their marriage when her English was limited and she relied on Li Wei to navigate American financial systems. However, as her confidence and language skills developed, she began feeling excluded from decisions that significantly affected their family's future.

"I realized I didn't even know how much money we had or where it was invested," Mei Lin explained. "When Amy started talking about college costs, I couldn't answer basic questions because Li Wei handled everything. I felt embarrassed and angry that I had let myself become so dependent on someone else for information about our own finances." Her secretive support for Amy represented an attempt to regain some financial agency, though it created new problems by violating trust and transparency within their marriage.

Amy, meanwhile, experienced her parents' conflict as fundamentally about her worth and autonomy. The financial arguments felt like judgments about her career aspirations and personal values, creating guilt about pursuing her interests when they seemed to threaten family harmony. She began working additional hours at a part-time job to save money for college expenses, hoping to reduce the financial pressure on her parents while also establishing some independence from their conflicts.

The situation reached a crisis point during a family argument where years of unspoken resentments surfaced alongside immediate college-related decisions. Li Wei accused Mei Lin of financial irresponsibility and undermining family unity. Mei Lin expressed anger about being excluded from financial planning while being expected to support decisions she hadn't participated in making. Amy declared her intention to take student loans and work her way through college rather than accept money that created such family turmoil.

"We were all talking about money, but really we were fighting about respect, control, and whose opinions mattered in our family," Amy later observed. "The financial issues were real, but they were also symbols of bigger problems in how we communicated and made decisions together." The immediate result was increased emotional distance between family members and practical confusion about how to proceed with college planning.

The turning point came when Mei Lin suggested they seek help from a family counselor who specialized in financial and cultural issues. Li Wei initially resisted, viewing external help as admission of failure and potentially shameful exposure of private family matters. However, the ongoing tension and its impact on everyone's well-being eventually convinced him to participate in counseling with the understanding that the focus would be on practical financial planning rather than deep psychological exploration.

Dr. Sarah Kim, a Licensed Marriage and Family Therapist with training in financial therapy, helped the family understand how their financial conflicts reflected intersections of cultural expectations, generational differences, gender roles, and communication patterns that had evolved throughout their marriage and Amy's development. Rather than taking sides about college choices or financial management approaches, Dr. Kim facilitated conversations where each family member could express their perspectives and underlying concerns while working toward collaborative solutions.

The process revealed that Li Wei's financial control stemmed partly from cultural expectations about paternal responsibility and partly from anxiety about economic security that had developed during their early years in America when employment was uncertain. Mei Lin's secretive behavior reflected not only her desire to support Amy but also her frustration about being excluded from financial decisions that affected her daily life and future security. Amy's career interests represented both normal adolescent development and her integration of American and Chinese cultural values that differed from her parents' perspectives.

"Dr. Kim helped us see that we all wanted the same things—financial security, family harmony, and Amy's success—but we had different ideas about how to achieve them," Li Wei reflected. "Instead of fighting about whose approach was right, we learned to talk about our fears and hopes and find ways to honor everyone's concerns." The therapeutic process involved both communication skills development and practical financial planning that incorporated everyone's input.

Six months later, the family had developed a collaborative approach to Amy's college financing that honored both Li Wei's emphasis on educational investment and Amy's career interests. They agreed on a state school choice that balanced cost with program quality, with Amy taking moderate student loans to demonstrate personal investment while her parents contributed what they had originally budgeted for education. More importantly, they established new patterns for family financial decisions that included regular discussions where all adult family members could express their perspectives and concerns.

Mei Lin became more actively involved in family financial management, with Li Wei teaching her about their investments and insurance while she took responsibility for researching and managing day-to-day household finances. Amy developed a realistic understanding of family financial capabilities and constraints while maintaining autonomy over her career choices. The family established regular "money meetings" where they could discuss financial goals, concerns, and decisions in structured, collaborative ways.

"We learned that good financial decisions require good relationships," Mei Lin observed a year later as Amy successfully completed her first year of college. "When we couldn't talk honestly about money, we made decisions that hurt each other and didn't really solve our problems. Now we can disagree about financial choices without feeling like we're attacking each other's character or cultural values."

The Chen family's experience illustrates several important principles about financial and social health. Their conflicts occurred not because they lacked financial resources or knowledge but because their financial decision-making processes had evolved in ways that excluded important family members and failed to accommodate changing needs and perspectives. The financial issues served as flashpoints for deeper questions about autonomy, respect, cultural identity, and family roles that required attention to both practical financial skills and underlying relationship dynamics.

Their resolution required recognizing that effective financial management within families involves both technical skills and relational competencies including communication, negotiation, and collaborative problem-solving. The cultural dimensions of their experience show how financial behaviors and expectations are embedded in social contexts that must be acknowledged and respected rather than dismissed or changed. Most importantly, their journey demonstrates how financial interdependence can become either a source of conflict that undermines relationships or a foundation for mutual support that enhances both financial outcomes and family well-being.

***

Unlike other behavioral health domains where connections may be primarily individual or psychological, social health also involves multiple people whose financial decisions, behaviors, and circumstances affect each other through various mechanisms including shared resources, mutual obligations, emotional contagion, and interdependent outcomes. Understanding these patterns requires examining both how financial factors influence relationship dynamics and how social relationships shape financial decision-making, activities, and outcomes.

6.2 Financial Abuse and Interpersonal Violence

Financial abuse represents a systematic pattern of behaviors designed to control, isolate, and maintain power over intimate partners, family members, or other vulnerable individuals through economic manipulation and coercion (Adams et al., 2020; Betz-Hamilton & Zurlo, 2019). Unlike isolated instances of financial disagreement or poor financial decision-making, financial abuse involves deliberate actions that limit another person's economic autonomy, creating conditions where victims become financially dependent on abusers and unable to maintain safety or independence without external support.

The tactics employed in financial abuse demonstrate sophisticated understanding of how financial dependence creates vulnerability and limits options for ending harmful relationships. Economic control manifests through restricting access to bank accounts, credit cards, or cash; monitoring all expenditures and requiring detailed justification for purchases; preventing employment or sabotaging work opportunities; hiding assets or financial information; and controlling major financial decisions including housing, insurance, and investments (Postmus, 2010). These behaviors systematically erode victims' financial agency while creating practical barriers to self-sufficiency that can persist long after relationships end.

Economic exploitation represents another dimension of financial abuse that involves actively harming victims' financial standing through identity theft, forced debt accumulation, credit damage, or theft of money and property. Abusers may open credit accounts in victims' names, force victims to sign financial documents under duress, use victims' financial resources for personal expenses, or damage victims' employment or education opportunities to prevent economic advancement (Adams et al., 2020). These actions create financial damage that can take years to repair while simultaneously demonstrating the abuser's power to harm victims' financial futures.

Financial abuse occurs across diverse populations and relationship types but disproportionately affects women, older adults, individuals with disabilities, and people from communities that have experienced historical economic marginalization (Hoge et al., 2019). The prevalence of financial abuse in intimate partner violence situations is nearly 99%, making it one of the most common tactics employed by abusers and often continuing long after physical violence has ended (National Network to End Domestic Violence, n.d.). This persistence reflects how financial abuse can maintain control even when victims have achieved physical separation from abusers.

The mental health impacts of financial abuse extend beyond the direct effects of economic harm to encompass profound psychological consequences including depression, anxiety, post-traumatic stress, and complex trauma responses. Victims often internalize shame and self-blame about their financial circumstances, particularly when abuse tactics involve forcing victims to participate in illegal activities or accumulate debt that feels like personal responsibility (Davila et al., 2021). The intersection of financial abuse with other forms of victimization creates complex trauma presentations that require specialized understanding and intervention approaches.

Recovery from financial abuse involves addressing both immediate practical needs for safety and economic stability and longer-term healing from financial trauma that may affect victims' relationships with money for years after abuse has ended. The financial damage created by abuse often includes poor credit, outstanding debt, lack of employment history, and limited financial efficacy that create ongoing barriers to autonomy (Hoge et al., 2019). Thus, developing financial empowerment is frequently a component of the strategy for leaving an abusive relationship.

6.3 Interpersonal Disagreements and Strife

Financial disagreements represent one of the most common sources of conflict in close relationships, consistently ranking among leading predictors of relationship dissatisfaction and dissolution across diverse populations and relationship types (Dew, 2007). These conflicts typically reflect deeper underlying issues related to power, trust, communication, values, and identity that become manifest through disagreements about spending, saving, debt, risk tolerance, and financial priorities. Understanding financial conflicts requires recognizing that they rarely occur solely about money but rather involve complex interactions between financial circumstances and relationship dynamics.

Different money scripts and financial socialization experiences create fertile ground for misunderstanding and conflict when partners bring fundamentally different beliefs about money into relationships. These unconscious beliefs about money's meaning, appropriate uses, and moral implications often remain invisible until specific situations trigger disagreements that reveal underlying philosophical differences (Mills & Solomon, 2012). For example, partners socialized in families that emphasized saving and security may experience anxiety and moral distress when their partners view debt as a useful financial tool, while partners from families that valued generosity and sharing may feel confused or hurt when their partners prioritize nuclear family financial security over extended family assistance.

Power imbalances within relationships significantly influence both the frequency and resolution of financial conflicts through mechanisms that affect who participates in financial decisions and whose preferences receive priority consideration. These imbalances may stem from income differences, financial knowledge disparities, cultural or gender role expectations, or personality differences that affect comfort with financial discussions and decision-making (LeBaron-Black et al., 2024). When power imbalances become entrenched, financial conflicts often escalate because they simultaneously represent disagreements about specific financial choices and challenges to established relationship hierarchies.

External financial pressures including income loss, unexpected expenses, economic recession, or life transitions create additional stress that can transform manageable financial differences into serious relationship conflicts. During these periods, normal financial disagreements may become amplified by anxiety, scarcity concerns, and reduced problem-solving capacity that accompanies financial stress. The timing of financial pressures relative to other relationship stressors can significantly influence whether couples develop collaborative approaches to financial challenges or experience conflict and blame that damages relationship quality (Rosino, 2016).

6.4 Money Disorders (Relational)

Relational money disorders represent dysfunctional patterns involving two or more people where financial behaviors serve to meet psychological needs or maintain relationship dynamics in ways that ultimately harm both financial and relational well-being (Canale et al., 2015). Unlike "individual" money disorders that primarily affect one person's financial and emotional functioning, relational money disorders emerge from and reinforce problematic interaction patterns between people who share financial responsibilities, obligations, or influence over each other's financial lives.

Financial Enabling involves repeatedly providing money or financial support to others despite evidence that this assistance perpetuates problematic behaviors or prevents the development of financial responsibility. The behavior typically stems from complex motivations including genuine care and concern, fear of conflict or rejection (including cultural obligation), guilt about past experiences, or personal needs to feel needed and important within relationships (Canale et al., 2015). Financial enabling often develops gradually as individuals discover that providing money temporarily reduces tension or crisis within relationships. This leads to increased provision of financial assistance as a problem-solving strategy even when it fails to address underlying issues.

The psychological functions served by financial enabling help explain why this behavior persists despite obviously negative consequences for both the enabler and the recipient. Enablers often experience temporary relief from anxiety when they "rescue" others from financial difficulties, feel an increased sense of control and importance when others depend on them for financial support, avoid confronting relationship problems or personal boundaries by focusing on financial assistance, and maintain connection with others who might otherwise become distant or angry (Canale et al., 2015). These immediate psychological benefits make enabling behaviors addictive in their own right, creating cycles where enablers become as dependent on providing assistance as recipients become on receiving it.

Financial Dependence represents the complementary pattern where individuals rely on others for financial support in ways that exceed temporary assistance during legitimate hardship and begin to replace personal responsibility for financial well-being. This dependence may manifest through chronic requests for money, inability or unwillingness to maintain employment adequate for basic expenses, manipulation of others' emotions to obtain financial assistance, or anger and withdrawal when financial support is refused or reduced (Canale et al., 2015). Like financial enabling, dependence often develops gradually through learned patterns where emotional distress or crisis reliably produces financial assistance from others.

The relationship dynamics that maintain financial enabling and dependence create circular patterns where each person's behavior reinforces the other's problematic responses. Enablers' willingness to provide financial assistance reduces incentives for dependents to develop financial skills or responsibility, while dependents' ongoing financial needs provide enablers with continued opportunities to feel helpful and important. These patterns often become deeply embedded in family systems where they serve multiple functions including avoiding conflict, maintaining closeness, and preserving established roles and hierarchies.

Financial Enmeshment occurs when appropriate financial boundaries between a parent and child become blurred or absent, creating situations that interfere with healthy development and autonomy. This pattern most commonly involves parents who overshare financial worries with children, include children inappropriately in adult financial decisions, or fail to establish age-appropriate financial boundaries that allow children to develop independent financial identities (Canale et al., 2015). The developmental impacts of financial enmeshment can persist throughout life as individuals who grew up in financially enmeshed families often struggle to establish appropriate financial boundaries in their own relationships. They may oscillate between financial over-involvement with others and rigid financial independence that prevents healthy interdependence, or experience anxiety about financial decision-making due to unclear sense of personal financial responsibility (Canale et al., 2015).

Financial Infidelity involves secrecy or deception about financial matters within relationships that explicitly or implicitly expect financial transparency and shared decision-making (Jeanfreau et al., 2018). Unlike occasional privacy about small purchases that most relationships accommodate, financial infidelity involves ongoing patterns of deception that violate relationship agreements and compromise partners' ability to make informed financial decisions. The behaviors range from hiding individual purchases or debts to maintaining secret accounts or making major financial decisions without consultation.

The impact of financial infidelity on relationships extends far beyond the immediate financial consequences to encompass broader trust injuries that can affect all aspects of partnership functioning. Partners who discover financial deception often experience betrayal trauma similar to other forms of infidelity, including questioning the foundation of their relationship, wondering what else they do not know about their partner, and struggling to rebuild trust and intimacy (Jeanfreau et al., 2018). The recovery process typically requires addressing both the practical financial issues involved and the relationship dynamics that contributed to and resulted from the deception.

6.5 Conclusion

Exploring the relationship between financial and social health reveals fundamental truths about human nature and the interconnected ways that financial and economic security and relationship quality influence each other throughout life. As the Chen family's experience illustrates, financial conflicts rarely emerge solely from practical disagreements about money management but rather reflect deeper issues about power, communication, cultural values, and family roles that require attention to both financial skills and relationship dynamics for sustainable resolution.

The issues explored in this chapter demonstrate how financial factors can impact social relationships depending on how they are managed within specific relationship and cultural contexts. Financial abuse represents the most extreme manifestation of how economic control can isolate and harm individuals while creating lasting trauma that affects both financial and social functioning. Interpersonal financial conflicts reveal how money serves as a flashpoint for broader relationship tensions around trust, power, and shared decision-making that must be addressed through improved communication and collaboration rather than simply better budgeting or financial knowledge. Relational money disorders including enabling, dependence, enmeshment, and infidelity illustrate how financial behaviors can become embedded in dysfunctional relationship patterns that serve psychological functions while creating practical problems requiring integrated interventions.

Interventions to address these complex interconnections require recognizing both individual psychological needs and relationship system dynamics. Professionals may use financial therapy modalities adapted for couples and families that provide frameworks for addressing the emotional underpinnings of financial relationship conflicts while building practical skills for collaborative financial management. Financial planning approaches that emphasize values alignment, communication improvement, and equitable role distribution can create structures for ongoing financial collaboration that strengthen rather than strain relationships. Approaches that leverage financial interdependence for resilience would harness financial relationships to serve as sources of strength and mutual support rather than only as potential sources of conflict and dependency.

Several key principles emerge from this exploration of financial-social health intersections that have implications for helping professionals across disciplines. Financial behaviors within relationships serve multiple functions beyond their apparent economic purposes and must be understood within relationship contexts rather than as individual choices occurring in isolation. Communication patterns, power distribution, and collaborative decision-making processes must be accounted for in any intervention approach. Cultural factors significantly influence appropriate approaches to financial relationships, requiring interventions that honor diverse values and practices rather than imposing uniform standards for healthy financial functioning.

The concept of financial interdependence provides a valuable framework for understanding how financial decisions occur within relationships where mutual influence, shared resources, and collectively impacting outcomes are normal rather than problematic aspects of financial life. This perspective challenges individualistic approaches that emphasize financial independence as an ideal while offering alternative models that leverage relationship strengths for enhanced financial and social well-being.

For helping professionals working with individuals, couples, and families, recognizing these interconnections enables more comprehensive assessment and intervention planning that addresses both financial concerns and relationship factors that may be maintaining or exacerbating financial difficulties. Mental health practitioners must understand how financial stress affects relationship dynamics while recognizing how relationship problems can impair financial management capacity. Financial professionals need awareness of how relationship factors influence their clients' financial behaviors and when collaborative or therapeutic approaches might enhance financial outcomes.

The financial domain of behavioral health provides a framework for understanding these complex relationships while supporting interventions that promote both financial stability and relationship well-being. By recognizing that financial health often develops within social contexts rather than through individual effort alone, practitioners can help clients build on existing relationship strengths while addressing problematic patterns that may be undermining both financial and social functioning. This integrated approach acknowledges the fundamental truth that sustainable financial well-being typically requires both individual capability and supportive relationships that honor mutual needs while promoting collective thriving.

References

Adams, A. E., Greeson, M. R., Littwin, A. K., & Javorka, M. (2020). The revised scale of economic abuse (SEA2): Development and initial psychometric testing of an updated measure of economic abuse in intimate relationships. *Psychology of Violence, 10*(3), 268–278. https://doi.org/10.1037/vio0000244

Anvari-Clark, J., & Miller, J. (2023). Financial interdependence: A social perspective. *Encyclopedia, 3*(3), 996–1008. https://doi.org/10.3390/encyclopedia3030072

Betz-Hamilton, A., & Zurlo, K. A. (2019). Financial abuse and victimization of older adults. In C. Callahan, J. J. Frey, & R. Imboden (Eds.), *The Routledge handbook on financial social work: Direct practice with vulnerable populations* (1st ed., pp. 26–37). Taylor & Francis. https://doi.org/10.4324/9781351165686

Canale, A., Archuleta, K. L., & Klontz, B. T. (2015). Money disorders. In B. T. Klontz, S. L. Britt, & K. L. Archuleta (Eds.), *Financial therapy: Theory, research, and practice* (pp. 35–68). Springer.

Choi, H., Irwin, M. R., & Cho, H. J. (2015). Impact of social isolation on behavioral health in elderly: Systematic review. *World Journal of Psychiatry, 5*(4), 432–438. https://doi.org/10.5498/wjp.v5.i4.432

Davila, A. L., Johnson, L., & Postmus, J. L. (2021). Examining the relationship between economic abuse and mental health among Latina intimate partner violence survivors in the United States. *Journal of Interpersonal Violence, 36*(1–2), NP287–NP310. https://doi.org/10.1177/0886260517731311

Dew, J. (2007). Two sides of the same coin? The differing roles of assets and consumer debt in marriage. *Journal of Family and Economic Issues, 28*(1), 89–104. https://doi.org/10.1007/s10834-006-9051-6

Heaney, C. A., & Israel, B. A. (2008). Social networks and social support. In K. Glanz, B. K. Rimer, & K. Viswanath (Eds.), *Health behavior and health education: Theory, research, and practice* (4th ed.). Jossey-Bass.

Hoge, G. L., Stylianou, A. M., Postmus, J. L., & Johnson, L. (2019). Domestic violence / intimate partner violence and issues of financial abuse and control: What does financial empowerment look like? In C. Callahan, J. J. Frey, & R. Imboden (Eds.), *The Routledge handbook on financial social work: Direct practice with vulnerable populations* (1st ed., pp. 15–25). Taylor & Francis. https://doi.org/10.4324/9781351165686

Hutchison, E. D., & Lee, S. M. (2015). Communities. In E. D. Hutchison (Ed.), *Dimensions of human behavior: Person and environment* (5th ed., pp. 447–478). SAGE Publications.

Jeanfreau, M., Noguchi, K., Mong, M. D., & Stadthagen, H. (2018). Financial infidelity in couple relationships. *Journal of Financial Therapy, 9*(1). https://doi.org/10.4148/1944-9771.1159

Jenkins, A. I. C., Le, Y., Surachman, A., Almeida, D. M., & Fredman, S. J. (2023). Associations among financial well-being, daily relationship tension, and daily affect in two adult cohorts separated by the great recession. *Journal of Social and Personal Relationships, 40*(4), 1103–1125. https://doi.org/10.1177/02654075221105611

LeBaron-Black, A. B., Dew, J. P., Wilmarth, M. J., Holmes, E. K., Serido, J., Yorgason, J. B., & James, S. (2024). Pennies and power: Finances, relational power, and marital outcomes. *Family Relations*. https://doi.org/10.1111/fare.12989

Mills, A., & Solomon, S. (2012). *Bringing money into the conversation: A quick start for therapists*. LifeWise Productions.

National Network to End Domestic Violence. (n.d.). About financial abuse. *NNEDV*. Retrieved June 7, 2025, from https://nnedv.org/content/about-financial-abuse/

Pellmar, T. C., Brandt, E. N., & Baird, M. A. (2002). Health and behavior: The interplay of biological, behavioral, and social influences: Summary of an Institute of Medicine report. *American Journal of Health Promotion, 16*(4), 206–219. https://doi.org/10.4278/0890-1171-16.4.206

Piuzzi, N. S., & Ring, D. (2021). American Academy of orthopaedic surgeons appropriate use criteria: Early screening for psychosocial risk and protective factors. *JAAOS—Journal of the American Academy of Orthopaedic Surgeons, 29*(15), e760. https://doi.org/10.5435/JAAOS-D-20-00810

Postmus, J. L. (2010, October). *Economic empowerment of domestic violence survivors*. Applied Research Forum, National Resource Center on Domestic Violence. http://www.ncdsv.org/images/VAWnet_EcoEmpowermentDVSurvivors_10-2010.pdf

Putnam, R. D. (2000). *Bowling alone: The collapse and revival of American community*. Simon & Schuster.

Rosino, M. (2016). ABC-X model of family stress and coping. In C. L. Shehan (Ed.), *The Wiley Blackwell encyclopedia of family studies*. John Wiley & Sons. https://doi.org/10.1002/9781119085621.wbefs313

Chapter 7
Orienting Your Professional Practice

7.1 Introduction

The journey from recognizing financial concerns as integral to behavioral health to implementing effective interventions requires careful consideration of professional roles, effective interventions, and collaborative approaches. As helping professionals increasingly encounter clients whose presenting concerns involve complex interactions between financial circumstances and other domains of well-being, the question becomes not whether to address financial factors, but how to do so effectively within one's scope of practice and professional competence.

This chapter provides guidance for translating the theoretical understanding of financial health presented in earlier chapters into practical professional action. It begins by examining why traditional approaches that rely solely on financial education often fall short of creating meaningful behavior change, highlighting the need for more sophisticated interventions that address psychological, social, and structural factors alongside financial knowledge. Understanding these limitations provides essential context for the more comprehensive approaches that follow.

The chapter then maps the landscape of professionals who work at the intersection of financial and behavioral health, from mental health practitioners and healthcare providers to financial professionals and specialized financial therapists. This overview helps practitioners understand not only their own role in addressing financial concerns but also when and how to collaborate with those from other fields. The complexity of financial health challenges often requires coordinated, collaborative care that leverages diverse expertise while respecting professional boundaries and maintaining client-centered approaches.

Supplementary Information The online version contains supplementary material available at https://doi.org/10.1007/978-3-032-02632-3_7.

J. Anvari-Clark, *Financial and Behavioral Health for Helping Professionals*,
https://doi.org/10.1007/978-3-032-02632-3_7

Finally, the chapter presents an overview of interventions across therapeutic, support, educational, and planning domains. Rather than providing exhaustive detail (which would be beyond the scope of this book), this overview helps practitioners understand the range of available approaches and their appropriate applications. This foundation prepares helping professionals to move beyond simple recognition of financial factors toward informed, ethical, and effective integration of financial considerations into their practice. The goal is not to transform every practitioner into a financial or mental health expert, but rather to develop the awareness, skills, and professional relationships necessary to address relevant factors competently within one's scope of practice while knowing when and how to engage appropriate collaborators. Those who are so inclined can then pursue further education in any of these areas.

***

Vignette 1: From Recognition to Referral
Dr. Sarah Kim, a clinical psychologist, noticed that her client Marcus frequently mentioned money worries during therapy sessions focused on his depression and anxiety. Initially, she suggested he "take a financial literacy class" and tried to redirect conversations back to his emotional symptoms. However, Marcus's anxiety worsened despite progress with other therapeutic goals, and he began missing sessions due to "work conflicts" that Dr. Kim suspected were actually financial pressures. Recognizing that her traditional approach wasn't addressing the interconnected nature of Marcus's concerns, Dr. Kim sought consultation with a financial social worker in her community and learned about the bidirectional relationship between financial stress and mental health. She realized that effective treatment required addressing both domains simultaneously, leading her to develop a collaborative relationship with a financial coach who specialized in anxiety-related money behaviors.

Vignette 2: From Individual to Collaborative Care
Jennifer, a financial planner, was working with the Rodriguez family on retirement planning when she noticed that their teenage daughter's college expenses were creating significant stress that went beyond normal financial planning concerns. Mrs. Rodriguez had developed insomnia and panic attacks when discussing college costs, while Mr. Rodriguez had become increasingly withdrawn and irritable during their meetings. Jennifer recognized that while she could address the technical aspects of education funding, the family's emotional responses suggested they might benefit from additional support. Rather than attempting to provide counseling outside her expertise, she referred them to a family therapist experienced with financial stress while maintaining her role in developing their financial strategy. The collaborative approach allowed the family to address both their practical planning needs and the anxiety that was interfering with their ability to make sound financial decisions.

***

7.2 Beyond Financial Education: The Limitations of Knowledge-Only Approaches

When faced with clients experiencing financial difficulties, the reflexive response for many helping professionals is to recommend financial education—a budgeting class, a financial literacy workshop, or simply "learning how to manage money better." While potentially well-intentioned, this approach often falls short because it addresses only one small aspect of financial capability while ignoring the complex psychological, social, and environmental factors that influence financial behaviors.

Research on Financial Education Effectiveness Research findings on the effectiveness of financial education reveal significant limitations to knowledge-only approaches. In a meta-analysis of 201 studies, Fernandes et al. (2014) found that interventions to improve financial literacy explained just 0.1% of the variance in financial behaviors observed, with even weaker effects seen in low-income samples. These findings suggest how minimal the impact of traditional financial education often is, and that other factors would presumably be much more influential. Their paper also proposed that feeling confident about financial concepts may be more important than actual technical knowledge in driving behavior change.

Some research does show more promising results. Kaiser et al. (2020) also conducted a meta-analysis and found positive causal effects of financial education programs on both financial knowledge and behaviors. However, even these more optimistic findings highlighted the importance of program design, timing, and integration with financial opportunities rather than education alone.

From Knowledge to Capability Financial knowledge alone is insufficient without opportunities to apply that knowledge. Friedline and West (2016) examined data from the National Financial Capability Study and found that Millennials who were "financially capable" (having both financial education and access to financial products like savings accounts) were 176% more likely to afford unexpected expenses and 224% more likely to save for emergencies compared to peers who were financially excluded. The researchers concluded that "interventions that focus solely on financial education or inclusion may be insufficient for facilitating Millennials' healthy financial behaviors" (p. 649).

This finding aligns with Sherraden's (2013) financial capability framework, which integrates financial access (opportunity to act) with financial literacy (ability to act). According to this framework, effective financial behavior requires both knowledge and appropriate financial products and services. For clients experiencing financial precarity, knowledge without accessible financial products or services creates frustration rather than improvement.

The Complex Psychology of Financial Education Financial education can have counter-intuitive effects on financial anxiety. White et al. (2024) examined how both the quantity and quality of financial education affect anxiety levels, finding complex relationships. More education sometimes reduced anxiety, possibly by providing a false sense of improved efficacy or by delivering "just-in-time" information that immediately helped with financial tasks. However, higher-quality financial education sometimes increased anxiety by giving people a clearer understanding of their financial situation—a situation of greater awareness of one's lack of knowledge.

Similarly, responses to financial literacy questions may not always reflect actual knowledge levels. Pearson et al. (2024) found that "don't know" responses to financial literacy questions may indicate lack of confidence or ambiguity rather than knowledge deficiency. This further complicates the relationship between financial education and behavior, as knowledge without confidence may not translate to action.

Cognitive Bandwidth and Scarcity Considerations According to Mullainathan and Shafir's (2013) research on scarcity, financial strain depletes cognitive resources, making it difficult for individuals to focus on learning new information or implementing complex financial strategies. When experiencing financial precarity, people often enter a "tunneling" state where immediate financial pressures dominate attention, leaving little cognitive bandwidth for educational content or long-term planning.

For clients experiencing acute financial stress, such as impending eviction or utility disconnection, expecting them to benefit from financial education is unrealistic. The scarcity mindset creates a psychological environment where learning is impaired and focus narrows to immediate survival needs. As Chen and Warmath (2022) found, acute scarcity affects problem-solving differently than chronic scarcity, suggesting interventions must be tailored to the client's specific situation.

Hamilton et al. (2019) noted that individuals under financial constraints develop coping mechanisms that can either support or undermine their financial well-being. Simply providing information fails to address these deeper psychological processes or build the resilience needed to navigate financial challenges effectively.

Financial Trauma and Emotional Barriers Many clients experiencing financial difficulties have histories of financial trauma that create powerful emotional barriers to engaging with financial information. For these clients, approaching financial topics can trigger shame, anxiety, or avoidance behaviors. Without addressing the emotional responses, financial education remains intellectually inaccessible even if physically available. Ross and Coambs (2018) highlight how psychological trauma significantly impacts financial decision-making across cognitive, behavioral, emotional, and relational dimensions. Simply providing information without addressing these underlying trauma responses is unlikely to produce meaningful change.

Inappropriate Referrals and Professional Responsibility Requiring clients to attend financial education as a prerequisite for receiving emergency financial assistance can be particularly problematic, often coming across as blaming the victim for circumstances over which they cannot control, such as systemic forces in society, or behaviors over which they have lost control. In crisis situations, simply providing financial information cannot facilitate the longer-term capability development required.

Furthermore, inappropriate referrals can waste both client and professional time while undermining credibility. Referring a client to "go see a financial planner" when they actually need a financial coach to develop financial efficacy reflects a lack of understanding of the different roles and approaches within financial services. Such referrals can lead to frustration when the client discovers the professional does not provide the needed service and ultimately damages the referring professional's credibility.

Cultural Contexts and Financial Interdependence Financial behaviors are deeply embedded in cultural contexts and social relationships that traditional financial education often fails to acknowledge. Gudmunson and Danes (2011) emphasize that financial socialization—how individuals develop financial values, attitudes, and behaviors—occurs primarily within families and cultural groups, shaping financial behaviors in ways that purely educational approaches cannot address.

Additionally, as Anvari-Clark and Miller (2023) note, financial interdependence—the interconnected nature of financial decisions within relationships and communities—significantly influences financial behaviors. Financial education taught from an individualist financial management paradigm (as most financial education is taught) may conflict with cultural values or family obligations that emphasize collective financial responsibility. For example, being able to calculate compounding interest holds little relevance when one feels safer placing their money in a mutually supportive rotating savings group.

Moving Beyond Education: A More Effective Approach Rather than simply recommending financial education, helping professionals need a more comprehensive approach in which they:

1. **Address immediate financial needs first**, ensuring basic security before attempting educational interventions.
2. **Recognize and work with emotional responses** to financial topics.
3. **Respect cultural contexts and patterns of financial interdependence.**
4. **Acknowledge structural barriers** while still empowering individual action.
5. **Combine subjective knowledge building and efficacy** with practical application opportunities.
6. **Integrate financial interventions** with other behavioral health supports.

This approach aligns with the financial capability framework (Sherraden, 2013), emphasizing that financial well-being arises from a combination of individual capability and appropriate environmental opportunities. It also reflects a holistic understanding of the relationships among the financial and other behavioral health domains, whereby financial precarity, financial efficacy, and financial well-being interact with mental, physical, social, and coping health.

Recognizing the limitations of education-only approaches creates the foundation for understanding why effective financial health interventions require collaboration among professionals with diverse expertise. To build these collaborative relationships effectively, practitioners must first understand the landscape of professionals who work with financial and behavioral health concerns.

7.3 Understanding the Professional Landscape

Knowing the various professionals who address financial and behavioral health issues helps practitioners make appropriate referrals and develop collaborative relationships. Although the following categories provide a general description of practice scope, it is important to note that individual practitioners may have additional specialized training or designations, and there may be overlap in services provided.

7.3.1 *Behavioral Health Professionals*

These professionals primarily address psychological, social, and physical aspects of health; some may also incorporate financial concerns within their approach:

Clinical Psychologists provide assessment, diagnosis, and treatment using evidence-based interventions. Refer when financial stress causes significant psychological distress requiring specialized mental health intervention.

Psychiatrists offer diagnosis and medication management for mental health conditions. Consider referral when financial stress or problem behaviors contribute to symptoms that may warrant medication evaluation.

Licensed Clinical Social Workers (LCSW) provide psychotherapy and case management with a person-in-environment perspective, particularly valuable when financial and mental health issues intertwine with social system challenges. Some social workers may also do financial therapy.

Licensed Professional Counselors (LPC) offer talk therapy for emotional, behavioral, and mental health issues. Helpful when clients need support processing feelings about financial challenges or when issues affect personal identity.

Marriage and Family Therapists (MFT) specialize in relationship dynamics and family systems. Appropriate when financial issues cause relationship conflict or threaten family stability.

Substance Use Disorder Counselors provide assessment and treatment for addiction. Essential when financial problems contribute to or result from substance use, or when financial recovery must integrate with addiction recovery.

Health Psychologists focus on how biological, psychological, and social factors influence health. Consider referral when financial stress manifests as physical symptoms or chronic illness impacts financial stability.

Primary Care Physicians provide comprehensive healthcare and serve as first contact points. May detect physical or mental manifestations of financial stress and offer initial screening and referrals.

7.3.2 *Financial Professionals*

These practitioners specialize in various aspects of financial management, planning, and behavior:

Financial Advisors provide investment advice and manage portfolios. Suitable when clients have investable assets requiring professional management or need investment or insurance selection guidance.

Certified Financial Planners (CFP®) create comprehensive plans and strategies to meet life goals. Most appropriate for long-term planning, wealth management, retirement planning, or tax optimization. The CFP designation is a professional certification held by financial planners and advisors for enhanced standards of practice.

Financial Coaches offer guidance on financial behaviors, habits, and mindset changes. Valuable when clients need accountability and behavior change support, especially when knowledge exists but implementation is challenging.

Financial Counselors (AFC®) provide education and guidance on budgeting, debt management, and goal setting. Particularly helpful when clients face immediate challenges requiring practical solutions.

Specialized Financial Counselors include credit, housing, bankruptcy, and student loan counselors addressing specific needs. Refer when clients face targeted challenges in these areas.

7.3.3 *Bridging Professionals*

Some professionals specifically work at the intersection of financial and behavioral health:

Financial Therapists integrate financial planning with therapeutic techniques to address money-related psychological issues. Appropriate when financial behaviors are driven by deep-seated psychological issues or money disorders are present (Britt et al., 2015).

Financial Social Workers integrate social work principles with financial guidance to address psychological and social aspects of money management. Effective when financial issues intersect with social service needs or trauma impacts financial behavior.

Financial Navigators help individuals access and coordinate financial resources and assistance programs, usually in a healthcare setting. Consider referral when clients need help identifying emergency assistance or navigating complex financial systems.

Integrated Care Providers work within healthcare systems that purposefully integrate behavioral health and financial support services, often collaborating across disciplines with specialized training in multiple domains (Mancini, 2021).

Understanding the roles and expertise of different professionals provides the foundation for developing effective collaborative relationships. However, knowing who does what is only the first step—the real challenge lies in structuring these professional partnerships to maximize client outcomes while respecting disciplinary boundaries and maintaining clear communication.

7.4 Collaboration Models for Effective Care

Addressing the complex interplay between financial and behavioral health concerns often requires collaboration among professionals with complementary expertise (Seay et al., 2015).

Sequential Collaboration Professionals address issues in coordinated sequence, with one practitioner completing work before another begins. This works well when one issue clearly needs addressing before others can be effectively attempted. For example, a psychologist might address acute anxiety symptoms before referring to a financial counselor for practical money management skills. Or a financial counselor might stabilize an immediate financial crisis before the client begins therapy on underlying financial trauma. This model requires clear communication about when the "handoff" should occur and what preparatory work has been completed. Callahan et al. (2019) note this approach ensures clients are emotionally ready to engage with financial concerns and practically ready to address psychological aspects.

Parallel Collaboration Multiple professionals work simultaneously with a client on different aspects of interconnected concerns, recognizing that financial and behavioral health issues often need concurrent attention (Seay et al., 2015). For instance, a financial coach might focus on budgeting skills while a substance abuse counselor simultaneously addresses addiction impacting spending. Or a marriage therapist might address relationship dynamics around money while a financial planner develops long-term investment strategy. Seay et al. (2015) emphasize that effective parallel collaboration requires regular communication between providers to ensure interventions complement rather than contradict each other, often including periodic joint meetings or structured information sharing with appropriate client consent.

Integrated Collaboration The most comprehensive approach involves professionals working jointly to address interconnected issues through formal partnerships, co-therapy models, or professionals with dual training (Seay et al., 2015). For example, a financial therapist with both clinical and financial training might address financial behaviors and underlying psychological factors in the same session. Or a financial planner and psychologist might conduct joint sessions to simultaneously address retirement planning and aging anxiety. Archuleta et al. (2015) found integrated solution-focused approaches particularly effective for issues where financial and psychological aspects are deeply intertwined, such as financial trauma or entrenched money disorders. This model requires professionals comfortable working across disciplinary boundaries and communicating effectively using both financial and psychological frameworks.

Building Effective Collaborative Relationships

Successful professional partnerships require several considerations (Seay et al., 2015):

1. **Clear Role Delineation**: Explicitly discuss and document each professional's responsibilities to avoid duplication or gaps in care, including how billing will be handled.
2. **Shared Language**: Develop common vocabulary bridging financial and behavioral health terminology to enhance communication.
3. **Formal Consent Processes**: Implement structured procedures allowing appropriate information sharing while protecting client confidentiality.
4. **Regular Communication**: Establish consistent communication channels and check-in points to ensure coordinated care.
5. **Client-Centered Approach**: Keep clients actively involved in the collaborative process, ensuring their goals and preferences guide the work.
6. **Cultural Humility**: Ensure collaborative approaches account for cultural differences in attitudes toward both money and mental health.

By intentionally building these collaborative relationships, professionals can offer more comprehensive support to clients navigating the complex intersection of financial and behavioral health challenges.

While collaboration models provide the structural framework for professional partnerships, the effectiveness of these relationships ultimately depends on the specific interventions employed and how well they address the complex interplay between financial circumstances and behavioral health. The following section outlines the range of evidence-based interventions available to practitioners working individually or in collaboration with others.

7.5 Interventions and Integration into Practice

Various interventions and approaches can address financial health, either independently or in conjunction with other therapeutic methods. These interventions are categorized by their primary focus, though many incorporate elements from multiple approaches. Many have been adapted by therapists or scholars for a financial context. Beyond these, other interventions may have a specific focus, such as on problem gambling or overshopping, are group-recovery models, or employ frameworks such as the transtheoretical stages of change (Prochaska & DiClemente, 2005) and motivational interviewing (Miller & Rollnick, 2013). Professionals should start by using the approaches with which they are already familiar and gradually aim to develop their competencies.

7.5.1 Therapeutic Financial Interventions

These interventions specifically address the psychological aspects of financial behaviors and are often delivered by professionals with mental health training or in collaboration with mental health professionals.

Experiential Financial Therapy This approach uses action-oriented techniques to address underlying emotional issues related to money through psychodrama, role-playing, and visualization (Klontz et al., 2015). Key elements include creating visual representations of money beliefs, role-playing financial scenarios to identify emotional triggers, developing embodied awareness of financial stress responses, and processing financial trauma through guided experiences. Research demonstrates significant reductions in psychological distress and financial anxiety while improving financial health behaviors.

Solution-Focused Financial Therapy (SFFT) SFFT adapts solution-focused therapy principles to financial concerns, helping clients identify and build upon existing strengths and resources rather than focusing extensively on problems (Archuleta et al., 2015). Core techniques include miracle questions that help clients envision ideal financial futures, exception-finding questions identifying when financial problems are less severe, scaling questions tracking progress toward financial goals, and compliment-giving to reinforce positive financial behaviors. A pilot study found SFFT participants experienced significant reductions in financial anxiety and improvements in financial well-being.

Cognitive-Behavioral Financial Therapy This approach applies cognitive-behavioral therapy principles to address dysfunctional financial thoughts and behaviors, helping clients identify and challenge automatic thoughts, underlying beliefs, and schemas related to money (Nabeshima & Klontz, 2015). Key interventions include identifying and restructuring irrational financial beliefs, monitoring and modifying financial thought patterns, conducting behavioral experiments around money, and developing coping strategies for financial triggers. Studies show effectiveness in treating money disorders such as compulsive buying and gambling.

Narrative Financial Therapy This approach helps clients externalize problematic financial stories and develop new, empowering narratives about money, recognizing how cultural, familial, and personal narratives shape financial behaviors and identity (McCoy et al., 2013). Core techniques include externalizing conversations that separate the person from the financial problem, exploring the influence of dominant cultural money narratives, developing alternative stories highlighting financial competence, and documenting and reinforcing new financial narratives.

Systemic Financial Therapy Systemic financial therapy addresses financial behaviors within the context of family and relationship systems, recognizing how money dynamics reflect and reinforce broader relationship patterns (Archuleta & Burr, 2015). Key interventions include family financial genograms and ecomaps to explore intergenerational money patterns, couples communication exercises around financial values and goals, boundary-setting work for financial enabling and dependence, and addressing financial infidelity through trust-rebuilding exercises. This approach is particularly valuable when financial problems reflect underlying relationship dynamics or when individual financial changes affect family systems.

While therapeutic interventions address the psychological underpinnings of financial behaviors, many clients also require more concrete support services to manage immediate financial challenges or maintain stability during periods of compromised functioning. These support interventions provide essential scaffolding that enables therapeutic work to be effective.

7.5.2 Support and Stability Interventions

These interventions provide structure and support for individuals and families whose financial management abilities are compromised by behavioral health-related complications.

Case Management This service provides critical support for individuals whose mental health or other conditions significantly impact financial management capacity, serving as essential safeguards against financial crises while promoting greater autonomy and recovery over time. Financial case management includes assessment of financial needs and capabilities, coordination of financial resources and services, benefits counseling, advocacy with creditors, and ongoing monitoring of financial goals (Malks et al., 2010). This approach is particularly valuable for individuals experiencing both mental health challenges and financial precarity, addressing practical aspects of financial stability that might otherwise overwhelm coping resources.

Representative Payee Services For individuals with severe mental health conditions significantly impairing financial management capacity, representative payee services may be appropriate. Representative payees receive and manage benefit payments on behalf of beneficiaries (often a family member), ensuring basic needs are met and funds are managed appropriately (Luchins et al., 2003). Research found that psychiatric patients with representative payees showed better money management skills, reduced substance use, and improved clinical outcomes compared to similar patients without this support (Kinsky et al., 2019). Recovery-oriented peer-provider approaches increasingly emphasize skill-building and gradual transition to greater financial responsibility when possible, including collaborative budget development, supervised practice with financial tasks, and gradual transfer of financial responsibilities as skills and stability improve (Jiménez-Solomon et al., 2016).

Financial Navigation Services Specialized navigation developed to help individuals traverse complex financial landscapes, particularly in healthcare settings. Financial navigators assist with insurance optimization, help access financial assistance programs including charity care (both within and outside the provider hospital) and pharmaceutical assistance, provide advocacy for prior authorization requests and appeals, and offer medical bill review and negotiation services (Doherty et al., 2021). This intervention proves particularly valuable for vulnerable populations navigating complex systems while managing health crises that compromise cognitive and emotional capacity for financial advocacy.

Relief Programs Medical debt relief programs represent systematic approaches to addressing the accumulated medical debt that can create lasting financial hardship following health crises. These interventions range from individual debt forgiveness programs offered by healthcare institutions and private foundations, to large-scale debt buy-up initiatives that purchase and forgive medical debt across entire communities. Hospital charity care programs provide debt relief for qualifying patients based on income and financial hardship criteria. These programs, often required by tax-exempt status regulations, can significantly reduce or eliminate medical debt for eligible individuals. However, awareness and access to these programs remain limited, and in many cases effectively hidden by omission, requiring advocacy and assistance to ensure that eligible patients receive available relief (Noguchi, 2022). Community-based medical debt relief initiatives have gained prominence through organizations that purchase medical debt portfolios at discounted rates and forgive the obligations without requiring individual applications or eligibility determinations. These programs demonstrate the potential for systematic approaches to addressing medical debt at population levels (Noguchi, 2022).

Resilience Through Financial Interdependence Individuals and families may also leverage social networks for financial cushioning and stability through structured resource sharing and mutual support systems (Schneider et al., 2017). Key components include contributing to and benefiting from economic activities in partnership with extended family members (such as trading childcare for help with a bill), accessing mutual aid networks providing emergency assistance, faith-based financial support ministries, and, as longer-term resilience strategies, participating in rotating savings and credit associations (ROSCAs) like tandas or susus, or engaging in community investment cooperatives (Anvari-Clark & Miller, 2023; Castro-Cosío, 2024; Quiñones & Grier-Reed, 2023). These approaches recognize financial issues are socially contextualized rather than purely individual affairs.

Support services provide crucial stability for clients in crisis or with significant functional limitations, but sustainable improvement often requires building practical knowledge and skills. Educational and skill-building interventions bridge the gap between immediate stabilization and long-term financial capability development.

7.5.3 Educational and Skill-Building Interventions

These interventions focus on developing practical financial knowledge and skills, with varying levels of efficacy-building and assistance provision, often incorporating elements that address psychological aspects of financial behavior.

Financial Education and Literacy Programs Structured financial education programs provide foundational knowledge about financial concepts, tools, and strategies. While traditional approaches focus primarily on information delivery, contemporary programs increasingly incorporate behavioral elements addressing psychological barriers to implementation (Kaiser et al., 2020). Effective programs typically include basic financial concepts and terminology, practical tools for budgeting and financial management, guidance on navigating financial systems and institutions, and resources for ongoing financial learning. While traditional financial education shows mixed effectiveness when delivered in isolation, Netemeyer et al. (2024) found that combining education with behavioral interventions significantly improves financial outcomes. Furthermore, just-in-time educational approaches connect relevant content to salient issues, enhancing participants' ability to immediately apply learnings, such as during benefit enrollment periods or during tax filing season (Newcomb & Cummings, 2019). Culturally tailored educational approaches that incorporate diverse financial values, family obligations, and community practices enhance relevance and engagement while validating participants' existing knowledge and experiences, ultimately improving both comprehension and implementation of financial concepts within participants' actual life contexts rather than imposing externally defined standards of "appropriate" financial behavior (Anvari-Clark & Miller, 2023).

Financial Capability Development Financial capability approaches focus on developing both the ability and opportunity to act in one's financial best interest. These programs address not only individual knowledge and skills but also access to appropriate financial products and services (Sherraden, 2013). Comprehensive financial capability interventions include financial education tailored to specific life circumstances, access to appropriate financial products, removal of structural barriers to financial action, and support for navigating complex financial systems. Studies suggest that financial capability approaches can be effective for marginalized populations facing both individual and structural barriers to financial health (Birkenmaier et al., 2022).

Financial Coaching Financial coaching provides structured support for developing and implementing financial goals and behaviors. Unlike financial advising, which often focuses on specific product recommendations, coaching emphasizes skill development, accountability, and behavioral change (Collins & Olive, 2016). Key components include collaborative goal-setting based on client values, development of concrete action plans, regular accountability check-ins, and celebration of progress and problem-solving for challenges. Research demonstrates that financial coaching can improve not only financial outcomes (Theodos et al., 2018) but also physical and mental health (White et al., 2022).

Financial Counseling Distinct from coaching, financial counseling typically focuses on immediate problem-solving for specific financial challenges through structured assessment, decision-making, and action planning (Delgadillo, 2014). Specialized forms address targeted needs including credit counseling for debt management, housing counseling for homeownership and rental issues, bankruptcy counseling for legal debt relief, and student loan counseling for education debt navigation. Key components include crisis assessment, options analysis, creditor negotiation, and referral coordination. This intervention emphasizes immediate stabilization and practical problem-solving rather than long-term behavioral change, making it useful for financial crises requiring rapid response.

Trauma-Informed Financial Empowerment Programming that develops financial literacy and efficacy in combination with trauma-healing approaches can improve the financial well-being of those whose financial behaviors have been shaped by traumatic experiences (Weida et al., 2024). Components include peer support groups that reduce isolation and shame, graduated exposure to financial tasks that build tolerance, integration of financial skill-building with emotional healing processes, and recognition of financial avoidance as adaptive responses to past harm (Phojanakong et al., 2020). This approach acknowledges that traditional financial education may be ineffective or harmful for trauma survivors without attention to underlying psychological impacts.

While education and skill-building interventions focus on developing individual capacity, some clients require additional safeguards and systematic planning approaches to protect their financial well-being over time. These planning and protection interventions are particularly valuable for individuals with conditions that may affect their financial decision-making capacity episodically or progressively.

7.5.4 Advance Planning and Protection Interventions

These interventions focus on establishing structures and safeguards to protect financial well-being, particularly for individuals with episodic or progressive mental health conditions.

Specialized Financial Planning Financial planning for individuals with mental health or other debilitating conditions addresses unique considerations including income volatility due to episodic symptoms, potential work limitations, higher healthcare costs, and planning for potential incapacity periods (Smith et al., 2000). Financial planners with expertise in this area help clients develop strategies that enhance financial security while accommodating specific challenges presented by the conditions. For individuals with bipolar disorder, planning might include establishing safeguards against impulsive spending during manic episodes, such as spending limits, cooling-off periods for large purchases, or two-signature requirements on major financial transactions (Mudigonda et al., 2016). For those with depression, planning might focus on taking direct actions (Asebedo & Wilmarth, 2017), such as automating essential financial tasks to ensure continuity during periods when executive function is compromised.

ABLE Accounts and Disability Financial Planning ABLE (Achieving a Better Life Experience) accounts provide U.S.-based tax-advantaged savings opportunities for individuals with disabilities that began before age 26, enabling them to accumulate resources for disability-related expenses without jeopardizing eligibility for means-tested public benefits (Briscese et al., n.d.). These accounts represent crucial financial tools for individuals whose health conditions create ongoing expenses while limiting earning capacity. ABLE accounts allow individuals to save up to $18,000 annually (as of 2024) for qualified disability expenses including healthcare, transportation, housing, education, and assistive technology (Briscese et al., n.d.). Account balances up to $100,000 do not affect eligibility for Supplemental Security Income (SSI), while higher balances may affect SSI but not Medicaid eligibility. This structure enables individuals with disabilities to build financial resources for health-related expenses without losing essential benefit coverage.

Legal and Fiduciary Arrangements Powers of attorney and other legal arrangements provide important protections when behavioral health conditions temporarily or permanently affect financial decision-making capacity. A financial power of attorney designates a trusted individual to make financial decisions when the principal is unable to do so, ensuring continuity during periods of acute mental health symptoms (Mudigonda et al., 2016). Advance financial directives outline specific wishes regarding financial management during periods of impaired capacity, providing guidance for designated agents and preserving autonomy (Mudigonda et al., 2016). For severe, persistent mental illness, legal arrangements like special needs trusts can protect access to essential benefits while providing supplemental financial support (Lacey & Nadler, 2012). These arrangements must balance protection with autonomy, using the least restrictive options necessary and incorporating the individual's preferences whenever possible. Regular review and adjustment of these arrangements is essential as the individual's condition, circumstances, and capabilities change over time.

7.6 Conclusion

Moving from recognizing the limitations of financial education to implementing effective financial health interventions requires a fundamental shift in how helping professionals conceptualize and address financial concerns. As this chapter demonstrates, simply recommending that clients "take a financial literacy class" fails because it ignores the complex psychological, social, and structural factors that drive financial behaviors. Knowledge alone cannot address financial trauma, cognitive bandwidth limitations during scarcity, or the cultural contexts that shape financial decision-making.

The scope of professional activities outlined in this chapter reveals why collaborative, interdisciplinary approaches prove more effective than isolated interventions. When Dr. Sarah Kim recognized that traditional therapy was not addressing Marcus's interconnected financial and mental health concerns, she discovered the value of partnering with financial coaches who understood anxiety-related money behaviors. Similarly, when Jennifer the financial planner encountered the Rodriguez family's emotional responses to college planning, she recognized that technical financial advice alone was insufficient without therapeutic support for their underlying anxiety.

These examples illustrate how the diverse professionals working at the intersection of financial and behavioral health—from clinical psychologists and financial therapists to financial coaches and navigators—each bring specialized expertise that addresses different aspects of the limitations inherent in education-only approaches. Mental health professionals can address the emotional barriers and trauma responses that prevent clients from engaging with financial information. Financial coaches provide the behavioral change support and accountability that knowledge transfer cannot deliver. Financial navigators help clients navigate complex systems when cognitive bandwidth is compromised by financial stress. Financial therapists integrate both domains to address the psychological functions that problematic financial behaviors serve.

The interventions presented throughout this chapter directly counter the specific limitations of traditional financial education. Where education assumes cognitive availability, therapeutic financial interventions address the emotional and psychological barriers that interfere with learning. Where education provides generic information, financial coaching offers individualized, culturally responsive support that works with clients' existing strengths and values. Where education treats financial behaviors as purely rational choices, support and stability interventions recognize when mental health conditions or trauma require external structure and specialized assistance.

Most importantly, this chapter demonstrates that effective financial health intervention is not about transforming every behavioral health professional into a financial expert (or vice-versa), but rather about developing the awareness, skills, and collaborative relationships necessary to address the health and financial factors competently within one's scope of practice. The collaborative models—sequential, parallel, and integrated—provide frameworks for coordinating care that leverages diverse expertise while maintaining appropriate professional boundaries.

The financial domain of behavioral health requires this kind of integrated thinking precisely because financial concerns rarely exist in isolation from other aspects of human experience. By moving beyond the limitations of education-only approaches toward collaborative, evidence-based interventions that address the full complexity of financial behaviors, helping professionals can provide more effective support for clients navigating the intricate relationships between their financial circumstances and overall well-being. This represents not just better practice, but a recognition that financial health, like all aspects of behavioral health, emerges from the dynamic interplay of individual, relational, and systemic factors that require comprehensive, collaborative attention.

References

Anvari-Clark, J., & Miller, J. (2023). Financial interdependence: A social perspective. *Encyclopedia, 3*(3), 996–1008. https://doi.org/10.3390/encyclopedia3030072

Archuleta, K. L., & Burr, E. A. (2015). Systemic financial therapy. In B. T. Klontz, S. L. Britt, & K. L. Archuleta (Eds.), *Financial therapy: Theory, research, and practice* (pp. 217–234). Springer.

Archuleta, K. L., Burr, E. A., Bell Carlson, M., Ingram, J., Irwin Kruger, L., Grable, J., & Ford, M. (2015). Solution focused financial therapy: A brief report of a pilot study. *Journal of Financial Therapy, 6*(1). https://doi.org/10.4148/1944-9771.1081

Asebedo, S. D., & Wilmarth, M. J. (2017). Does how we feel about financial strain matter for mental health? *Journal of Financial Therapy, 8*(1), 62–80. https://doi.org/10.4148/1944-9771.1130

Birkenmaier, J., Rothwell, D., Frey, J. J., & Coffey, D. S. (2022). Introduction to the special issue on "financial capability and asset building for family financial wellbeing". *Journal of Family and Economic Issues, 43*(4), 647–653. https://doi.org/10.1007/s10834-022-09871-y

Briscese, G., Levere, M., & Pollack, H. (n.d.). *Improving financial security for people with disabilities: The promise of ABLE accounts.* Center for Financial Security, University of Wisconsin-Madison. Retrieved June 5, 2025, from https://minds.wisconsin.edu/bitstream/handle/1793/85399/WI23-10_Working-Paper_Pollack-et-al_4.24.pdf?sequence=1

Britt, S. L., Klontz, B. T., & Archuleta, K. L. (2015). Financial therapy: Establishing an emerging field. In B. T. Klontz, S. L. Britt, & K. L. Archuleta (Eds.), *Financial therapy: Theory, research, and practice* (pp. 3–14). Springer. https://www.scopus.com/inward/record.uri?eid=2-s2.0-84955124051&doi=10.1007%2f978-3-319-08269-1_1&partnerID=40&md5=25dc4f757ae8205de468f111dc295a43

Callahan, C. (2019). Overview of interventions. In J. J. Frey & R. Imboden (Eds.), *The Routledge handbook on financial social work: Direct practice with vulnerable populations* (1st ed.). Taylor & Francis. https://doi.org/10.4324/9781351165686

Castro-Cosío, A. (2024). 'Informal' financial practices in the south Bronx: Family, compadres, and acquaintances. *Journal of Family and Economic Issues, 45*, 327–342. https://doi.org/10.1007/s10834-023-09912-0

Chen, P.-J., & Warmath, D. (2022). Maintaining financial well-being: Differences in response to acute versus chronic scarcity. *Consumer Interests Annual, 68*.

Collins, J. M., & Olive, P. (2016). Financial coaching: Defining an emerging field. In J. J. Xiao (Ed.), *Handbook of consumer finance research* (2nd ed.). Springer International Publishing. Retrieved February 19, 2022, from http://link.springer.com/10.1007/978-3-319-28887-1

Delgadillo, L. M. (2014). Financial clarity: Education, literacy, capability, counseling, planning, and coaching. *Family and Consumer Sciences Research Journal, 43*(1), 18–28. https://doi.org/10.1111/fcsr.12078

Doherty, M. J., Thom, B., & Gany, F. (2021). Evidence of the feasibility and preliminary efficacy of oncology financial navigation: A scoping review. *Cancer Epidemiology, Biomarkers & Prevention, 30*(10), 1778–1784. https://doi.org/10.1158/1055-9965.EPI-20-1853

Fernandes, D., Lynch, J. G., & Netemeyer, R. G. (2014). Financial literacy, financial education, and downstream financial behaviors. *Management Science, 60*(8), 1861–1883. https://doi.org/10.1287/mnsc.2013.1849

Friedline, T., & West, S. (2016). Financial education is not enough: Millennials may need financial capability to demonstrate healthier financial behaviors. *Journal of Family and Economic Issues, 37*(4), 649–671. https://doi.org/10.1007/s10834-015-9475-y

Gudmunson, C. G., & Danes, S. M. (2011). Family financial socialization: Theory and critical review. *Journal of Family and Economic Issues, 32*(4), 644–667. https://doi.org/10.1007/s10834-011-9275-y

Hamilton, R. W., Mittal, C., Shah, A., Thompson, D. V., & Griskevicius, V. (2019). How financial constraints influence consumer behavior: An integrative framework. *Journal of Consumer Psychology, 29*(2), 285–305. https://doi.org/10.1002/jcpy.1074

Jiménez-Solomon, O. G., Méndez-Bustos, P., Swarbrick, M., Díaz, S., Silva, S., Kelley, M., et al. (2016). Peer-supported economic empowerment: A financial wellness intervention framework for people with psychiatric disabilities. *Psychiatric Rehabilitation Journal, 39*(3), 222–233. https://doi.org/10.1037/prj0000210

Kaiser, T., Lusardi, A., Menkhoff, L., & Urban, C. J. (2020). *Financial education affects financial knowledge and downstream behaviors* (Working Paper 27057). National Bureau of Economic Research. http://www.nber.org/papers/w27057

Kinsky, S. M., Creasy, S. L., & Hawk, M. (2019). A systematic review of health outcomes associated with provision of representative payee services. *Psychiatric Services, 70*(8), 714–727. https://doi.org/10.1176/appi.ps.201800320

Klontz, B. T., Klontz, P. T., & Tharp, D. (2015). Experiential financial therapy. In B. T. Klontz, S. L. Britt, & K. L. Archuleta (Eds.), *Financial therapy: Theory, research, and practice* (pp. 103–120). Springer.

Lacey, R. P., & Nadler, H. D. (2012). *Special needs trusts*. Family Law Quarterly, 46(2), 247–267. Retrieved June 2, 2025, from https://www.jstor.org/stable/23526329

Luchins, D. J., Roberts, D. L., & Hanrahan, P. (2003). Representative payeeship and mental illness: A review. *Administration and Policy in Mental Health and Mental Health Services Research, 30*(4), 341–353. https://doi.org/10.1023/A:1024089317630

Malks, B. F., Strobel, D. M., Leung, Y., Court, M. W., Morris, J. R., May, G., et al. (2010). Changing systems to address elder abuse: Examples from aging services, the courts, the long-term care ombudsman, and the faith community. *Journal of Elder Abuse & Neglect, 22*(3–4), 306–327. https://doi.org/10.1080/08946566.2010.490159

Mancini, M. A. (2021). *Integrated behavioral health practice*. Springer International Publishing. https://doi.org/10.1007/978-3-030-59659-0

McCoy, M., Ross, D., & Goetz, J. (2013). Narrative financial therapy: Integrating a financial planning approach with therapeutic theory. *Journal of Financial Therapy, 4*(2). https://doi.org/10.4148/1944-9771.1052

Miller, W. R., & Rollnick, S. (2013). *Motivational interviewing: Helping people change*. Guilford.

Mudigonda, M., Bartlett, P., Morriss, R., Chopra, A., & Jones, S. (2016). *Advance planning for people with bipolar disorder*. Unpublished. https://doi.org/10.13140/RG.2.1.1932.1209

Mullainathan, S., & Shafir, E. (2013). *Scarcity: Why having too little means so much*. Times Books, Henry Holt.

Nabeshima, G., & Klontz, B. T. (2015). Cognitive-behavioral financial therapy. In B. T. Klontz, S. L. Britt, & K. L. Archuleta (Eds.), *Financial therapy: Theory, research, and practice* (pp. 143–160). Springer.

Netemeyer, R. G., Lynch, J. G., Lichtenstein, D. R., & Dobolyi, D. (2024). Financial education effects on financial behavior and well-being: The mediating roles of improved objective and subjective financial knowledge and parallels in physical health. *Journal of Public Policy & Marketing, 07439156241228197*. https://doi.org/10.1177/07439156241228197

Newcomb, S., & Cummings, B. F. (2019). Making the science practical: Behavioral interventions in practice. In D. B. Durband, R. H. Law, & A. K. Mazzolini (Eds.), *Financial Counseling* (pp. 141–151). Springer International Publishing. https://doi.org/10.1007/978-3-319-72586-4_10

Noguchi, Y. (2022, August 16). After wiping out $6.7 billion in medical debt, this nonprofit Is just getting started. *KFF Health News*. Retrieved June 5, 2025, from https://kffhealthnews.org/news/article/nonprofit-medical-debt-buy-forgive/

Pearson, B., Korankye, T., Liu, Y., & Qing, D. (2024). Knowing the "don't knows" to financial literacy questions in the U.S. national financial capability study. *Journal of Financial Counseling and Planning, 35*(2), 292–304. https://doi.org/10.1891/JFCP-2023-0067

Phojanakong, P., Welles, S., Dugan, J., Booshehri, L., Brown Weida, E., & Chilton, M. (2020). Trauma-informed financial empowerment programming improves food security among families with young children. *Journal of Nutrition Education and Behavior, 52*(5), 465–473. https://doi.org/10.1016/j.jneb.2020.02.008

Prochaska, J. O., & DiClemente, C. C. (2005). The transtheoretical approach. In J. C. Norcross & M. R. Goldfried (Eds.), *Handbook of psychotherapy integration* (2nd ed., pp. 147–171). Oxford University Press.

Quiñones, M., & Grier-Reed, T. (2023). The Tanda: An informal financial practice at the intersection of culture and financial management for Mexican American families. *Journal of Family and Economic Issues*. https://doi.org/10.1007/s10834-023-09913-z

Ross, D., & Coambs, E. (2018). The impact of psychological trauma on finance: Narrative financial therapy considerations in exploring complex trauma and impaired financial decision making. *Journal of Financial Therapy, 9*(2). https://doi.org/10.4148/1944-9771.1174

Schneider, C. R., Fehrenbacher, D. D., & Weber, E. U. (2017). Catch me if I fall: Cross-national differences in willingness to take financial risks as a function of social and state 'cushioning'. *International Business Review, 26*(6), 1023–1033. https://doi.org/10.1016/j.ibusrev.2017.03.008

Seay, M., Goetz, J. W., & Gale, J. (2015). Collaborative relational model. In B. T. Klontz, S. L. Britt, & K. L. Archuleta (Eds.), *Financial therapy: Theory, research, and practice* (pp. 161–172). Springer International Publishing. https://doi.org/10.1007/978-3-319-08269-1_10

Sherraden, M. (2013). Building blocks of financial capability. In J. Birkenmaier, M. Sherraden, & J. Curley (Eds.), *Financial capability and asset development: Research, education, policy, and practice* (pp. 3–43). Oxford University Press.

Smith, G. C., Hatfield, A. B., & Miller, D. C. (2000). Planning by older mothers for the future care of offspring with serious mental illness. *Psychiatric Services, 51*(9), 1162–1166. https://doi.org/10.1176/appi.ps.51.9.1162

Theodos, B., Stacy, C. P., & Daniels, R. (2018). Client led coaching: A random assignment evaluation of the impacts of financial coaching programs. *Journal of Economic Behavior & Organization, 155*, 140–158. https://doi.org/10.1016/j.jebo.2018.08.019

Weida, E. B., Carroll-Scott, A., Le-Scherban, F., Bloom, S., & Chilton, M. (2024). Trauma-informed financial empowerment programming associated with improved financial well-being. *Journal of Child and Family Studies, 33*(11), 3541–3550. https://doi.org/10.1007/s10826-024-02927-7

White, K., Olajide, O., Watkins, K., Reiter, M., Johnson, P., & McCoy, M. (2024). Financial education and financial anxiety: Do quality and quantity differ? *Journal of Financial Counseling and Planning, 35*(2), 276–291. https://doi.org/10.1891/JFCP-2023-0022

White, N., Packard, K., Kalkowski, J., Walters, R., Haddad, A. R., Flecky, K., et al. (2022). Improving health through action on economic stability: Results of the finances first randomized controlled trial of financial education and coaching in single mothers of low-income. *American Journal of Lifestyle Medicine, 17*, 424. https://doi.org/10.1177/15598276211069537

Chapter 8
Implementing a Financial Health Informed Practice

8.1 Introduction

An important step toward implementing effective ethical practice is careful attention to both personal and professional development. This chapter provides concrete considerations for implementing financial health-informed practice across diverse professional settings. It begins with essential self-work that helps practitioners understand their own relationship with money and how personal financial experiences shape their professional responses to clients' financial concerns. This foundation of self-awareness proves crucial for competent practice that respects both professional boundaries and client needs.

The chapter then guides practitioners through the process of integrating financial considerations into their existing practice in ways that honor professional scope while building competence over time. Rather than requiring practitioners to become financial experts overnight or expanding beyond one's professional boundaries, this approach emphasizes starting where you are and building skills systematically through training, collaboration, and reflective practice.

8.2 Working on the Self: Exploring Personal Financial Beliefs and Biases

Before professionals can effectively help clients improve their financial health and behaviors, they must first understand and address their own relationship with money (Goetz et al., 2019; Holden & Jeanfreau, 2023). This critical self-work serves as the foundation for competent practice, just as it does in other areas of behavioral health

Supplementary Information The online version contains supplementary material available at https://doi.org/10.1007/978-3-032-02632-3_8.

J. Anvari-Clark, *Financial and Behavioral Health for Helping Professionals*,
https://doi.org/10.1007/978-3-032-02632-3_8

intervention. As helping professionals, we bring our own financial socialization, beliefs, traumas, and biases into our work with clients, often unconsciously.

8.2.1 Understanding Personal Financial Socialization

One's approach to money was shaped long before professional training began. As Gudmunson and Danes (2011) describe, financial socialization is the process through which financial values, attitudes, knowledge, and behaviors develop, primarily through family interactions and experiences. These early influences create deeply held beliefs about money that may remain largely unconscious yet powerfully influence your comfort and effectiveness in addressing financial concerns with clients.

Consider how discussions about money were handled in your family of origin:

- Were financial topics openly discussed or considered taboo?
- What messages did you receive about debt, saving, spending, or giving?
- How was financial success defined or portrayed?
- Were there cultural or religious values that shaped financial practices?

Research by LeBaron et al. (2019) found that parental financial modeling and explicit financial teaching and experiences significantly impact financial attitudes and behaviors in adulthood. Understanding how one's own financial socialization influences the professional perspective is an essential first step in developing competence to address clients' financial concerns.

8.2.2 Understanding Money Beliefs and Behaviors

Furthermore, before helping others navigate their financial journeys, helping professionals must understand their own relationship with money. Because our personal financial socialization influences our beliefs and behaviors, it creates powerful lenses through which we then interpret financial situations and make decisions. These unconscious patterns can significantly impact how we relate to clients, what solutions we propose, and even which financial topics we feel comfortable addressing. Without this self-awareness, professionals risk projecting their own financial values onto clients or missing important cultural nuances that shape clients' financial lives (Goetz et al., 2019). Recognizing one's own money attitudes serves as an essential foundation for authentic, effective, and ethical practice that respects the diverse experiences and goals of those we serve (Anvari-Clark & Rose, 2023).

One approach is to use the Klontz Money Script Inventory (B.T. Klontz & Britt, 2012; Taylor et al., 2016a). Money scripts are unconscious beliefs about money that drive financial behaviors. These scripts typically develop in childhood and operate below conscious awareness, yet they significantly influence financial decisions, professional comfort with financial topics, and biases in working with clients. According to Klontz and Britt (2012), four common categories of money scripts include:

- **Money avoidance**: Beliefs that money is bad, wealthy people are greedy, or that one does not deserve money.
- **Money worship**: Beliefs that more money will solve all problems or that one can never have enough.
- **Money status**: Beliefs that self-worth is tied to net worth and that outward displays of wealth confer status.
- **Money vigilance**: Beliefs emphasizing frugality, secrecy, and concern about finances.

To begin, one must first identify one's own money scripts and recognize how they might influence work with clients (Goetz et al., 2019). For example, a therapist holding money avoidance beliefs may unconsciously lead to abstaining from discussing financial topics with clients or feeling uncomfortable when clients express aspirations for wealth. Alternatively, advisors operating from money vigilance scripts can lead to judging clients who don't adhere to strict budgeting or saving practices, and missing important cultural or contextual factors that influence their financial behaviors.

Another tool for understanding financial behaviors is Money Habitudes, which helps individuals explore their financial habits, attitudes, and motivations with the goal of facilitating money conversations (Anvari-Clark & Betz-Hamilton, 2024; Solomon, 2022). Drawing upon insights from research in neuro-finance, psychology, and behavioral economics, Money Habitudes categorizes financial beliefs and behaviors into six distinct domains. Each habitude represents a specific orientation toward money:

- **Security** associates money with feelings of safety and control.
- **Planning** views money as a tool to achieve future goals.
- **Status** uses money to create a positive image of oneself.
- **Giving** derives satisfaction from sharing money with others.
- **Spontaneous** employs money to enjoy the present moment.
- **Carefree** sees money as a low priority in decision-making.

Money Habitudes is predicated on a recognition that these orientations exist on a continuum and that a person will identify with each habitude to varying extents. Notably, both overuse and underuse of a given habitude can potentially be problematic depending on context. For example, excessive status orientation might lead to overspending or financial infidelity, while insufficient attention to status could result in lost professional opportunities due to inappropriate presentation (Anvari-Clark & Betz-Hamilton, 2024).

Money Habitudes is not a diagnostic tool but rather a personal reflection tool and conversation starter that helps users understand their financial motivations and behaviors in a nonjudgmental framework. This approach allows professionals to engage clients in meaningful discussions about financial behaviors while considering the emotional and psychological dimensions that drive those behaviors (Solomon, 2022).

[Author Disclosure: I have used Money Habitudes with clients and my social work students since 2010. Since 2023, I have consulted for Money Habitudes, LLC to design a training program and, following an unfunded research study into the psychometric properties of the tool, received compensation to design improvements.]

By identifying dominant money scripts and behaviors and recognizing their interplay, professionals and clients both can develop greater self-awareness about their financial decision-making and tailor interventions to address specific behavioral patterns.

8.2.3 Examining Financial Privilege and Bias

Financial privilege and bias often remain unexamined aspects of professional practice. Many helping professionals have attained educational privilege and may hold assumptions about "normal" or "responsible" financial behaviors that reflect their own values rather than the lived realities of clients. Morduch and Schneider (2017) found in their financial diaries research that low-income families often employ sophisticated financial strategies to manage volatile incomes and expenses, challenging stereotypes about financial irresponsibility. Similarly, Stack's (1974) classic research on survival strategies in low-income Black communities revealed complex networks of resource sharing that function as alternative financial systems.

Helping professionals should reflect on their own background and how it shapes their assumptions:

- What financial resources, education, or safety nets have been available to you?
- How might your expectations about "appropriate" financial behaviors reflect privilege?
- In what ways might your professional training have reinforced your financial norms?
- How do you respond to clients whose financial priorities differ from conventional financial advice?

It should be noted that professionals can exhibit bias toward clients whose financial values seem to align with their own, not just bias against those with different values. Neither bias for nor bias against allows the professional to accurately assess the client's reality, strengths, and challenges in their true context; bias obscures what the client actually needs with what the professional assumes the client needs. This distortion extends to the assessment tools and materials professionals select, which may inherently favor certain financial value structures while marginalizing others. Recognizing one's own financial privilege and biases thus allows approaching clients with greater humility and cultural responsiveness, acknowledging the validity of diverse financial practices and priorities shaped by different life circumstances and developing more inclusive approaches to financial intervention.

8.2.4 Practical Self-Assessment Activities

To develop greater self-awareness regarding financial beliefs and biases, helping professionals should consider engaging in the following reflective activities:

1. **Take a financial attitudes assessment**: Utilize empirically validated assessments such as the Klontz Money Script Inventory (Taylor et al., 2016a) or Money Habitudes (Anvari-Clark & Betz-Hamilton, 2024) to identify one's own financial attitudes and potential areas of bias.
2. **Complete a financial genogram**: Map one's family financial history, beliefs, and patterns across at least three generations. Note significant financial events, patterns of financial success or struggle, and intergenerational messages about money. Holden and Jeanfreau (2023) describe how creating a financial genogram can reveal inherited patterns and beliefs that influence current financial attitudes. (Conducting the financial attitudes assessment prior to completing the genogram will lend important insight into patterns of socialization and divergence.)
3. **Track one's own financial behaviors**: For at least two months, record income, allocate money in anticipation of spending, track actual expenditures, and note the emotional responses to financial decisions. Notice patterns of avoidance, anxiety, satisfaction, or other emotions related to money. Pay attention to discrepancies between stated personal values and actual behaviors.
4. **Examine the credit report**: Review the credit report and reflect on emotional responses to the retrieval process and the information contained in the report. Consider how emotional reactions might parallel clients' experiences and what this reveals about financial comfort zones.
5. **Reflect on cultural influences**: Write about how one's own cultural background has shaped one's financial values and behaviors. Consider religious teachings, ethnic traditions, family expectations, and generational experiences that influence the resulting financial worldview.
6. **Practice discussing money**: Many helping professionals avoid personal financial discussions due to discomfort. Practice appropriate self-disclosure about financial topics with trusted colleagues to develop greater ease in addressing these issues professionally. And, as one begins to engage in self-reflection and to improve the personal financial situation, it is natural to experience a greater ease in discussing money.

8.2.5 From Self-Awareness to Professional Effectiveness

This self-work directly translates to improved professional effectiveness in several ways (Goetz et al., 2019):

1. **Reduced countertransference**: Understanding one's own financial triggers and biases helps prevent countertransference reactions when working with clients whose financial circumstances or choices align or differ from the professional's.
2. **Authentic engagement**: Professionals who have examined their own financial beliefs and practiced using the range of assessments, tools, and processes can engage more authentically with clients around financial concerns, modeling appropriate comfort with these often-sensitive topics.
3. **Cultural humility**: Awareness of one's own financial socialization fosters greater appreciation for diverse financial values and practices, enabling culturally responsive approaches to financial intervention.
4. **Enhanced financial communication skills**: Personal financial exploration helps develop comfort with financial terminology and concepts, making it easier to discuss these topics clearly with clients, in language that resonates with their worldview.
5. **Experiential knowledge**: Having engaged in these activities for themselves, professionals can better guide clients through similar processes with firsthand understanding of both the practical and emotional dimensions involved.

As McCoy et al. (2024) found in their research on financial planning education, students who experienced being "clients" themselves developed greater empathy and understanding of the client experience. Similarly, the helping professional's personal engagement with these activities will enhance their effectiveness in addressing financial behaviors with clients.

By investing in this foundational self-work, professionals establish the personal awareness and comfort necessary to help clients navigate their own complex relationships with money. This preparation allows them to move beyond simply recommending financial education to engaging meaningfully and with greater competence with the psychological, social, and practical dimensions of financial behavior change.

8.3 Integrating Financial and Behavioral Support Within the Professional Role

After examining one's own financial attitudes and biases, consider how to appropriately address financial behaviors within the professional scope of practice:

8.3.1 Recognizing Professional Boundaries and Scope of Practice

Different helping professions have varying scopes of practice regarding health and financial matters. Review the professional code of ethics and scope of practice to understand appropriate boundaries.

Social Workers Have a broad scope for addressing financial concerns, particularly within case management, community practice, and clinical roles. The profession's person-in-environment perspective naturally encompasses financial dimensions of client well-being (Callahan et al., 2019). The Grand Challenges for Social Work identify financial capability as a core area of social work practice (American Academy of Social Work & Social Welfare, 2021) and the Financial Social Work Initiative (n.d.) provides continuing education and certification. Social workers can engage in various financial interventions, from helping clients access benefits to addressing financial trauma, while remaining within their scope of practice.

Mental Health Counselors and Psychologists Can address psychological aspects of financial behaviors, including financial anxiety, money-related relationship conflicts, and compulsive financial behaviors. While not providing specific financial advice, they can help clients understand emotional triggers for financial decisions and develop healthier financial coping strategies. As Klontz et al. (2015) note, money disorders frequently co-occur with other mental health issues, making financial concerns legitimate therapeutic targets.

Healthcare providers Increasingly recognize financial toxicity as affecting health outcomes. Providers can screen for financial concerns impacting healthcare decisions, connect patients with financial navigation services, and consider financial implications when developing treatment plans. Tucker-Seeley and Yabroff (2016) highlight how financial hardship affects cancer treatment outcomes, demonstrating the relevance of financial considerations in healthcare settings.

Financial Planners, Coaches, and Counselors Provide direct financial guidance but often encounter psychological and behavioral barriers to implementation. Understanding the psychological dimensions of financial behaviors can enhance their effectiveness and allow them to recognize when psychological referrals might be appropriate. The emerging field of financial therapy bridges these domains, as described by Klontz et al. (2015). The Certified Financial Planner Board of Standards explicitly details guidance in the Code of Ethics for engaging with other people to provide professional services (CFP Board 2018), and the Association for Financial Counseling & Planning Education® (AFCPE®; 2023) underscores the importance of referring clients when outside the bounds of one's limitations.

Understanding the latitude and boundaries helps determine when to address financial matters directly, when to refer to other professionals, and how to collaborate effectively across disciplines.

8.3.2 Three Levels of Financial Integration

Financial integration can occur at different levels of intensity and intervention, depending on professional training, setting constraints, and client needs. Understanding these levels helps practitioners identify appropriate entry points while building competence over time.

Level 1: Basic Financial Awareness

This foundational level involves recognizing financial factors that may be affecting clients and incorporating basic financial screening into assessment and treatment planning. All helping professionals can develop this level of awareness regardless of their primary discipline.

Financial Screening and Assessment Basic screening involves asking simple questions about financial stress, stability, and concerns during routine intake processes. Questions might include: "Are financial concerns affecting your stress level?" "Have money worries been keeping you awake at night?" or "Are financial pressures affecting your relationships?" These questions normalize financial discussions while identifying when deeper exploration might be warranted. More comprehensive evaluation should be conducted when initial screening reveals financial concerns. Various scales and assessment tools are available to measure objective and/or subjective aspects of a person's financial state, including: APR Financial Stress Scale (Heo et al., 2020), Consumer Financial Protection Bureau Financial Well-Being Scale (2017), Financial Anxiety Scale (Archuleta et al., 2013), Financial Self-Efficacy Scale (Lown, 2011), InCharge Financial Distress/Financial Well-Being Scale (Prawitz et al., 2006), Klontz Money Behavior Inventory (Klontz et al., 2012; Taylor et al., 2016b), Money Habitudes (Solomon, 2022), Perceived Financial Well-Being Scale (Netemeyer et al., 2018), Scale of Economic Self-Efficacy (Hoge et al., 2020), and Socio-Economic Empowerment Assessment (Hawkins & Kim, 2012). Information on these and others is available in the online electronic supplementary materials that accompany this chapter (see Financial and Behavioral Health Tools, Assessments, and Resources).

Treatment Planning Integration Practitioners can incorporate financial goals and considerations into existing treatment plans without providing direct financial intervention. A mental health counselor might include financial stress reduction as a treatment goal while referring to financial counseling services. A healthcare provider might consider financial barriers when discussing treatment adherence and connect patients with financial navigation services.

Education and Resource Connection If done in a contextually appropriate and informed manner, basic financial education and connecting clients with appropriate financial resources can be helpful. This might involve maintaining lists of reputable financial counselors, knowing about local financial assistance programs, or providing basic information about financial topics relevant to the client population.

Level 2: Financial Conversations

This intermediate level involves more sophisticated understanding of financial behaviors and the ability to have meaningful conversations about money within one's professional context. Practitioners at this level have developed comfort with financial topics and basic skills for addressing financial concerns.

Financial Coaching Skills Professionals develop basic coaching skills that can be applied to financial behaviors, including motivational interviewing techniques, goal-setting frameworks, and behavioral change strategies. These skills enable practitioners to help clients explore their relationship with money, identify financial goals, and develop action plans within the context of their primary professional relationship.

Understanding Financial Psychology Practitioners understand how psychological factors influence financial behaviors and can help clients recognize connections between emotions and financial decisions. They can identify when financial behaviors may be serving psychological functions (such as emotional regulation or control) and incorporate this understanding into their work.

Collaborative Goal Setting Rather than simply referring clients to financial professionals, practitioners at this level can work collaboratively with clients to set financial goals that support broader behavioral health objectives. This might involve helping a client understand how debt reduction could decrease anxiety or how budgeting skills could enhance their sense of personal efficacy.

Integration with Primary Practice Financial conversations become integrated into the practitioner's primary work rather than being treated as a separate concern. A therapist might explore how financial stress affects relationship dynamics, while a healthcare provider might discuss how financial planning could support long-term healthcare goals.

Level 3: Integrated Financial Interventions

This advanced level involves providing specialized interventions that integrate financial and behavioral health approaches. Practitioners at this level have received additional training and may hold specialized credentials or certifications.

Financial Therapy Mental health and financial professionals with additional training can provide financial therapy that addresses both psychological and practical aspects of financial concerns. This might involve treating money disorders, addressing financial trauma, or helping couples work through financial conflicts using therapeutic techniques adapted for financial contexts.

Specialized Assessment and Treatment Practitioners can conduct comprehensive assessments of financial behaviors and provide specialized interventions tailored to specific populations or conditions. This might include financial empowerment groups for trauma survivors, financial planning for individuals with serious mental illness, or financial literacy programs adapted for specific cultural communities.

Program Development and Leadership The development of new programs or services that integrate financial and behavioral health approaches is much needed. These could entail training programs for other practitioners, research on integrated approaches, or advocacy for internal policy changes that support comprehensive care.

Supervision and Consultation Experienced practitioners can provide supervision and consultation to others developing financial integration skills, helping to build organizational capacity for addressing financial concerns within broader behavioral health contexts.

Illustrations

Level 1: Basic Financial Awareness

Case 1: Primary Care Physician—Dr. Sarah Chen
Dr. Chen has been treating Maria Santos, a 42-year-old teacher, for recurring headaches and elevated blood pressure over six months. Despite appropriate medical treatment, Maria's symptoms persist. During a routine follow-up, Dr. Chen incorporates basic financial screening into her assessment. "Maria, sometimes physical symptoms like yours can be related to stress. Are financial concerns affecting your stress level or keeping you awake at night?" Maria reveals significant anxiety about mounting medical bills and her husband's recent job loss. Dr. Chen validates these concerns while maintaining her medical focus, noting in her treatment plan that financial stress may be contributing to Maria's hypertension. She provides information about the hospital's financial assistance program and refers Maria to a

nonprofit credit counselor. This basic financial awareness integration allows Dr. Chen to address underlying contributors to Maria's medical condition while staying within her scope of practice and connecting her patient with appropriate financial resources.

Case 2: Credit Counselor—James Rodriguez
James works at a nonprofit credit counseling agency and meets with Patricia Williams, a 35-year-old marketing manager seeking help with credit card debt. During his standard financial assessment, James incorporates basic behavioral health screening questions: "Have money worries been affecting your sleep or relationships?" Patricia reveals that debt stress has been causing panic attacks and marital tension. While James focuses on debt management strategies—creating a realistic budget, negotiating with creditors, and developing a debt repayment plan—he recognizes the psychological impact of financial stress. He normalizes the emotional aspects of financial difficulties and provides educational information about the stress-debt cycle. James documents Patricia's progress on both financial metrics and self-reported stress levels, and when her panic symptoms persist despite debt reduction progress, he refers her to a mental health counselor. This approach demonstrates how financial professionals can integrate basic awareness of behavioral health factors while maintaining their primary focus on financial solutions.

Level 2: Financial Conversations

Case 3: Addiction Psychologist—Dr. Michael Torres
Dr. Torres is treating Kevin Murphy, a 28-year-old in recovery from gambling addiction, who reports increasing anxiety about finances despite being debt-free. Using motivational interviewing techniques, Dr. Torres explores Kevin's relationship with money: "Tell me about what having money in your savings account means to you." Kevin reveals that having any available money triggers urges to gamble, leading him to spend impulsively on unnecessary items as a "safer" way to eliminate the temptation. Dr. Torres helps Kevin recognize how his avoidance of financial planning serves as a psychological coping function but ultimately undermines his recovery goals. Together, they develop collaborative financial goals that support Kevin's sobriety—such as setting up automatic transfers to a restricted savings account and creating spending categories that align with his values. Dr. Torres integrates these financial conversations into their ongoing therapy work, helping Kevin understand the emotional functions of his financial behaviors while building healthier money management skills that support his overall recovery.

Case 4: Financial Coach—Lisa Park
Lisa works with Thomas and Sandra Kim, a couple in their early 50 s struggling with retirement planning. During their coaching sessions, Lisa uses a money beliefs and behaviors assessment, debriefing with open-ended questions to explore the results. She discovers that Thomas grew up in poverty and hoards money out of fear, while Sandra witnessed her parents' divorce over financial disagreements and

avoids money discussions entirely. Rather than simply providing retirement calculations, Lisa helps the couple recognize how their different money histories create conflict in their financial partnership. She facilitates conversations about their individual financial fears and collaboratively establishes goals that address both their practical retirement needs and their emotional money concerns. Lisa integrates goal-setting frameworks that consider both partners' psychological comfort levels, helping them develop a retirement plan that feels emotionally sustainable. Their financial progress is measured not just in dollars saved, but in improved communication about money and reduced financial anxiety, demonstrating how Level 2 integration addresses both practical and psychological aspects of financial health.

Level 3: Integrated Financial Interventions

Case 5: Financial Social Worker—Dr. Rachel Bennett
Dr. Bennett, who holds both a DSW and a certificate in financial social work, works with the Jones family following their teenage daughter's diagnosis with cancer. The family faces overwhelming medical costs while processing trauma related to their daughter's life-threatening diagnosis. Dr. Bennett conducts comprehensive assessment that reveals financial trauma responses—the father has developed compulsive spending on supplies "just in case," while the mother has become paralyzed by financial decisions. Using specialized psychotherapy techniques, Dr. Bennett addresses both the practical financial challenges and the underlying trauma responses. She employs narrative therapy approaches to help the family reframe their financial story from "financial victim" to "adaptive survivors," while simultaneously connecting them with cancer financial assistance programs and helping them develop sustainable medical budgeting strategies. Treatment goals include trauma symptom reduction, improved family financial communication, and practical financial stability. Dr. Bennett tracks outcomes across multiple domains—decreased anxiety, improved family cohesion, and progress toward financial goals—demonstrating how Level 3 integration addresses complex interactions between financial and behavioral health concerns.

Case 6: Financial Planner—Robert Chang, CFP®, CFT™
Robert holds both Certified Financial Planner® and Certified Financial Therapist™ credentials and works with Jennifer Walsh, a 40-year-old executive who survived childhood financial abuse. Jennifer has achieved significant career success but sabotages her financial security through impulsive spending and investment avoidance. Robert conducts a specialized assessment that reveals how Jennifer's financial behaviors serve protective functions—spending provides temporary relief from financial anxiety, while avoiding investments prevents potential "failure" that triggers childhood trauma memories. Using integrated financial therapy approaches, Robert addresses both the psychological and practical aspects

of Jennifer's financial concerns. He employs trauma-informed financial planning techniques that respect Jennifer's need for control while gradually building her capacity for financial risk-taking. Their work includes processing financial trauma through narrative approaches, developing self-compassion practices, and creating a comprehensive financial plan that accommodates her psychological needs while building long-term security. Robert measures success through both traditional financial metrics and trauma recovery indicators, such as decreased financial anxiety and increased sense of financial agency, illustrating how Level 3 practitioners can provide sophisticated interventions that integrate financial and mental health expertise.

8.3.3 Diagnostic Frameworks and Billing Considerations

The intersection of financial behaviors and mental health diagnoses creates both challenges and opportunities for mental health professionals. Understanding how to appropriately document, treat, and bill for services addressing financial concerns requires careful consideration of diagnostic frameworks, scope of practice, and reimbursement requirements. While not intending to be comprehensive, and considering ongoing changes to the frameworks and codes, the following can help mental health practitioners see where such alignment may exist and how to address documentation and billing requirements. Note that specific codes may be outdated or inaccurate. Use professional judgment when integrating them into your work.

The DSM-5-TR™ and ICD-10-CM codes can provide valuable supplementary documentation for addressing financial concerns in practice settings where diagnostic coding drives reimbursement (American Psychiatric Association [APA], 2022; ICD10Data.com, 2025). In particular, Z-codes such as Z59.86 (Financial insecurity), Z59.5 (Extreme poverty), Z59.6 (Low income), Z62.814 (Personal history of child financial abuse), and Z59.9 (Problem related to housing and economic circumstances, unspecified) can be used alongside primary diagnoses to document financial factors affecting treatment (ICD10Data.com, 2025). However, it is important to recognize that relegating financial concerns exclusively to Z-code status may perpetuate the misconception that financial behaviors are only external social determinants rather than intrinsic aspects of behavioral health. The integrative approach presented throughout this book encourages recognizing financial behaviors as fundamental to behavioral functioning, with financial efficacy, precarity, and well-being directly impacting and being impacted by other health domains. Z-codes and other coding and diagnosing should therefore be viewed as practical billing tools that complement, rather than replace, the more comprehensive understanding of financial health presented here.

Aligning Financial Concerns with Diagnostic Frameworks

Financial health concerns can be aligned with diagnoses in three primary ways:

1. Financial behaviors as primary diagnostic criteria.
2. Financial concerns trigger or exacerbate a disorder.
3. Financial concerns manifest as symptoms of or treatment complexities to an underlying disorder.

Financial Behaviors as Primary Diagnostic Criteria

Several diagnoses directly involve problematic financial behaviors, such as:

- **Gambling Disorder (F63.0)**: Characterized by persistent and recurrent problematic gambling behavior leading to clinically significant impairment or distress (APA, 2022). This disorder has been clearly associated with a range of poor physical, social, and psychological health issues, as well as increased prevalence of bankruptcy (Canale et al., 2015; Grant et al., 2010).
- **Other Specified Disruptive, Impulse-Control, and Conduct Disorder (F91.8)**: These may include compulsive buying/over-shopping, which involves recurrent and uncontrollable buying episodes that extend beyond normal shopping behavior and create significant distress or impairment (Mueller et al., 2010).
- **Hoarding Disorder (F42.3)**: While primarily focused on difficulty discarding possessions, this disorder often has financial implications through excessive acquisition and clutter that impairs financial functioning (Klontz et al., 2012).

Financial Concerns as Triggers

Financial stressors can precipitate or exacerbate various mental health conditions. For example:

- **Adjustment Disorders (F43.xx)**: Financial stressors such as job loss, eviction, or significant debt can trigger adjustment reactions featuring anxiety, depression, or conduct disturbances. Richardson et al. (2013) found a significant relationship between debt and mental health issues, including depression and anxiety.
- **Generalized Anxiety Disorder (F41.1)**: Persistent worry about finances is explicitly mentioned as a diagnostic feature, often accompanied by concerns about job security, debt management, and present or future financial precarity (Archuleta et al., 2013).
- **Major Depressive Disorder (F32.x)**: Financial strain has been associated with depressive symptoms, with income volatility showing particularly strong connections to depression (Prause et al., 2009; Starkey et al., 2013).
- **Trauma and Stressor-Related Disorders (F43.xx)**: Financial traumas like foreclosure, bankruptcy, or economic abuse can trigger trauma responses (Downing, 2016) and other emotional distress (Maher & Hayes, 2024).

Financial Concerns as Symptoms or Treatment Complexities

Financial behaviors may also appear alongside other primary disorders. Some examples include:

- **Bipolar and Related Disorders with Manic Episodes (F31.xx)**: Often feature impaired financial judgment, unrestrained spending sprees, and foolish business investments that can lead to significant financial losses (APA, 2022).
- **Borderline Personality Disorder (F60.3)**: May include impulsive spending as part of the broader pattern of impulsivity (APA, 2022).
- **Obsessive-Compulsive Personality Disorder (F60.5)**: Often characterized by excessive devotion to work, inability to discard worn or worthless objects, and a "miserly spending style" where money is hoarded for future catastrophes (APA, 2022).
- **Dependent Personality Disorder (F60.7)**: While not explicitly financial in the DSM-5-TR™, this can manifest as financial dependence (Canale et al., 2015), where individuals belittle their own financial capabilities and excessively rely on others for financial support and decision-making. Notably, an extreme carefree money habitude personality can exhibit as dependence upon others for money or to meet basic needs (Solomon, 2022).
- **Gender Dysphoria (F64.x)**: While not symptoms per se, financial aspects of gender dysphoria create significant treatment complexities that warrant clinical attention. Individuals may develop problematic financial coping mechanisms such as excessive shopping as a way to manage dysphoria-related distress (Budge et al., 2013). Additionally, the significant costs associated with gender-affirming care create unique financial stressors. Insurance coverage may be limited, and some funding agencies require demonstrated financial capability before covering treatments. This creates a complex relationship between financial health and treatment access that can exacerbate psychological distress (White et al., 2022). Documentation should focus on how financial interventions directly support the treatment of dysphoria and associated distress.
- **Attention-Deficit/Hyperactivity Disorder (F90.x)**: Financial impairment is often overlooked but significant in ADHD. Symptoms directly affecting financial management and other executive functioning include forgetfulness in paying bills (explicitly mentioned in diagnostic criteria), difficulty with organization of financial records, impulsive spending, and challenges sustaining attention during financial planning activities (APA, 2022; Barkley & Murphy, 2010). Research shows adults with ADHD experience higher rates of financial distress and lower financial self-efficacy compared to peers (Icick et al., 2020).
- **Problems Related to Abuse or Neglect (T74.x)**: Financial abuse can manifest in various forms, including identity theft, coerced debt, controlling access to resources, or exploitation of financial resources. While not a standalone diagnosis, experience of these behaviors could potentially be documented under psychological abuse or neglect codes. Financial enmeshment, enabling, and financial dependence (Canale et al., 2015) may occur within these relational patterns, significantly impacting psychological well-being.

- **Other Problems Related to Employment (Z56.x)**: Significant income reduction, job loss, or employment instability can trigger considerable psychological distress without necessarily meeting criteria for a specific disorder. These occupational problems can be coded when they are a focus of clinical attention, recognizing the substantial impact of income volatility on mental health (Kopasker et al., 2018; Wilkinson, 2016).

Regarding "Unspecified" categories: These can be used legitimately when there is sufficient evidence of a disorder within a category but insufficient information to make a more specific diagnosis. For financial concerns, consider "Unspecified Anxiety Disorder" (F41.9) or "Unspecified Trauma-and Stressor-Related Disorder" (F43.9) when financial stressors clearly cause clinically significant distress but do not fully meet criteria for more specific diagnoses. However, clinicians should attempt to gather enough information for more specific diagnosis whenever possible.

Additional Billing Considerations for Financial Interventions

Mental health professionals must carefully consider reimbursement requirements when addressing financial behaviors in clinical practice:

1. **Connection to diagnosed conditions**: Financial interventions should be clearly linked to treatment goals for diagnosed conditions. For example, addressing financial avoidance behaviors can be framed as part of treatment for anxiety disorders, while helping a client establish a sustainable spending plan may be part of recovery from a manic episode or gambling disorder.
2. **Medical necessity**: Documentation should clearly articulate how financial interventions address impairment or dysfunction related to the diagnosed condition. This includes explaining how financial behaviors contribute to or result from the clinical presentation.
3. **Relevant codes**: Select diagnostic codes where financial behaviors are explicitly relevant to the clinical presentation. Common categories include: Adjustment Disorders, Anxiety Disorders, Depressive Disorders, Trauma and Stressor-Related Disorders, Obsessive-Compulsive and Related Disorders, and Impulse Control Disorders. They can also be used to document problems and mitigating factors impacting the condition (Centers for Medicare & Medicaid Services, 2024).
4. **Collaborative care codes**: In integrated care settings, collaborative care billing codes may allow for more comprehensive approaches to addressing financial and mental health concerns simultaneously.

Illustrative Examples

Example 1: Anxiety Disorder with Financial Triggers A client presents with Generalized Anxiety Disorder (F41.1) with significant worry focused on finances despite objective financial stability. Treatment includes cognitive behavioral ther-

apy around catastrophic financial thoughts, gradual exposure to reviewing financial statements, and developing healthy financial monitoring habits. Documentation links these interventions to reducing financial anxiety symptoms and improving functioning.

Example 2: Recovery from Manic Episode *Following a Bipolar I Disorder (F31.x) manic episode with significant financial consequences, treatment includes establishing financial safeguards to prevent future impulsive spending, processing shame around financial decisions made during the episode, and rebuilding financial confidence through small, manageable tasks. These interventions are documented as relapse prevention and functional recovery strategies.*

8.3.4 Ethical Considerations

Addressing financial concerns within helping relationships raises several important ethical considerations that practitioners must navigate carefully to maintain professional standards while providing effective support (Barsky, 2019; Klontz et al., 2015; Newcomb & Cummings, 2019). At the most fundamental, in almost all cases, it is important to let a client make their own financial choices. For them to feel recognized and supported—even when acting in ways that undermine long-term financial health—bases the professional relationship on trust and unconditional positive regard. Change cannot be forced, but conditions for it to take place when the client is ready can be created. This aligns with the social work principle of self-determination (National Association of Social Workers 2017) and public health approach of harm reduction (Mancini, 2021).

Scope of Practice The fundamental ethical principle guiding financial integration is practicing within one's scope of practice and professional competence. This means understanding the boundaries of your professional training and expertise while recognizing when referrals to other professionals are appropriate. For mental health professionals, this might mean addressing the psychological aspects of financial behaviors while referring to financial counselors for technical money management advice. For financial professionals, this could involve recognizing when psychological factors are interfering with financial decision-making and referring to mental health professionals.

The development of competence is an ongoing ethical obligation. Practitioners incorporating financial considerations into their work should seek appropriate training, supervision, and consultation to ensure they can address these concerns effectively. This might involve continuing education in financial therapy, participating in interdisciplinary case consultation, or developing collaborative relationships with professionals from complementary disciplines.

Dual Relationships and Boundaries Financial discussions can create unique boundary challenges, particularly in smaller communities where practitioners and clients may encounter each other in public. Practitioners must be careful to avoid dual relationships that could compromise professional judgment or exploit the therapeutic relationship. This includes declining to provide personal financial advice to clients outside of the professional relationship, avoiding financial transactions with clients, and maintaining clear boundaries between professional and personal financial discussions.

The inherent power differential in helping relationships requires particular attention when financial topics arise. Practitioners must avoid abusing their professional position to influence clients' financial decisions in ways that unduly benefit the practitioner or that reflect the practitioner's values rather than the client's best interests.

Confidentiality and Documentation Financial information often feels particularly sensitive to clients, requiring careful attention to confidentiality protections. Practitioners must clearly explain how financial information will be documented, who will have access to this information, and what confidentiality protections apply. This is particularly important in collaborative care situations where information may be shared across disciplines.

Documentation should focus on clinically relevant information while avoiding unnecessary detail about specific financial circumstances. The focus should be on how financial factors affect the client's behavioral health and treatment rather than detailed financial reporting that serves no clinical purpose.

Cultural Humility and Financial Values Ethical practice requires recognition that financial values and practices vary significantly across cultural contexts. Practitioners must approach clients' financial choices with cultural humility, recognizing that their own financial values may not be appropriate for all clients. This includes understanding how financial interdependence operates in different cultural contexts, respecting diverse approaches to family financial obligations, and avoiding the imposition of individualistic financial planning models on clients whose cultures emphasize collective financial decision-making.

Religious and spiritual considerations also play important roles in many clients' financial values and behaviors. Practitioners must respect these influences while helping clients navigate any conflicts between spiritual teachings and practical financial needs.

Self-Awareness and Countertransference The earlier discussion of personal financial self-awareness serves important ethical functions by helping practitioners recognize and manage their own reactions to clients' financial circumstances and choices. Practitioners must monitor their responses to clients' financial behaviors, particularly when these behaviors differ significantly from their own values or experiences.

Countertransference around financial issues can manifest in various ways: judging clients for financial choices, feeling anxious about clients' financial situations, wanting to rescue clients from financial difficulties, or becoming overly invested in clients' financial outcomes. Regular supervision and consultation help practitioners recognize and address these reactions appropriately.

8.4 Implementation Strategies

Moving from conceptual understanding to practical implementation requires systematic approaches that build competence over time while maintaining ethical standards. The following strategies help practitioners integrate financial health considerations into their work in sustainable, effective ways.

Start Small and Build Partnerships Implementation begins with modest steps that build confidence and competence gradually. Rather than attempting comprehensive financial integration immediately, practitioners can start by incorporating basic financial screening into their existing assessment processes. This might involve adding one or two financial stress questions to intake forms or spending a few minutes in sessions exploring how financial concerns might be affecting clients' presenting problems.

Building professional partnerships provides essential support for implementation efforts. Establishing relationships with financial counselors, coaches, planners, and therapists in your community creates referral resources while providing opportunities for consultation and learning. These relationships can begin informally through professional networking events, continuing education programs, or interdisciplinary case consultations.

Effective partnerships require clear communication about roles, boundaries, and expectations. Developing written agreements about how referrals will be handled, what information will be shared, and how communication will be maintained helps ensure smooth collaboration while protecting client interests.

Seek Training and Build Competence Formal training opportunities help practitioners develop the knowledge and skills needed for effective financial integration. This might include:

- **Continuing education workshops** on topics like financial psychology, financial trauma, or money disorders.
- **Certificate programs** in financial social work, financial therapy, or specialized financial counseling.
- **Interdisciplinary training** that brings together professionals from different fields to learn collaborative approaches.
- **Supervision and consultation** from experienced practitioners who have integrated financial considerations into their work.

Professional organizations increasingly offer training opportunities at the intersection of financial and behavioral health. The Financial Therapy Association (FTA), Association for Financial Counseling & Planning Education (AFCPE), and National Association of Social Workers (NASW), as well as other professional associations and academic institutions all provide relevant continuing educational offerings. Self-directed learning through reading, webinars, and online courses can supplement formal training opportunities. The references throughout this book provide starting points for deeper exploration of specific topics relevant to your practice context.

Document and Evaluate Outcomes Implementing financial integration requires appropriate documentation that captures both the financial factors affecting clients and the interventions provided. This documentation should focus on clinically relevant information while avoiding unnecessary financial detail. Key elements might include:

- Financial stress levels and their impact on presenting problems.
- Financial goals and their relationship to broader treatment objectives.
- Financial interventions provided and their outcomes.
- Referrals made to financial professionals and their results.

Outcome evaluation helps practitioners understand the effectiveness of their financial integration efforts while identifying areas for improvement. This might involve tracking client progress on financial goals, measuring changes in financial stress levels, or evaluating client satisfaction with integrated approaches.

Simple evaluation measures can be incorporated into existing clinical practices without creating a significant additional burden. Pre-and post-treatment administration of financial questions or well-being scales, client feedback surveys about integrated approaches, or tracking of referral completion rates provide valuable information about implementation effectiveness.

8.5 Conclusion

Implementing a financial health-informed practice may represent a transformative shift in how helping professionals conceptualize and address client well-being. This chapter has provided considerations for moving beyond simple recognition of financial factors toward sophisticated integration of financial considerations into professional practice. The journey requires both personal reflection and professional development, beginning with practitioners' own financial self-awareness and extending through systematic skill building and collaborative partnership development.

The three-level implementation framework offers flexibility for practitioners across diverse professional contexts while establishing clear progression pathways for building competence. Rather than requiring immediate expertise in financial domains outside one's training, this approach enables practitioners to start where they are and grow systematically. Level 1 integration can immediately enhance practice effectiveness by incorporating basic financial screening and resource connection, while Levels 2 and 3 provide pathways for more specialized development as interest and opportunity allow.

The case examples illustrate how financial health integration enhances rather than complicates existing practice relationships. Successful implementation requires ongoing attention to professional boundaries, ethical considerations, and collaborative relationships. The diagnostic and billing frameworks presented provide guidance for mental health professionals navigating documentation requirements, while the emphasis on partnership development ensures that clients receive appropriate expertise rather than practitioners extending beyond their competence. These safeguards protect both clients and practitioners while enabling meaningful integration of financial considerations.

As the field continues to evolve, practitioners implementing financial health-informed approaches become pioneers in more comprehensive, effective behavioral health practice. Their documentation of outcomes, refinement of approaches, and development of innovative interventions will contribute to the growing evidence base supporting integrated financial and behavioral health services. This implementation work represents not just individual professional development, but a contribution to a broader transformation in how helping professions address the complex, interconnected nature of human well-being.

References

American Academy of Social Work and Social Welfare. (2021). Grand challenges. *Grand challenges for social work.* https://grandchallengesforsocialwork.org/

American Psychiatric Association. (2022). *Diagnostic and statistical manual of mental disorders* (5th, Text Revision ed.). Arlington, VA: American Psychiatric Association. https://dsm.psychiatryonline.org/doi/book/10.1176/appi.books.9780890425787

Anvari-Clark, J., & Betz-Hamilton, A. (2024). Factor analyses of a money beliefs and behaviors assessment tool. *Journal of Financial Counseling and Planning., 36.* https://doi.org/10.1891/JFCP-2023-0144

Anvari-Clark, J., & Rose, T. (2023). Financial behavioral health and investment risk willingness: Implications for the racial wealth gap. *International Journal of Environmental Research and Public Health, 20*(10), 5835. https://doi.org/10.3390/ijerph20105835

Archuleta, K. L., Dale, A., & Spann, S. M. (2013). College students and financial distress: Exploring debt, financial satisfaction, and financial anxiety. *Journal of Financial Counseling and Planning, 24*(2), 50–62. https://eric.ed.gov/?id=EJ1043230

Association for Financial Counseling & Planning Education®. (2023). AFCPE® code of ethics. Retrieved June 10, 2025, from https://www.afcpe.org/certification/professional-standards/code-of-ethics/

Barkley, R. A., & Murphy, K. R. (2010). Impairment in occupational functioning and adult ADHD: The predictive utility of executive function (EF) ratings versus EF tests. *Archives of Clinical Neuropsychology, 25*(3), 157–173. https://doi.org/10.1093/arclin/acq014

Barsky, A. E. (2019). *Ethics and values in social work: An integrated approach for a comprehensive curriculum* (2nd ed.). Oxford University Press Canada. Retrieved June 2, 2025, from. https://www.oupcanada.com/catalog/9780190678111.html

Budge, S. L., Katz-Wise, S. L., Tebbe, E. N., Howard, K. A. S., Schneider, C. L., & Rodriguez, A. (2013). Transgender emotional and coping processes: Facilitative and avoidant coping throughout gender transitioning. *The Counseling Psychologist, 41*(4), 601–647. https://doi.org/10.1177/0011000011432753

Callahan, C., Frey, J. J., & Imboden, R. (Eds.). (2019). *The Routledge handbook on financial social work: Direct practice with vulnerable populations* (1st ed.). Taylor & Francis. https://doi.org/10.4324/9781351165686

Canale, A., Archuleta, K. L., & Klontz, B. T. (2015). Money disorders. In B. T. Klontz, S. L. Britt, & K. L. Archuleta (Eds.), *Financial therapy: Theory, research, and practice* (pp. 35–68). Springer.

Centers for Medicare & Medicaid Services. (2024). *Improving the collection of social determinants of health (SDOH) data with ICD-10-CM Z Codes*. U.S. Department of Health and Human Services. https://www.cms.gov/files/document/cms-2023-omh-z-code-resource.pdf

Certified Financial Planner Board of Standards, Inc. (2018). *Code of ethics and standards of conduct*. CFP Board. Retrieved June 10, 2025, from, https://www.cfp.net/-/media/files/cfp-board/standards-and-ethics/cfp-code-and-standards.pdf

Consumer Financial Protection Bureau. (2017). *CFPB Financial well-being scale: Scale development technical report*. https://www.consumerfinance.gov/data-research/research-reports/financial-well-being-scale/

Downing, J. (2016). The health effects of the foreclosure crisis and unaffordable housing: A systematic review and explanation of evidence. *Social Science & Medicine, 162*(2016), 88–96. https://doi.org/10.1016/j.socscimed.2016.06.014

Financial Social Work Initiative. (n.d.). Education. *Financial social work initiative*. Retrieved October 7, 2021, from https://www.ssw.umaryland.edu/fsw/education/

Goetz, J. W., Durband, D. B., & Mazzolini, A. K. (2019). The importance of self-awareness for financial counselors and clients. In D. B. Durband, R. H. Law, & A. K. Mazzolini (Eds.), *Financial Counseling* (pp. 65–76). Springer International Publishing. https://doi.org/10.1007/978-3-319-72586-4_5

Grant, J. E., Schreiber, L., Odlaug, B. L., & Kim, S. W. (2010). Pathological gambling and bankruptcy. *Comprehensive Psychiatry, 51*(2), 115–120. https://doi.org/10.1016/j.comppsych.2009.04.002

Gudmunson, C. G., & Danes, S. M. (2011). Family financial socialization: Theory and critical review. *Journal of Family and Economic Issues, 32*(4), 644–667. https://doi.org/10.1007/s10834-011-9275-y

Hawkins, R. L., & Kim, E. J. (2012). The socio-economic empowerment assessment: Addressing poverty and economic distress in clients. *Clinical Social Work Journal, 40*(2), 194–202. https://doi.org/10.1007/s10615-011-0335-4

Heo, W., Cho, S. H., & Lee, P. (2020). APR financial stress scale: Development and validation of a multidimensional measurement. *Journal of financial Therapy, 11*(1). https://doi.org/10.4148/1944-9771.1216

Hoge, G. L., Stylianou, A. M., Hetling, A., & Postmus, J. L. (2020). Developing and validating the scale of economic self-efficacy. *Journal of Interpersonal Violence, 35*(15–16), 3011–3033. https://doi.org/10.1177/0886260517706761

Holden, C. L., & Jeanfreau, M. (2023). The self-reflective financial therapist: Creating a financial genogram. *Journal of Financial Therapy, 14*(2). https://doi.org/10.4148/1944-9771.1339

ICD10Data.com. (2025). 2025 ICD-10-CM Codes Z55-Z65: Persons with potential health hazards related to socioeconomic and psychosocial circumstances. *ICD10Data.com*. Reference website. Retrieved May 5, 2025, from https://www.icd10data.com/ICD10CM/Codes/Z00-Z99/Z55-Z65

Icick, R., Moggi, F., Slobodin, O., Dom, G., Mathys, F., Van Den Brink, W., et al. (2020). Attention deficit/hyperactivity disorder and global severity profiles in treatment-seeking patients with substance use disorders. *European Addiction Research, 26*(4–5), 201–210. https://doi.org/10.1159/000508546

Klontz, B., Britt, S. L., Archuleta, K. L., & Klontz, T. (2012). Disordered money behaviors: Development of the Klontz money behavior inventory. *Journal of Financial Therapy, 3*(1), 17–42. https://doi.org/10.4148/jft.v3i1.1485

Klontz, B. T., & Britt, S. L. (2012). How clients' money scripts predict their financial behaviors. *Journal of Financial Planning*, 25(11), 33–43. Retrieved November 16, 2023, from https://www.financialplanningassociation.org/article/journal/NOV12-how-clients-money-scripts-predict-their-financial-behaviors

Klontz, B. T., Britt, S. L., & Archuleta, K. L. (2015). *Financial therapy: Theory, research, and practice*. Springer.

Kopasker, D., Montagna, C., & Bender, K. A. (2018). Economic insecurity: A socioeconomic determinant of mental health. *SSM–Population Health, 6*, 184–194. https://doi.org/10.1016/j.ssmph.2018.09.006

LeBaron, A. B., Runyan, S. D., Jorgensen, B. L., Marks, L. D., Li, X., & Hill, E. J. (2019). Practice makes perfect: Experiential learning as a method for financial socialization. *Journal of Family Issues, 40*(4), 435–463. https://doi.org/10.1177/0192513X18812917

Lown, J. M. (2011). 2011 outstanding AFCPE® conference paper: Development and validation of a financial self-efficacy scale. *Journal of Financial Counseling and Planning, 22*(2), 11.

Maher, C. A., & Hayes, B. E. (2024). Nonfinancial consequences of identity theft revisited: Examining the association of out-of-pocket losses with physical or emotional distress and behavioral health. *Criminal Justice and Behavior, 51*(3), 459–481. https://doi.org/10.1177/00938548231223166

Mancini, M. A. (2021). *Integrated behavioral health practice*. Springer International Publishing. https://doi.org/10.1007/978-3-030-59659-0

McCoy, M., Watkins, K., White, K., Kahler, R., & Reiter, M. (2024). The importance of the "client" experience for financial planning students: A qualitative inquiry of themes. *Journal of Financial Counseling & Planning, 35*(2), 264–275. https://doi.org/10.1891/JFCP-2022-0077

Morduch, J., & Schneider, R. (2017). *The financial diaries*. Princeton University Press.

Mueller, A., Mitchell, J. E., Black, D. W., Crosby, R. D., Berg, K., & de Zwaan, M. (2010). Latent profile analysis and comorbidity in a sample of individuals with compulsive buying disorder. *Psychiatry Research, 178*(2), 348–353. https://doi.org/10.1016/j.psychres.2010.04.021

National Association of Social Workers. (2017, August 4). Code of ethics. *NASW-National Association of Social Workers*. Retrieved August 6, 2020, from https://www.socialworkers.org/about/ethics/code-of-ethics

Netemeyer, R. G., Warmath, D., Fernandes, D., & Lynch, J. G. (2018). Perceived financial well-being scale. From: How am I doing? Perceived financial well-being, its potential antecedents, and its relation to overall well-being. *Journal of Consumer Research, 45*(1), 68–89. https://doi.org/10.1093/jcr/ucx109. https://sjdm.org/dmidi/Perceived_Financial_Well_Being_Scale.html

Newcomb, S., & Cummings, B. F. (2019). Making the science practical: Behavioral interventions in practice. In D. B. Durband, R. H. Law, & A. K. Mazzolini (Eds.), *Financial Counseling* (pp. 141–151). Springer International Publishing. https://doi.org/10.1007/978-3-319-72586-4_10

Prause, J., Dooley, D., & Huh, J. (2009). Income volatility and psychological depression. *American Journal of Community Psychology, 43*(1–2), 57–70. https://doi.org/10.1007/s10464-008-9219-3

Prawitz, A. D., Garman, E. T., Sorhaindo, B., O'Neill, B., Kim, J., & Drentea, P. (2006). InCharge financial distress/financial well-being scale: Development, administration, and score interpretation. *Journal of Financial Counseling and Planning, 17*(1), 34–50. https://doi.org/10.1037/t60365-000

Richardson, T., Elliott, P., & Roberts, R. (2013). The relationship between personal unsecured debt and mental and physical health: A systematic review and meta-analysis. *Clinical Psychology Review, 33*(8), 1148–1162. https://doi.org/10.1016/j.cpr.2013.08.009

Solomon, S. (2022). *Money habitudes professional guide*. Money Habitudes.

Stack, C. (1974). *All our kin*. Basic Books.

Starkey, A. J., Keane, C. R., Terry, M. A., Marx, J. H., & Ricci, E. M. (2013). Financial distress and depressive symptoms among African American women: Identifying financial priorities and needs and why it matters for mental health. *Journal of Urban Health, 90*(1), 83–100. https://doi.org/10.1007/s11524-012-9755-x

Taylor, C., Klontz, B., & Britt, S. (2016a). Reliability and convergent validity of the Klontz money script inventory-revised (KMSI-R). *Journal of Financial Therapy, 6*(2). https://doi.org/10.4148/1944-9771.1100

Taylor, C., Klontz, B., & Britt, S. (2016b). Internal consistency and convergent validity of the Klontz money behavior inventory (KMBI). *Journal of Financial Therapy, 6*(2). https://doi.org/10.4148/1944-9771.1101

Tucker-Seeley, R. D., & Yabroff, K. R. (2016). Minimizing the "financial toxicity" associated with cancer care: Advancing the research agenda. *Journal of the National Cancer Institute, 108*(5). https://doi.org/10.1093/jnci/djv410

White, K. J., Love, K., McCoy, M., Reiter, M., Seponski, D. M., Koposko, J., & Regan, E. (2022). Factors associated with the financial strain of transgender and gender diverse college students. *Journal of Consumer Affairs, 56*(4), 1617–1637. https://doi.org/10.1111/joca.12483

Wilkinson, L. R. (2016). Financial strain and mental health among older adults during the great recession. *The Journals of Gerontology Series B: Psychological Sciences and Social Sciences, 71*(4), 745–754. https://doi.org/10.1093/geronb/gbw001

Chapter 9
Improving Client Financial Behaviors: On Goal Setting

9.1 Introduction

Effective goal-setting represents one of the most fundamental yet sophisticated skills helping professionals can develop when working with clients facing financial challenges. Collaborating with clients in establishing clear, achievable, and meaningful financial objectives fosters financial efficacy and behavioral change, drawing upon multiple theoretical frameworks presented throughout this book (Anvari-Clark & Rose, 2023; Hoge et al., 2020). Financial efficacy—the ability and confidence to manage financial challenges—fundamentally involves setting and achieving goals that build both practical competence and psychological resilience.

The guidance on goal-setting presented in this chapter is universally appropriate across all helping disciplines, including social work, psychology, addiction counseling, healthcare, financial planning, financial coaching, and financial counseling. However, professionals must adapt these principles for their specific contexts, scope of practice, and the nature of their client relationships. Whether working with clients in single-session consultations, brief interventions, or ongoing therapeutic relationships, the core principles remain consistent while implementation varies based on professional setting and client needs.

When professionals apply stress and resilience theory to financial goal-setting, they recognize that mastering financial challenges builds resilience and coping mechanisms that can be applied to future situations (Allen & Henderson, 2017; Rosino, 2016). Similarly, understanding financial scarcity's impact on cognitive bandwidth highlights the importance of breaking complex financial goals into manageable steps that reduce cognitive load and increase the likelihood of success (Mullainathan & Shafir, 2013). The framework presented also acknowledges financial interdependence—how social relationships and support networks influence financial behaviors and goal achievement (Anvari-Clark & Miller, 2023). This

Supplementary Information The online version contains supplementary material available at https://doi.org/10.1007/978-3-032-02632-3_9.

J. Anvari-Clark, *Financial and Behavioral Health for Helping Professionals*,
https://doi.org/10.1007/978-3-032-02632-3_9

recognition is particularly important as professionals help clients navigate financial goals that interinfluence not only individual circumstances but also with family relationships, social connections, and community obligations. These theoretical insights inform practical approaches that address multiple dimensions of financial behavior change.

Financial goals exist within the broader behavioral health framework, creating opportunities for professionals to address multiple domains simultaneously. A savings goal may enhance mental health by reducing financial anxiety (Archuleta et al., 2020), a debt reduction plan may improve physical health by reducing stress-related symptoms (Sweet, 2021), and improved financial management routines can strengthen both social health and coping mechanisms (Canale et al., 2015). By helping clients establish concrete, achievable financial goals that align with their values and priorities, professionals provide pathways toward improved financial and overall well-being that address the interrelated domains of behavioral health.

9.2 The Psychology of Financial Goal Achievement

Understanding the psychological factors that influence goal achievement provides the foundation for effective financial goal-setting interventions. Confidence in one's ability to achieve goals significantly influences both goal selection and goal attainment. This relationship becomes particularly important in financial contexts, where past experiences of financial difficulty or failure can undermine efficacy and lead clients to set goals that are either unrealistically modest or unrealistically ambitious.

The concept of mastery through experiences proves central to building financial efficacy via goal achievement (Bandura, 1977). Clients who have successfully achieved goals in any domain of their lives possess transferable skills and psychological resources that may be applied to financial challenges. The familiar observation that "it is so much easier to do something the second time than the first" reflects the power of proven competence to build confidence for future endeavors. This principle suggests two important considerations when designing financial goals with clients: (1) starting with achievable objectives that build momentum, and (2) helping clients recognize existing strengths and successful experiences they can transfer to financial contexts.

Emotional momentum via feedback represents another crucial psychological dimension of goal achievement (Bandura, 1977). When clients struggle through and achieve one financial goal, the knowledge that they can change, improve their situation, and exercise agency over their circumstances carries forward into subsequent goals and challenges. This psychological phenomenon underlies the effectiveness of debt reduction strategies such as the "snowball method," which prioritizes paying off smaller debts first to create early victories that build motivation for tackling larger obligations. The emotional weight of uncertainty—where clients lack clarity about their situation and how to handle it—can be substantially reduced through the goal-setting process itself, which provides structure, direction, and concrete next steps.

Furthermore, the importance of focus and attention in goal achievement cannot be overstated, particularly for clients experiencing financial stress or scarcity. Research on productivity and attention suggests that dividing focus among multiple simultaneous projects reduces overall effectiveness and increases completion time (Newport, 2024). This insight supports prioritizing single goals or carefully sequenced goal achievement rather than attempting multiple financial objectives simultaneously. While clients may have several financial priorities they want to address, working intensively on one goal (or two complementary goals) at a time typically produces better outcomes than spreading attention across multiple objectives.

9.3 The Enhanced SMART Goals Framework

The SMART goals framework provides a systematic approach to goal design that addresses the psychological and practical dimensions of behavior change. While variations exist in the acronym's components, the enhanced framework presented here includes: Specific, Measurable, Action-oriented, Accountable, Realistic, Relevant, and Time-bound elements. Each component serves important psychological and practical functions that increase the likelihood of goal achievement.

Specific Goals
Specificity in goal-setting requires clarity about exactly what the client wants to achieve, eliminating ambiguity that can undermine motivation and progress monitoring. Vague financial goals such as "I want to be better with money" or "I want to save more" lack the precision necessary for effective planning and progress assessment. Specific goals identify concrete outcomes, precise amounts, and clear definitions of success.

The process of making goals specific often requires iterative conversation and exploration of underlying intentions and values. A client's initial statement about wanting to "save money" might evolve through discussion into a specific goal of "saving $5000 to purchase a reliable used car." This specificity enables both professional and client to understand exactly what success looks like and to develop appropriate strategies for achievement.

Specificity also requires consideration of the goal's relationship to broader life objectives and values. The most effective financial goals connect specific outcomes to meaningful life priorities, creating emotional investment that sustains motivation through inevitable challenges. A savings goal is more compelling when connected to career advancement, family well-being, or personal responsibility rather than existing as an abstract financial objective.

Measurable Progress
Measurability allows both clients and professionals to track progress, celebrate milestones, and adjust strategies based on actual results. Financial goals lend themselves well to typical quantitative measurement—dollar amounts saved, debt balances reduced, income increased—but measurement can also include behavioral indicators such as frequency of budgeting activity, number of days without overspending, or completion of financial education modules. The measurement approach should match the goal's nature and the client's preferences for tracking progress. The key is establishing clear criteria for progress that enable both recognition of achievements and identification of obstacles requiring strategy adjustment. Measures could be defined as (1) an amount (e.g., number of dollars saved or of debt paid, or a credit score number), (2) a binary counting of outcome (e.g., an account was opened [Yes/No]), or (3) a counting of process (e.g., number of times in a month an impulse purchase was made). Having a clear quantitative measure will provide the evidence of progress and help answer the question "…And how is that approach working for you?" unequivocally. Digital tools and apps can facilitate measurement, but traditional methods such as written tracking or visual progress indicators can also prove effective. The measurement system should be simple enough to maintain consistently while providing sufficient detail to support decision-making and motivation.

Action-Oriented Strategies
Effective goals specify not only desired outcomes but also the concrete actions required to achieve them. Action-oriented goal-setting breaks large objectives into manageable steps, identifies specific behaviors that need to change, and creates implementation plans that connect daily decisions to long-term objectives.

For a savings goal, action-oriented planning might include setting up automatic transfers, identifying specific expenses to reduce, or establishing new income sources. The action component transforms the goal from an aspiration into a practical plan with clear behavioral requirements. Action plans should account for potential obstacles and include contingency strategies. Clients benefit from thinking through common scenarios that might derail progress and developing specific responses for these situations. This preparation reduces the likelihood that unexpected events will completely disrupt goal achievement.

Accountability Structures
Accountability involves identifying who will support, monitor, and encourage goal achievement. While some clients have strong internal motivation and self-monitoring capacity, most benefit from external accountability that provides encouragement, objective feedback, and gentle pressure to maintain momentum.

Accountability can come from various sources: family members, friends, professional relationships, support groups, or formal coaching arrangements. The key is identifying accountability sources that feel supportive rather than judgmental, and that have the capacity and willingness to provide consistent engagement. Professional relationships often provide crucial accountability, particularly for clients who lack supportive social networks or whose families may not understand or support their financial goals. Regular check-ins with helping professionals create structure for reviewing progress, problem-solving obstacles, and adjusting strategies based on experience.

Realistic Expectations
Realistic goals balance ambition with achievability, considering both the client's current circumstances and their capacity for change. Unrealistic goals often lead to discouragement and abandonment of change efforts, while overly modest goals may fail to create sufficient motivation or meaningful improvement. Determining realistic expectations requires careful assessment of the client's financial resources, time availability, competing priorities, and past experiences with similar challenges. Goals should stretch the client's current capacity while remaining achievable with reasonable effort and commitment. The "start small and build" principle proves particularly valuable for clients with limited goal-achievement experience or low confidence. Initial goals can focus on building goal-setting skills and creating success experiences that support larger objectives over time.

Relevance to Life Values
Relevant goals connect financial objectives to the client's broader values, priorities, and life circumstances. Goals that align with meaningful personal objectives generate more sustainable motivation than those imposed by external expectations or generic financial advice. Exploring relevance often requires helping clients articulate their values and examine how financial goals support their most important life objectives. A debt reduction goal becomes more compelling when connected to career flexibility, relationship stability, or personal peace of mind rather than simply improving credit scores. Cultural considerations play an important role in goal relevance, as financial priorities and definitions of success vary significantly across different cultural contexts. Professionals must help clients identify goals that align with their own values rather than imposing culturally specific assumptions about appropriate financial objectives.

Time-Bound Implementation
Time-bound goals establish clear deadlines that create urgency and enable progress monitoring. Deadlines should be realistic but firm enough to provide structure and motivation. Open-ended goals often lack the pressure necessary to drive consistent action and behavior change. Effective time frames consider both the goal's scope and the client's other commitments and constraints and set the endpoint at the day level (e.g., March 25, 2027). Short-term goals might span several weeks to a few months, while longer-term objectives may require a year or more. Breaking larger goals into time-bound milestones creates opportunities for celebration and strategy adjustment throughout the achievement process. Flexibility with timelines remains important, as life circumstances may require adjustments to original deadlines. The key is maintaining forward momentum while adapting timelines to realistic circumstances rather than abandoning goals when initial deadlines prove unworkable.

9.4 Facilitating Goal-Setting Conversations

The process of facilitating effective goal-setting conversations can utilize motivational interviewing techniques and requires careful attention to the client's emotional responses and systematic exploration of each SMART component. Successful goal-setting conversations create collaborative partnerships where clients maintain ownership of their goals while receiving professional support for effective planning and implementation.

Beginning goal-setting conversations often involves helping clients recognize their existing capacity for achievement by exploring successful goal attainment in other life domains. Rather than focusing immediately on financial objectives, professionals can ask clients to identify goals they have successfully achieved in areas such as health, education, relationships, or career development. This exploration serves multiple purposes: it builds confidence by highlighting existing competencies, it identifies transferable skills and strategies, and it provides a template for applying systematic approaches to financial goals. The conversation should allow clients to identify their own success experiences rather than having professionals suggest examples. This approach ensures that the client's unique strengths and experiences guide the discussion, avoiding potentially limiting assumptions about what types of achievements might be relevant.

When clients have identified a successful goal achievement experience, professionals can systematically explore how that success maps onto the SMART framework. Questions might include: "What specifically was your goal at the time?" "How did you measure your progress along the way?" "What steps did you take to achieve this goal?" "To whom were you accountable during this process?" "How did you determine that this was a realistic goal for you?" "What relevance did this goal have to your life?" "How long did it take you to achieve the outcome, and did you need to adjust your timeline for any reason?"

This exploration helps clients recognize that they already possess goal-setting and achievement skills while simultaneously introducing the SMART framework in a concrete, experiential way. Clients often express increased confidence when they realize that their financial goals can utilize the same systematic approach that created success in other life areas. Transitioning from successful experiences to financial goal-setting requires careful attention to the client's emotional responses and any limiting beliefs about their financial capacity. Professionals should acknowledge that financial goals may feel different or more challenging than other objectives while emphasizing the transferable nature of goal-setting skills and strategies.

The collaborative development of specific financial goals begins with broad exploration of the client's financial priorities and concerns. Rather than immediately pushing for specificity, professionals can help clients identify general areas where they want to see improvement and then gradually work toward more precise objectives. This process often requires several conversations as clients clarify their intentions and consider the implications of different goal options.

Throughout the goal-setting process, professionals should remain alert to signs that goals may not align with the client's actual values or circumstances. Goals that emerge from external pressure, unrealistic expectations, or insufficient self-knowledge often fail to generate sustainable motivation. The collaborative process should help clients identify goals that feel personally meaningful and achievable rather than simply checking boxes on generic financial planning checklists.

9.4.1 Adapting Goal-Setting Across Professional Contexts

While the core principles of effective goal-setting remain consistent across helping professions, implementation must be adapted for different professional contexts, scope of practice limitations, and client relationship parameters. Understanding these adaptations enables professionals to use goal-setting approaches effectively within their specific practice settings while maintaining appropriate professional boundaries.

Single-Session Consultations
Professionals working with clients in single-session contexts, such as financial counselors providing brief consultations or healthcare providers addressing financial barriers to treatment, must adapt goal-setting approaches for limited time and relationship constraints. In these contexts, goal-setting often focuses on immediate stabilization needs and connecting clients with ongoing support resources. Single-session goal-setting typically emphasizes one clear, achievable objective that can create early momentum while addressing the client's most pressing concern. The professional's role involves helping the client identify this priority goal, providing basic framework for achievement, and connecting the client with resources for ongoing support and accountability. Follow-up mechanisms become particularly important in single-session contexts, as clients need ongoing support for goal achievement but may not have continued access to the professional who helped establish the goal. Referrals to appropriate ongoing services, peer support resources, or self-monitoring tools can bridge this gap while respecting the limitations of brief professional relationships.

Ongoing Therapeutic Relationships
Mental health professionals, social workers, and others working with clients over extended periods can integrate goal-setting into broader therapeutic or supportive relationships. In these contexts, financial goals often connect to larger therapeutic objectives around anxiety reduction, trauma recovery, relationship improvement, or life skills development. The extended relationship allows for more comprehensive goal exploration, regular progress monitoring, and strategy adjustment based on the client's evolving circumstances and insights. Financial goals can be coordinated with other therapeutic goals to create integrated approaches that address multiple behavioral health domains simultaneously. Professional boundaries remain important even in extended relationships, as most helping professionals are not trained

financial experts and should not provide specific financial advice beyond their scope of practice. The focus remains on the behavioral and psychological dimensions of goal-setting while connecting clients with appropriate financial expertise when needed.

Healthcare Settings
Healthcare professionals may encounter financial concerns primarily as health toxicity, barriers to treatment adherence, medication compliance, or accessing necessary care. Goal-setting in these contexts often focuses on addressing immediate financial obstacles to health care while connecting patients with broader financial support resources. Financial goals in healthcare settings typically emphasize practical problem-solving around specific medical expenses, insurance navigation, or accessing financial assistance programs. The goals are often short-term and directly related to health care needs rather than comprehensive financial planning. Collaboration with financial counselors, social workers, or patient navigation services becomes particularly important in healthcare settings, as medical professionals typically lack the time and training to provide comprehensive financial goal-setting support while maintaining focus on clinical care.

Financial Services Contexts
Financial planners, coaches, and counselors work most directly with comprehensive financial goal-setting, though they must adapt their approaches based on their specific training and the complexity of their clients' psychological needs. These professionals often have the time and expertise for detailed goal development and ongoing support. Integration with mental health considerations becomes important when financial professionals recognize that clients' financial behaviors are significantly influenced by psychological factors, trauma histories, or mental health conditions. Goal-setting approaches must account for these factors while remaining within the financial professional's scope of practice. Referral relationships with mental health professionals enable financial service providers to address the full complexity of their clients' needs while maintaining appropriate professional boundaries and ensuring clients receive comprehensive support.

9.4.2 Common Goal-Setting Challenges and Solutions

Despite the systematic approach provided by the SMART framework, goal-setting conversations often encounter predictable challenges that require skilled professional responses. Understanding these common obstacles and effective strategies for addressing them enables helping professionals to maintain productive goal-setting relationships even when clients experience difficulties.

Overwhelming Financial Complexity
Many clients present with complex financial situations involving multiple pressing needs: overwhelming debt, inadequate income, housing instability, lack of

emergency savings, and family financial obligations. The complexity can feel paralyzing, leading clients to avoid goal-setting altogether or to attempt simultaneous progress on multiple fronts that ultimately undermines success in any single area.

Effective responses to overwhelming complexity involve helping clients identify their most urgent priority while acknowledging that other concerns will be addressed in sequence. Professionals can use triage principles to help clients distinguish between immediate crises requiring urgent attention and important but less time-sensitive objectives that can be addressed after initial stabilization. The "one goal at a time" principle becomes particularly important for clients experiencing financial overwhelm. Focusing intensive attention on a single objective allows clients to experience success and build confidence while reducing the cognitive burden associated with managing multiple complex goals simultaneously.

Conflicting Values and Priorities

Goal-setting conversations sometimes reveal conflicts between the client's stated financial objectives and their deeper values, family obligations, or cultural expectations. These conflicts can emerge when clients feel pressure to pursue goals that don't align with their authentic priorities or when competing values create internal tension about appropriate financial choices.

Exploring value conflicts requires sensitive conversation about what truly matters to the client versus what they feel they "should" want to achieve. Professionals must help clients identify goals that align with their authentic values while acknowledging external pressures and expectations that may influence their thinking. Cultural humility becomes particularly important when value conflicts arise, as financial goals that seem obviously beneficial from one cultural perspective may conflict with important values or obligations from another perspective.

External Resistance and Lack of Support

Clients' financial goals sometimes encounter resistance from family members, friends, or community members who may feel threatened by changes in financial behavior or who have competing interests in the client's financial decisions. This external resistance can undermine goal achievement even when clients have strong personal motivation.

Addressing external resistance requires helping clients develop strategies for managing these relationships while maintaining commitment to their goals. This might involve communication skills for discussing goals with family members, boundary-setting strategies for managing financial pressure from others, or identifying alternative sources of support and accountability. In some cases, clients may need to pursue financial goals despite family opposition, requiring careful attention to safety considerations and support system development. Professionals must help clients assess the risks and benefits of goal pursuit in challenging relational contexts while providing emotional support for difficult decisions.

9.5 Examples of Financial Goals

Practical application of the enhanced SMART framework benefits from concrete examples that demonstrate how abstract principles translate into specific, actionable goals. The following examples illustrate effective goal-setting across common financial health objectives while highlighting the flexibility needed to adapt approaches for different client circumstances and priorities. Three different types of goals are featured—financial, behavioral, and procedural—that align with various financial health outcomes. These correspond with three different approaches to measurement:

- A counted amount: "Do I have $___, Yes/No?"
- A process: number of times in a given period or percentage change.
- A binary outcome achieved: "Have I opened the account, Yes/No?"

See electronic supplementary materials online for a worksheet template (see My SMART Goal).

Financial Example: Emergency Savings Goal

Specific: Save $1000 for an emergency fund to cover unexpected expenses without using credit cards [$ count].

Measurable: Track progress through monthly account balance reviews, with milestone celebrations at $250, $500, and $750.

Action-oriented: Transfer $125 to savings account automatically on the first and 15th of each month by setting up automatic bank transfers.

Accountable: Weekly check-ins with financial coach and monthly progress reports to accountability partner (spouse/trusted friend).

Realistic: Based on careful budgeting analysis showing ability to redirect $250 monthly from dining out expenses without significantly impacting quality of life.

Relevant: Directly addresses anxiety about financial emergencies and supports goal of reducing dependence on credit cards for unexpected expenses.

Time-bound: Achieve full $1000 emergency fund within 4 months (by [specific day/month/year]).

Financial Example: Debt Reduction Goal

Specific: Pay off $3500 credit card debt completely, starting with the highest interest rate card [$ count].

Measurable: Amount of credit card balance will ultimately become $0.

Action-oriented: Pay $350, plus minimum payments on all other cards, each month by reducing entertainment budget and increasing freelance income.

Accountable: Monthly progress reviews with financial counselor and debt tracking shared with accountability partner.

Realistic: Plan accounts for maintaining minimum payments on all other debts while focusing extra payments on target card.

Relevant: Eliminating high-interest debt will reduce financial stress and free up money for other important goals like emergency savings.

Time-bound: Complete payoff within 12 months ([day/month/year]), with interim goal of 50% reduction by 6 months.

Note: Due to ongoing accumulating interest, the total amount of debt to be paid will rise during the payoff period. Use an online debt-payoff calculator to account for extra interest costs in the overall timeline to reach $0.

Behavioral Example: Addressing Problem Gambling

Specific: To completely stop online gambling activities [0 times].

Measurable: Engage in no gambling activity, as evidenced by no related transactions on my bank, credit card, cash withdrawals, or any other statements.

Action-oriented: Install gambling-blocking software on all technology devices and attend at least four Gamblers Anonymous (GA) meetings each week.

Accountable: Weekly check-ins and as-needed calls with addiction counselor and GA sponsor.

Realistic: With professional help and support groups, quitting gambling is achievable.

Relevant: Stopping gambling will significantly improve financial situation, coping health, and family relationships.

Time-bound: Maintain gambling abstinence for 1 year, until (day/month/year).

Note: For true addictions and significant problem behaviors, although the client has identified wanting a year of abstinence, this goal should be balanced with the mental and emotional tool of "taking it one day at a time" and a harm reduction approach. As a coping mechanism, it is important to also explore and address with the client the underlying emotional issues prompting this particular coping behavior. Otherwise, there will always be loopholes around successful abstinence—getting around software blockers, gambling in-kind rather than online, hiding transactions (e.g., with a new or someone else's credit card), "white-knuckling" the abstinence until the 1-year anniversary and then treating oneself to a gambling binge, or even swapping the gambling disorder for another harmful coping behavior. As with all behavioral and substance use disorders, the true issue at hand is not the harmful activity itself, but a deeper need for healing and connection. Thus, this work on the emotional self should be the broader context within which the SMART goal is situated.

Behavioral Example: Budget Implementation Goal

Specific: Allocate all income and then record all expenses in a written monthly budget that includes necessary expenses plus savings and discretionary spending [frequency count].

Measurable: To allocate all current money and income as it is earned, to record all of expenses daily, and to review them weekly.

Action-oriented: Use a budgeting app for daily expense tracking, conduct weekly budget review meetings on Sundays, and adjust categories monthly based on actual spending patterns.

Accountable: Weekly budget reviews with spouse/partner and monthly check-ins with financial coach for strategy refinement.

Realistic: With a user-friendly budget app and consistent schedule for activity (including times of day/week), developing a budgeting habit is achievable.

Relevant: Consistent budgeting will reduce financial anxiety, improve communication with partner about money, and support achievement of other financial goals.

Time-bound: Establish a consistent budgeting habit within 1 month, with weekly assessments and monthly budget refinements. Track 100% of daily expenses and conduct weekly reviews for 6 consecutive months (by day/month/year) using a budgeting app to improve awareness of spending habits and financial decision-making.

Note: The goal could still be improved by identifying *which* app they will use, otherwise potentially leading to a paralysis-by-analysis situation in which they never get started actually doing the budgeting work. Clients will likely have a preferred budgeting approach and technology. A good prerequisite procedural goal is to select an app (or other format) that will work best to facilitate the allocate-spend-track-review process. Upon successful completion of the overall budget tracking goal, it will be important to evaluate how to maintain the activity in perpetuity and with what modifications.

Procedural Example: Opening a Retirement Account

Specific: Open and fund a Roth IRA retirement account to begin building tax-advantaged retirement savings [achievement Y/N].

Measurable: Successfully establish an active Roth IRA with an initial investment of $1000.

Action-oriented: Research three (3) different providers to compare fees and investment options, complete the application with the chosen provider, and transfer funds from savings account.

Accountable: Monthly check-ins with financial coach to ensure completion and discuss next steps for ongoing contributions.

Realistic: Client has necessary documentation, initial funding available, and meets income requirements for Roth IRA eligibility.

Relevant: Opening retirement account addresses long-term financial security goals and provides tax advantages for future wealth building.

Time-bound: Complete entire process within 30 days, with provider research completed within the first 2 weeks.

Note: Successful completion of procedural goals often creates momentum for related objectives. Upon opening the Roth IRA, professionals should help clients immediately establish automatic monthly contributions while motivation remains high. Even modest regular contributions prove more beneficial than waiting for increased income, as procrastination often undermines future goal implementation. Other procedural goals may similarly benefit from immediate follow-through on related activities to maintain progress momentum.

Procedural Example: Automated Bill Payment Goal

Specific: Set up automatic payments for all monthly recurring bills to ensure timely payment and reduce financial management burden [achievement Y/N].

Measurable: All monthly bills including utilities, rent, insurance, and subscriptions will be paid automatically without manual intervention.

Action-oriented: Create comprehensive list of all recurring bills, gather necessary account information and payment details, and configure automatic payments through bank's online portal or individual creditor websites.

Accountable: Progress shared with accountability partner (roommate) who benefits from timely utility payments and will help monitor successful implementation.

Realistic: Client has online access to banking services, necessary account information readily available, and sufficient monthly income to cover automated payments.

Relevant: Payment automation prevents late fees, improves credit score through consistent payment history, and reduces monthly financial stress and cognitive burden.

Time-bound: Complete setup for all bills within 14 days (by day/month/year), with verification of successful first automated payments within 45 days.

9.6 Special Considerations for Complex Situations

While the SMART framework provides a solid foundation for most financial goal-setting situations, some client circumstances require additional considerations and adaptations. Understanding these special situations enables helping professionals to maintain effective goal-setting approaches even when clients face complex challenges that might otherwise undermine traditional goal-setting strategies.

Trauma-Informed Goal Setting
Clients with histories of financial trauma, domestic violence involving financial abuse, or other traumatic experiences may approach goal-setting with heightened anxiety, hypervigilance about control, or deeply ingrained beliefs about their inability to achieve financial stability. Trauma-informed goal-setting requires careful attention to safety, choice, and empowerment principles. Safety considerations in goal-setting include ensuring that financial goals do not inadvertently create additional safety risks, particularly for clients leaving abusive relationships. Goals might need to prioritize immediate safety and independence over optimal financial strategies, such as focusing on access to separate bank accounts rather than investment returns. Choice and control become paramount in trauma-informed goal-setting, with professionals taking extra care to ensure that clients maintain ownership of their goals rather than feeling pressured into objectives that don't feel personally meaningful. The goal-setting process itself should demonstrate respect for client autonomy and decision-making capacity. Empowerment through goal achievement can provide powerful healing experiences for trauma survivors, but goals must be

carefully calibrated to create success experiences rather than repeated failures that reinforce trauma-related beliefs about helplessness or inadequacy.

Mental Health Considerations

Clients experiencing depression, anxiety, bipolar disorder, ADHD, or other mental health conditions may require adapted goal-setting approaches that account for how symptoms affect motivation, executive functioning, and behavioral consistency. These adaptations should not lower expectations but rather modify strategies to work with rather than against mental health symptoms.

Depression often affects goal-setting through reduced motivation, difficulty experiencing pleasure from achievements, and negative thought patterns that undermine confidence. Goal-setting approaches might emphasize smaller, more frequent achievements that provide regular positive feedback, integration with mental health treatment goals, and careful attention to realistic timelines that account for symptom fluctuations.

Anxiety can create either perfectionist goal-setting that sets unrealistic standards or avoidant patterns that prevent goal engagement altogether. Balanced approaches help anxious clients set appropriately challenging goals while building in flexibility and self-compassion for inevitable setbacks.

ADHD and executive functioning challenges may require enhanced structure, external accountability, strategies for managing attention and organization, and longer timelines to establish behavioral patterns. Goals might emphasize systems and habits rather than specific numerical targets, with particular attention to implementation strategies that work with ADHD symptoms rather than against them, such as including a line in one's budget for impulsive purchases.

Substance Use and Addiction Recovery

Clients in recovery from substance use disorders and problem behaviors face unique financial challenges that require specialized goal-setting approaches. Active addiction often creates significant financial damage through job loss, legal expenses, medical costs, and impulsive spending. Goal-setting in early recovery may focus on immediate stabilization: securing housing, addressing legal and medical debts, establishing basic budgeting systems, and avoiding financial triggers for relapse. These goals often require coordination with addiction treatment providers and may need to be subordinated to recovery maintenance when conflicts arise. Later recovery allows for more comprehensive financial goal-setting, but professionals must remain aware of how financial stress might affect recovery stability. Goals should support rather than undermine recovery by reducing rather than increasing stress and by building efficacy in multiple life domains.

Family and Relationship Dynamics

Financial goals exist within relationship contexts that significantly influence both goal-setting and achievement processes. Couples and other family members may have different financial values, priorities, or approaches to money management that create conflict around goal-setting. Effective goal-setting in relationship contexts requires understanding and addressing these dynamics rather than assuming that individual motivation alone determines goal achievement. This might involve helping couples develop shared financial goals that honor both partners' values, supporting individuals in setting goals that account for family obligations, or helping clients navigate cultural expectations around financial responsibilities.

Communication skills become particularly important when financial goals affect relationships, as goal achievement often requires relationship conversations about priorities, boundaries, and mutual support. Professionals may need to provide guidance on financial communication or refer clients to relationship counseling when financial goal conflicts reflect deeper relationship issues.

9.7 Integration with Broader Behavioral Health Treatment

Financial goal-setting gains maximum effectiveness when integrated with broader behavioral health treatment approaches rather than being addressed in isolation. This integration recognizes that financial behaviors both affect and are affected by mental health, physical health, coping strategies, social relationships, and other factors. Effective integration requires understanding these connections and designing goal-setting approaches that support clients' overall health and well-being rather than focusing narrowly on financial metrics.

Coordinating with Mental Health Treatment
Mental health professionals working with clients facing financial challenges can integrate financial goal-setting into broader therapeutic goals around anxiety reduction, depression treatment, trauma recovery, or life skills development. Financial goals might serve as behavioral activation strategies for depressed clients, anxiety management tools for worried clients, or empowerment experiences for trauma survivors.

Coordination requires clear communication between financial and mental health professionals when clients are receiving services from multiple providers. This collaboration ensures that financial goals support rather than undermine mental health treatment objectives while preventing contradictory advice or overwhelming clients with competing priorities. Assessment of mental health symptoms and their relationship to financial behaviors informs goal-setting strategies. Clients experiencing severe depression might need smaller, more immediate goals that provide frequent positive feedback, while clients with anxiety might benefit from goals that build confidence through graduated success experiences.

Supporting Physical Health Objectives
Financial stress significantly affects physical health through multiple pathways including cardiovascular impacts, immune system suppression, sleep disruption, and health behavior changes. Financial goal-setting can support physical health by reducing financial stress, enabling better healthcare access, and creating resources for health-promoting activities.

Healthcare professionals can integrate financial goal-setting into treatment planning by helping patients address financial barriers to medication adherence, lower stress-inducing debts, or facilitate lifestyle changes. Financial stability goals might directly support diabetes management, cardiac rehabilitation participation, or cancer treatment completion. Preventive health considerations also inform financial goal-setting, as securing emergency funds, health savings accounts, or health, disability, and long-term care insurance coverage can prevent future health crises from creating financial catastrophes. These connections help clients understand how financial goals serve broader health and well-being objectives rather than existing as separate concerns or just another added expense.

Building Healthy Coping Strategies

Financial goal achievement often requires developing healthy coping strategies to manage stress, anxiety, and frustration that arise during behavior change processes. Clients accustomed to using spending, gambling, or other financial behaviors as emotional regulation strategies need alternative coping mechanisms to support goal achievement.

Goal-setting conversations can explicitly address coping strategy development by helping clients identify emotional triggers for problematic financial behaviors, developing alternative responses to stress and difficult emotions, and building support systems that provide emotional resources during challenging periods. Integration with substance use treatment becomes particularly important when financial stress serves as a relapse trigger or when financial goals conflict with recovery maintenance. Goal-setting approaches must prioritize recovery stability while addressing financial concerns in ways that support rather than undermine healing.

Strengthening Social Connections

Financial goals affect and are affected by social relationships in complex ways, and achievement often requires support from family members, friends, or professional relationships. Yet, financial stress can strain social connections and reduce access to social support. Effective goal-setting addresses these social dimensions rather than treating financial behavior change as purely an individual endeavor.

Building social support for financial goals might involve helping clients communicate with family members about their objectives or including them in the planning process, developing accountability relationships with trusted friends, or connecting with peer support groups of others working on similar challenges. These social connections provide both practical support and emotional encouragement during difficult periods.

Cultural considerations become particularly important in social integration, as different cultural contexts have varying expectations around financial responsibility, family financial obligations, and appropriate sources of financial support. Goal-setting approaches must honor these cultural contexts while supporting clients in achieving their individual objectives.

9.8 Professional Development and Competency Building

Effective financial goal-setting requires helping professionals to develop specific competencies that bridge financial knowledge and behavioral change skills. While professionals need not become financial experts to utilize goal-setting approaches effectively, they must develop sufficient knowledge and skills to facilitate productive goal-setting conversations.

Core Competencies for Goal-Setting

Basic financial literacy provides the foundation for understanding clients' financial situations and the feasibility of different goal options. Professionals need not be able to provide comprehensive financial advice, but they should understand fundamental concepts such as budgeting, debt management, saving strategies, and the relationship between different financial goals.

Motivational interviewing skills enable professionals to facilitate collaborative goal-setting conversations that maintain client ownership and motivation while providing structure and guidance. These skills include open-ended questioning, reflective listening, summarizing, and supporting client efficacy and motivation for change (Miller & Rollnick, 2013). Understanding of behavior change principles helps professionals design goal-setting approaches that account for psychological factors affecting motivation, habit formation, and relapse prevention. This includes knowledge of how to break complex goals into manageable steps, build accountability structures, and support clients through setbacks and obstacles. Assessment skills enable professionals to evaluate clients' readiness for goal-setting, identify potential obstacles to goal achievement, and recognize when clients might benefit from additional services or support beyond goal-setting interventions.

Scope of Practice Considerations

Each helping profession has specific scope of practice guidelines that affect how professionals can engage in financial goal-setting. Mental health professionals can address the psychological and behavioral dimensions of financial goal-setting while referring clients to financial professionals for specific investment advice, tax planning, or complex financial product recommendations. Healthcare professionals can help patients set goals around managing medical expenses and accessing financial assistance while connecting them with financial counselors for comprehensive financial planning. Social workers often have the broadest scope for addressing financial goal-setting as part of comprehensive case management and advocacy services. However, they must still recognize the limits of their financial expertise and collaborate with or refer to financial professionals when clients need specialized financial advice beyond basic goal-setting support. Financial professionals have the most comprehensive training in financial knowledge, but when setting goals that the individual carries out, they must recognize when clients' psychological barriers, mental health concerns, or complex life circumstances require collaboration with behavioral health professionals. The most effective financial goal-setting often occurs through collaborative relationships that combine financial expertise with behavioral health knowledge.

Training and Continuing Education
Professional development in financial goal-setting benefits from formal training opportunities that address both financial literacy and behavioral change skills.

Financial literacy training should cover fundamental concepts relevant to goal-setting without requiring professionals to become financial experts. This includes understanding different types of financial goals, basic strategies for achieving common objectives, and recognition of when clients need specialized financial advice beyond goal-setting support.

Motivational interviewing training provides crucial skills for facilitating collaborative goal-setting conversations. These skills transfer effectively from other behavioral health applications and enhance professionals' ability to support client motivation and ownership of financial goals. Trauma-informed care training also becomes increasingly important as professionals recognize the prevalence of financial trauma and its effects on goal-setting capacity.

Supervision and Consultation
Supervisors can help professionals navigate scope of practice boundaries, develop competency in goal-setting conversations, and identify when referrals or collaboration might benefit clients. Consultation relationships with financial professionals enable behavioral health practitioners to access financial expertise while maintaining their primary focus on psychological and behavioral dimensions of goal achievement. These relationships can provide guidance on goal feasibility, appropriate referral resources, and strategies for addressing common financial challenges.

9.9 Case Examples and Practice Applications

The following case examples illustrate how theoretical frameworks translate into practical interventions across different client populations and professional settings, while highlighting adaptations needed for specific circumstances and challenges.

Case Example 1: Single Mother Facing Housing Instability
Maria, a 28-year-old single mother of two young children, seeks help from a social worker at a family service agency. She recently left an abusive relationship and is staying in transitional housing while working part-time at a retail job. Her immediate concerns include securing stable housing, managing limited income, and building financial responsibility to prevent future dependency on abusive partners.

Initial Assessment Maria expresses feeling overwhelmed by financial demands and uncertain about her ability to achieve stability. She has no savings, limited credit history, and fears about her capacity to support her children on her own. However, she demonstrates strong motivation and has successfully navigated other challenging life transitions.

Goal-Setting Process The social worker begins by exploring Maria's successful experience of leaving the abusive relationship, highlighting the planning, courage, and resource-gathering skills she demonstrated. This exploration builds confidence while introducing the systematic approach that can be applied to financial goals.

Collaborative Goal Development **Specific:** Save $3000 for the first month's rent, last month's rent, and security deposit for a two-bedroom apartment.

Measurable: Track savings weekly with goal of $200 per month over 15 months.

Action-oriented: Apply for earned income tax credit, sell unused household items, reduce transportation costs by using public transit, participate in food assistance programs to free up grocery budget.

Accountable: Weekly check-ins with social worker and monthly progress sharing with trusted friend from support group.

Realistic: Goal timeline accounts for income limitations while utilizing available community resources and assistance programs.

Relevant: Stable housing directly supports children's school stability and Maria's long-term well-being goals.

Time-bound: Achieve full savings goal within 15 months (by day/month/year) with quarterly milestones for progress assessment.

Adaptations and Support: The goal-setting process acknowledges trauma history through emphasis on choice and control, integration with safety planning, and coordination with domestic violence advocacy services. Progress tracking includes attention to emotional well-being and stress management alongside financial metrics.

Case Example 2: Young Adult with Student Debt and Lifestyle Inflation
David, a 26-year-old recent graduate working in marketing, approaches a financial coach feeling overwhelmed by student loan debt while struggling to control spending on social activities and lifestyle expenses. He earns a good salary but feels unable to make progress on debt while maintaining social connections and professional appearance expectations.

Initial Assessment David demonstrates high financial knowledge but struggles with implementation and feels conflicted between short-term social needs and long-term financial objectives. He expresses anxiety about missing out on social opportunities while simultaneously worrying about his financial future.

Goal-Setting Process The financial coach helps David explore his successful completion of graduate school, highlighting his ability to delay gratification, manage complex projects, and maintain motivation toward long-term objectives. This exploration reveals transferable skills and builds confidence for financial goal achievement.

Collaborative Goal Development **Specific:** Reduce student loan balance by $8000 through extra payments over and above minimum requirements.

Measurable: Track monthly extra payments of $445.

Action-oriented: Redirect 50% of entertainment budget toward loan payments, develop lower-cost social alternatives, negotiate one freelance project monthly to increase income.

Accountable: Monthly check-ins with financial coach and quarterly progress sharing with accountability partner (colleague with similar goals).

Realistic: Plan maintains reasonable social budget while creating meaningful debt reduction progress.

Relevant: Debt reduction supports long-term goals of homeownership and career flexibility.

Time-bound: Achieve $8000 debt reduction within 18 months (by day/month/year).

Social Integration: Goal achievement includes developing skills for communicating with friends about budget constraints, identifying low-cost social alternatives, and building social connections that support rather than undermine financial objectives.

Case Example 3: Older Adult Managing Fixed Income and Healthcare Costs
Eleanor, a 67-year-old retiree, works with a healthcare social worker to address mounting medical expenses that are straining her fixed income. She takes multiple medications, requires regular specialist visits, and worries about affording future healthcare needs while maintaining independence in her home.

Initial Assessment Eleanor demonstrates strong organizational skills and has successfully managed household finances for decades. However, healthcare cost inflation has outpaced her income increases, creating new financial pressures she has not previously experienced.

Goal-Setting Process The healthcare social worker explores Eleanor's successful household management history, highlighting her budgeting skills, resourcefulness, and advocacy abilities. The conversation focuses on applying these existing strengths to navigate healthcare financial challenges.

Collaborative Goal Development **Specific:** Reduce monthly healthcare out-of-pocket expenses by $150 through prescription assistance programs, generic substitutions, and Medicare benefit optimization.

Measurable: Track ongoing monthly healthcare expenses and savings achieved through various assistance programs, totaling $150 per month.

Action-oriented: Research and apply for pharmaceutical company assistance programs, schedule Medicare benefits review, request generic alternatives from physicians, and investigate community health resources.

Accountable: Monthly check-ins with healthcare social worker and quarterly reviews with Medicare counselor.

Realistic: Goal builds on optimizing existing Medicare benefits while accessing available assistance programs appropriate for her income level.

Relevant: Healthcare cost reduction maintains independence and reduces anxiety about future medical needs.

Time-bound: Implement all cost-reduction strategies within 6 months (by day/month/year) with ongoing monitoring for additional opportunities.

Healthcare Integration: Goal achievement coordinates with medical care providers to ensure cost reduction strategies do not compromise health outcomes, and includes advocacy with insurance companies and assistance program administrators.

Case Example 4: Family Recovering from Financial Crisis

The Johnson family—parents Mike and Sarah with three teenagers—works with a financial therapist after Mike's job loss created severe financial stress that strained family relationships and required them to access emergency assistance programs. Mike has found new employment at reduced income, and the family wants to rebuild both financial stability and healthy communication patterns around money that were disrupted during the crisis period.

Initial Assessment The family demonstrates strong relationships and mutual support but struggles with guilt, blame, and different approaches to financial recovery. The teenagers experienced stress from the financial crisis and have concerns about family stability and their own future opportunities. Family members report avoiding financial conversations due to anxiety and conflict, while financial decisions are being made without adequate communication or input from affected family members.

Goal-Setting Process The financial therapist facilitates family conversations that highlight their successful navigation of the crisis period, emphasizing teamwork, resourcefulness, and resilience. The process explores how financial stress disrupted previously effective family communication patterns and identifies opportunities to develop healthier approaches to financial discussions and decision-making.

Collaborative Goal Development **Specific:** Implement weekly family financial meetings that include structured communication, shared decision-making, and conflict resolution around money topics.

Measurable: Conduct family financial meetings 90% of scheduled weeks with all family members participating, tracked through meeting logs and family feedback.

Action-oriented: Establish meeting structure with rotating leadership roles, develop family financial communication guidelines, practice active listening and conflict resolution skills during sessions.

Accountable: Weekly progress review with financial therapist and monthly family assessment of meeting effectiveness and communication improvements.

Realistic: Meeting structure accounts for teenagers' schedules and developmental needs while building on family's existing strengths in teamwork and mutual support.

Relevant: Improved financial communication addresses family's core concern about preventing future financial stress from damaging relationships while building collective capacity for financial decision-making.

Time-bound: Establish consistent meeting pattern within 8 weeks (by day/month/year), with ongoing evaluation and refinement of communication processes every 3 months.

Therapeutic Integration: Goal achievement addresses underlying emotional dynamics around money, processes guilt and blame related to the financial crisis, and builds family resilience for future financial challenges while strengthening overall relationship functioning.

9.10 Conclusion

The enhanced SMART framework presented in this chapter provides a systematic approach and tool that addresses both the psychological and practical dimensions of financial behavior change while remaining adaptable to diverse professional contexts and client circumstances.

The guidance offered here recognizes that financial goal-setting exists within the broader framework of behavioral health, where financial objectives both influence and are influenced by mental health, physical health, coping strategies, and social relationships. This integrated perspective enables helping professionals to support clients in achieving financial goals that enhance overall health and well-being rather than treating financial concerns in isolation.

Whether working with clients in single-session consultations or ongoing therapeutic relationships, the core principles of effective goal-setting remain consistent: collaborative development that maintains client ownership, systematic attention to each component of the SMART framework, recognition of psychological factors that influence goal achievement, and integration with broader treatment objectives when appropriate. Professional competency in facilitating these conversations develops through training, supervision, and practice while respecting scope of practice boundaries and the need for appropriate referrals and collaboration.

The case examples presented illustrate how these principles translate into real-world practice across diverse client populations and circumstances. Effective goal-setting requires flexibility and adaptation while maintaining systematic attention to the components that research demonstrates increase the likelihood of goal achievement. Success is measured not only by achievement of specific financial objectives but also by clients' increased confidence, competence, and sense of agency over their financial circumstances.

As the field of financial health continues to evolve, goal-setting approaches will undoubtedly become more sophisticated and evidence-based. However, the fundamental recognition that sustainable financial behavior change requires attention to both practical strategies and psychological factors will remain central to effective practice. Helping professionals who develop competency in financial goal-setting position themselves to provide more comprehensive, effective support to clients facing the complex financial challenges that characterize contemporary life.

The financial challenges clients face are ultimately about much more than money—they reflect fundamental human needs for security, dignity, choice, and hope for the future. Effective goal-setting honors these deeper needs while providing practical pathways for achieving them. In doing so, helping professionals contribute not only to their clients' financial stability but to affect the trajectory of their overall health, resilience, and well-being across all domains of life. The transformation achieved when reaching goals represents the ultimate objective of financial goal-setting within the behavioral health context: enabling clients to develop efficacy to navigate future challenges and opportunities with resilience and hope.

References

Allen, K. R., & Henderson, A. C. (2017). *Family theories: Foundations and applications*. Wiley-Blackwell.

Anvari-Clark, J., & Miller, J. (2023). Financial interdependence: A social perspective. *Encyclopedia, 3*(3), 996–1008. https://doi.org/10.3390/encyclopedia3030072

Anvari-Clark, J., & Rose, T. (2023). Financial behavioral health and investment risk willingness: Implications for the racial wealth gap. *International Journal of Environmental Research and Public Health, 20*(10), 5835. https://doi.org/10.3390/ijerph20105835

Archuleta, K. L., Mielitz, K. S., Jayne, D., & Le, V. (2020). Financial goal setting, financial anxiety, and solution-focused financial therapy (SFFT): A quasi-experimental outcome study. *Contemporary Family Therapy, 42*(1), 68–76. https://doi.org/10.1007/s10591-019-09501-0

Bandura, A. (1977). Self-efficacy: Toward a unifying theory of behavioral change. *Psychological Review, 84*(2), 191–215. https://doi.org/10.1037/0033-295X.84.2.191

Canale, A., Archuleta, K. L., & Klontz, B. T. (2015). Money disorders. In B. T. Klontz, S. L. Britt, & K. L. Archuleta (Eds.), *Financial therapy: Theory, research, and practice* (pp. 35–68). Springer.

Hoge, G. L., Stylianou, A. M., Hetling, A., & Postmus, J. L. (2020). Developing and validating the scale of economic self-efficacy. *Journal of Interpersonal Violence, 35*(15–16), 3011–3033. https://doi.org/10.1177/0886260517706761

Miller, W. R., & Rollnick, S. (2013). *Motivational interviewing: Helping people change*. Guilford.

Mullainathan, S., & Shafir, E. (2013). *Scarcity: Why having too little means so much*. Times Books, Henry Holt.

Newport, C. (2024). *Slow productivity*. Portfolio / Penguin Random House. Retrieved June 11, 2025, from https://www.penguinrandomhouse.com/books/722732/slow-productivity-by-cal-newport/

Rosino, M. (2016). ABC-X model of family stress and coping. In C. L. Shehan (Ed.), *The Wiley Blackwell Encyclopedia of family studies*. John Wiley & Sons. https://doi.org/10.1002/9781119085621.wbefs313

Sweet, E. (2021). Debt-related financial hardship and health. *Health Education & Behavior, 48*(6), 885–891. https://doi.org/10.1177/1090198120976352

Chapter 10
Conclusion

10.1 Introduction

Throughout this book, the financial domain of behavioral health has been explored as an essential component of human well-being. The framework presented demonstrates how financial precarity, financial efficacy, and financial well-being interact with mental, physical, coping, and social health domains to create a more comprehensive picture of behavioral health. As the exploration concludes, it is clear that the integration of financial concerns into behavioral health practice has transformative potential for both research and practical applications.

The inclusion of the financial domain represents a paradigm shift in how to conceptualize the relationship between money and well-being. Rather than viewing financial issues as only external stressors that impact health, or framing their relationship as a simple health-wealth connection, financial concerns are now understood as intrinsic components of health itself—with subjective perceptions often proving as influential as objective circumstances (Anvari-Clark & Rose, 2023; Asebedo & Wilmarth, 2017). This integrated perspective enables more holistic approaches to assessment and intervention across helping professions.

This concluding chapter examines three critical areas for advancing financial health: research directions to deepen understanding of this emerging field, policy implications that can create supportive environments for financial health, and future directions for practice integration. By addressing these areas, a robust foundation for the continued development of financial health is established as both a theoretical framework and practical approach to improving lives.

To conclude the exploration of financial health, several key themes emerge that can guide future development of this field. Financial concerns cannot be effectively addressed in isolation from other behavioral health domains, as financial challenges cascade across multiple dimensions of well-being. The vignettes and research

Supplementary Information The online version contains supplementary material available at https://doi.org/10.1007/978-3-032-02632-3_10.

J. Anvari-Clark, *Financial and Behavioral Health for Helping Professionals*,
https://doi.org/10.1007/978-3-032-02632-3_10

presented throughout this book illustrate how financial precarity impacts mental health, physical well-being, coping behaviors, and social relationships. This holistic perspective suggests that integrated approaches considering the interplay between all behavioral health domains offer the greatest potential for meaningful impact. Furthermore, interventions that strengthen financial efficacy can create positive ripple effects throughout an individual's life, enhancing not only financial outcomes but overall well-being (Netemeyer et al., 2018a).

The bidirectional nature of relationships between financial concerns and other behavioral health domains represents another crucial insight. While financial factors influence health outcomes, health conditions also profoundly shape financial circumstances and behaviors. Medical diagnoses can trigger catastrophic expenses and lost income, while mental health challenges may impair financial decision-making and management. Supportive relationships can enhance financial resilience, while physical well-being contributes to earning capacity and financial stability.

10.2 Research Strategies and Emerging Directions

10.2.1 Current Research Landscape

Research in financial health currently exists in fragmented forms across multiple disciplines. While substantial literature examines relationships between financial stress and psychological outcomes (American Psychiatric Association, 2020; Asebedo & Wilmarth, 2017), medical debt and physical health (Richardson et al., 2013; Zafar, 2016), financial strain and coping behaviors (Åslund et al., 2014), and financial circumstances and social relationships (Dew, 2007; Jeanfreau et al., 2018), fewer studies adopt a comprehensive behavioral health approach that examines these domains holistically (Anvari-Clark & Rose, 2023).

The emerging behavioral health framework presented in this book provides an organizational structure for integrating these disparate research streams. This framework conceptualizes financial health as "a person's capacity to wield material means in support of their overall well-being," recognizing that this capacity emerges from the dynamic interaction between financial precarity, financial efficacy, and financial well-being. This definition aligns with complexity theory's emphasis on emergence and system-level properties arising from component interactions (Theise, 2023; Turner & Baker, 2019), providing a theoretical foundation for future research.

10.2.2 Measurement Tools and Approaches

Several validated instruments exist to measure components of financial health, though none adequately capture the construct in its entirety. For financial precarity, objective measures include the ability to cover unexpected expenses ($400–$2000)

(Gaffney et al., 2020; Lusardi et al., 2011), while subjective aspects can be assessed with measures of financial anxiety (Archuleta et al., 2013) and financial stress (Heo et al., 2020). Financial efficacy can be measured using tools like the Scale of Economic Self-Efficacy (Hoge et al., 2020) and the Financial Self-Efficacy Scale (Lown, 2011), which assess confidence in financial decision-making, problem-solving abilities, and emotional regulation around financial matters. For financial well-being, the Consumer Financial Protection Bureau's (CFPB) Financial Well-Being Scale (CFPB, 2017) and the Perceived Financial Well-Being Scale (Netemeyer et al., 2018b) provide validated measures of subjective financial security and freedom of choice in the present and future.

Future research should develop integrative measurement approaches that capture interactions among these components. The study from which this book originated provides one starting point in this process (Anvari-Clark & Rose, 2023). Mixed-methods designs that combine quantitative scales with qualitative explorations of lived experiences are particularly valuable for understanding the complex, context-dependent nature of financial health. Longitudinal studies that track changes in financial health and behaviors over time, especially during life transitions or economic disruptions, can provide insights into developmental trajectories and protective factors (Willson et al., 2007).

10.2.3 Methodological Considerations

Advancing financial health research demands innovative methodological approaches that can capture the nuanced, dynamic interactions between financial circumstances and multiple health domains. Traditional research methods, while valuable, often struggle to reflect the complex reality of how financial factors influence and are influenced by various aspects of behavioral health. As the field evolves, several methodological approaches show promise for deepening our understanding of financial health phenomena.

Systems modeling offers powerful tools for exploring how financial health emerges from interactions between multiple factors over time. Agent-based models and system dynamics approaches allow researchers to simulate complex feedback loops between financial and health domains, testing hypotheses about how changes in one area might cascade through the system (Cassidy et al., 2019). For example, these models could illustrate how an intervention targeting financial efficacy might influence not only financial behaviors but also mental health outcomes, physical health decisions, and social relationships. By making these complex interactions visible, systems modeling can help researchers identify leverage points for intervention and anticipate unintended consequences of well-intentioned programs.

The temporal dimension of financial health behaviors calls for methods that capture real-time experiences rather than relying solely on retrospective self-reports. Ecological momentary assessment (Shiffman & Hufford, 2008), typically implemented through smartphone applications, allows researchers to collect multiple brief assessments throughout participants' daily lives. This approach can reveal the immediate impacts of financial stressors, decision points, and coping responses as they unfold in natural contexts. For instance, researchers might track how a financial setback affects stress levels, health behaviors, and social interactions in the hours and days that follow, providing granular insights into processes that might be missed by conventional surveys. These methods are particularly valuable for understanding within-person variations in financial health that may be obscured by between-person comparisons.

The lived experiences of financial health are deeply embedded in specific social, cultural, and economic contexts. Community-based participatory research approaches recognize this reality by involving community members as co-researchers throughout the research process (Collins et al., 2018; West & Castro, 2023). By engaging those with direct experience of financial challenges in question formulation, study design, data collection, and interpretation, this methodology ensures that research reflects community priorities and produces findings that resonate with lived realities. For marginalized populations whose financial experiences may be shaped by structural inequities and cultural factors often overlooked in mainstream research, participatory approaches can yield insights that might otherwise remain hidden. Moreover, this methodology builds community capacity while generating knowledge, creating the foundation for sustainable change.

The digital transformation of financial services has created new opportunities to study financial behaviors through the traces they leave in transaction data. When conducted with appropriate privacy protections and ethical safeguards, big data approaches can reveal patterns in financial behavior that self-report measures might miss due to recall limitations, social desirability bias, or lack of awareness (Baker & Kueng, 2021; McKnight & Rucci, 2020). Analysis of financial transaction data can illuminate spending patterns, saving behaviors, and financial decision-making in naturalistic contexts across large, diverse populations. When combined with health records or other behavioral data, these approaches could uncover relationships between financial patterns and health outcomes that inform both individual interventions and policy development.

As behavioral-level financial health interventions develop, implementation science becomes increasingly crucial for translating research findings into effective practice across diverse settings. This methodological approach examines how interventions can be successfully implemented in real-world contexts, considering factors such as organizational readiness, workforce capacity, and adaptation to local conditions (Long et al., 2018). Implementation research can identify barriers to and facilitators of financial health integration across diverse service systems, from healthcare settings to financial institutions to community organizations. By studying implementation processes alongside intervention outcomes, researchers can develop strategies that enhance the reach, adoption, and sustainability of evidence-based approaches to financial health.

Mixed-methods designs that integrate quantitative and qualitative approaches offer particularly valuable frameworks for financial health research (Morduch & Schneider, 2017; Sánchez-Román et al., 2022). Quantitative methods can identify patterns and test relationships across populations, while qualitative approaches illuminate the meanings, processes, and contexts that shape financial experiences and behaviors. For example, a study might combine validated scales measuring financial stress and health outcomes with in-depth interviews exploring how individuals interpret and respond to financial challenges within their cultural contexts. This integration produces a more complete understanding than either approach alone could provide, capturing both the scale of financial-behavioral health issues and the lived experiences behind the statistics.

10.2.4 Research Directions

As financial health matures as a field, several key research directions offer particularly promising avenues for advancing both theoretical understanding and practical applications. The complex, interconnected nature of financial health challenges researchers to move beyond simplistic cause-and-effect models toward more sophisticated conceptualizations that capture real-world complexity.

Understanding bidirectional relationships between financial factors and other behavioral health domains represents an important frontier. While considerable research has documented how financial stress affects mental and physical health, a more nuanced grasp is needed of how health conditions influence financial behaviors and outcomes. Recent work by Swensen and Urban (2023) reveals that physical health shocks can significantly impact financial well-being—not just through direct medical costs but also through reduced work capacity, cognitive impairment, and changed financial priorities. These bidirectional effects create feedback loops that can either amplify negative outcomes or, with appropriate intervention, facilitate improvement across multiple domains.

The role of socioeconomic and cultural contexts in shaping financial health also warrants deeper investigation. Financial behaviors are not merely individual choices but rather practices embedded in specific cultural, social, and economic environments. Warmath et al. (2021) demonstrated this principle by revealing significant differences in how financial stress relates to well-being across collectivistic versus individualistic cultures. In collectivistic contexts, social support often serves as a buffer against financial hardship, moderating the relationship between objective financial circumstances and subjective well-being. Similarly, Park et al. (2019) identified substantial racial differences in family financial assistance patterns, with Black families often maintaining more extensive financial support networks that influence both financial security and relationship dynamics. Understanding these cultural variations is essential for researching and developing contextually appropriate interventions that respect and leverage existing adaptive processes.

Financial health also benefits from a developmental lens that considers how financial capabilities, attitudes, and behaviors evolve across the lifespan. Gudmunson and Danes (2011) established that early financial socialization experiences—how children learn about money through observation, instruction, and practice within families—significantly shape adult financial behaviors and attitudes. This perspective suggests opportunities for early intervention but also raises questions about sensitive periods for financial capability development and the potential for remediation later in life. Longitudinal research by Shippee et al. (2012) provides compelling evidence that accumulated financial strain over decades has significant impacts on women's health outcomes, highlighting the cumulative nature of financial health processes. These findings suggest the need for more life-course-oriented research and interventions that address both immediate financial concerns and longer-term developmental trajectories.

The effectiveness of financial capability interventions represents another critical research area, particularly when evaluating impacts across multiple behavioral health domains. While numerous financial education and capability-building programs exist, systematic reviews by Birkenmaier et al. (2021a, 2022a, 2022b, 2023) revealed mixed evidence for financial capability and asset-building initiatives, suggesting that intervention models may need refinement to achieve reliable outcomes. Future research should examine which intervention components most effectively address the psychological and social dimensions of financial health, rather than focusing solely on financial knowledge, skills, or asset amounts. This work requires nuanced outcome measures that capture changes in financial efficacy, perceived financial well-being, and associated health indicators, moving beyond simplistic financial metrics to holistic assessment of intervention impacts.

Technological innovations are transforming financial services and behaviors, yet research on their behavioral health implications remains limited. Digital financial tools—from budgeting apps to automated savings platforms to alternative lending services—are changing how people interact with money, creating both opportunities and risks for financial health. Research examining how these tools affect financial stress, efficacy, and overall well-being could inform better design of financial technology that supports rather than undermines behavioral health. Studies that explore how technology might bridge gaps in financial inclusion, provide just-in-time financial guidance, or create digital communities that enhance financial efficacy through social support and shared learning would be particularly useful.

Workplace applications of financial health concepts offer significant potential for broad population impact. Financial concerns significantly affect employee productivity, absenteeism, and health care costs, with Meuris and Leana (2017a, 2017b) demonstrating that financial precarity impacts organizational performance through both reduced cognitive bandwidth and increased stress. Research on workplace financial wellness programs can identify effective approaches for supporting employee financial health while addressing concerns about privacy, stigma, and equitable access. Particular attention should be given to evaluating structural workplace factors—including compensation, scheduling practices (O'Neil, 2017), and benefit design—and their effects on employee financial health alongside individual-level interventions.

Finally, community-level factors in financial health represent an understudied but crucial area for research development. Most existing research focuses on individual or household levels, neglecting the broader financial interdependence paradigm and how community financial resources, norms, and institutions shape individual financial health, beyond being a social determinant or driver. Community-based participatory research approaches (Collins et al., 2018) could illuminate how local financial systems—from banking access to informal lending networks to community development initiatives—influence residents' financial experiences and behaviors. This ecological perspective could inform community-level approaches that create environments conducive to financial health while addressing structural inequities through policy advocacy.

10.3 Policy Implications

The deeper framing of financial health presents significant opportunities for policy development that can support well-being across multiple domains simultaneously. As research in financial health continues to evolve, several policy directions show promise for addressing both financial stability and associated health outcomes. These approaches reflect a growing recognition that financial and health policies, traditionally developed in separate spheres, might achieve greater impact through intentional integration.

Guaranteed income programs represent one of the most direct policy approaches to addressing financial precarity and its behavioral health consequences. Recent pilot programs have yielded encouraging results that extend beyond economic metrics to include meaningful health improvements (Hamilton et al., 2024). The Stockton Economic Empowerment Demonstration (SEED), which provided $500 monthly to randomly selected residents in Stockton, California, demonstrated that guaranteed income reduced income volatility while simultaneously improving mental health and enhancing participants' overall financial well-being (West & Castro, 2023).

Emergency savings initiatives represent another promising policy direction with potential for broad population impact. Research consistently demonstrates that emergency savings provide both financial protection and psychological benefits, reducing anxiety and enhancing perceived financial security even among those who never need to use their reserves (Despard & Roll, 2024; Stavins, 2020). Automatic enrollment approaches, which include employees in emergency savings programs unless they actively opt out, can significantly increase participation rates compared to opt-in approaches. Research on retirement savings suggests such programs significantly increase participation rates compared to opt-in approaches, potentially extending these benefits to emergency savings contexts (Frydman & Camerer, 2016; Thaler & Sunstein, 2008). Matched saving incentives, whether provided by government programs or employers, can accelerate emergency fund development, particularly for lower-income households that might otherwise struggle to build meaningful reserves. Programs like Individual Development Accounts have demonstrated the potential of matching approaches to promote saving behavior, with possible applications to emergency savings contexts (Birkenmaier et al. 2022a).

Innovative approaches like sidecar savings accounts that link emergency savings to retirement accounts offer another promising direction, allowing individuals to build both long-term security and short-term buffers simultaneously (Prabhakar, 2021). Having both notably prevents tapping retirement accounts for hardship purposes, frequently undermining long-term stability and necessitating the burden of repayment or tax penalties. Additionally, policies that eliminate minimum balance requirements, maintenance fees, and withdrawal penalties for basic savings accounts can make emergency saving more accessible, particularly for unbanked or underbanked populations who currently face significant barriers to formal financial services.

The regulatory environment governing financial products and services significantly impacts financial health by shaping the fairness and transparency of financial transactions. Predatory financial products can exacerbate financial precarity through high fees, deceptive terms, and exploitative practices that target vulnerable populations (Ekman & Coleman, 2012). Consumer protection policies can counter these effects through measures like interest rate caps that prevent debt spirals leading to financial distress and associated health impacts. Plain language requirements for financial products help consumers make informed decisions that align with their long-term well-being, while restrictions on unfair debt collection practices can reduce stress and preserve dignity for those experiencing financial difficulties. Alternative credit scoring models that expand evaluation beyond traditional metrics to include rental payments, utility bills, and other indicators can increase access to affordable credit for those with limited credit histories, potentially reducing reliance on high-cost alternative financial services that can exacerbate financial precarity.

Workplace policies represent another promising avenue for supporting financial health, given that most adults spend substantial time at work and derive much of their financial resources through employment. Living wage requirements that ensure compensation provides for basic needs create a foundation for financial stability and reduce chronic financial stress that can undermine health across domains (Werner & Lim, 2016). For hourly workers, predictable scheduling policies that provide consistent and advance notice of work hours enable better financial planning and reduce income volatility that contributes to financial precarity (Berman & Gorlin, 2018). Employer-sponsored emergency funds that facilitate savings through payroll deduction, possibly with employer matching, can build financial resilience while demonstrating organizational commitment to employee well-being. Financial wellness benefits including education, counseling, budgeting, and planning services can build financial knowledge and efficacy when designed with behavioral health principles in mind. Paid leave policies that provide access to sick, family, and medical leave prevent income disruption during health challenges, reducing the financial impact of illness or caregiving responsibilities.

As policies to support financial health evolve, several considerations should guide their development. First, an explicit equity focus is essential, as disparities in financial health by race, gender, disability status, and other factors reflect broader patterns of structural inequality. Policies should address these disparities through targeted approaches rather than one-size-fits-all solutions that may inadvertently reinforce existing inequities, despite efforts at universal inclusion. Second, integration across domains offers potential for synergistic effects, suggesting the value of coordinated approaches that consider multiple behavioral health dimensions simultaneously rather than addressing financial or health outcomes in isolation. Third, evidence-based design incorporating findings from financial health research, particularly regarding psychological and social dimensions of financial experiences, can enhance policy effectiveness. Fourth, participatory processes that include diverse stakeholders, especially those with lived experience of financial precarity, in policy development can ensure that interventions address actual needs and resonate with target populations. Finally, implementation support deserves particular attention, as even well-designed policies may fail without adequate systems alignment, workforce capacity, and accessibility for target populations.

10.4 Future Directions for Practice Integration

Integrating financial health into existing professional practice represents both a significant opportunity and a complex challenge. The framework presented throughout this book offers a theoretical foundation for understanding how financial concerns intersect with other behavioral health domains, but translating this understanding into effective practice requires thoughtful implementation strategies across diverse service contexts. Several key areas deserve particular attention as the field moves forward.

Professional training and education stand at the forefront of successful integration efforts. Currently, most helping professionals receive minimal education about financial concerns, while financial professionals receive little training in behavioral health. Indeed, in many cases, it is an optional elective. This siloed approach to professional development creates barriers to comprehensive care. Graduate programs in social work, counseling, psychology, financial planning, and healthcare can address this gap by incorporating financial health content into their core curricula (Anvari-Clark, 2022; Birkenmaier et al., 2021b; Huang et al., 2021). Rather than treating financial concerns as a specialized niche, programs can integrate financial dimensions throughout coursework on assessment, intervention, and human development. This integration helps future practitioners recognize financial issues as fundamental components of client well-being rather than secondary concerns to be addressed only after "more important" needs are met.

For practitioners already in the field, continuing education opportunities focused on financial health can expand competencies and update approaches based on emerging research (Asset Building Clinic, 2020; Callahan et al., 2022). Furthermore, licensing boards may require educational hours related to cultural competence; learning how different populations approach and experience financial matters can fall squarely into this area. These educational offerings should move beyond basic financial literacy to address the complex interplay between financial circumstances and other behavioral health domains. Professional associations have begun developing specialized certifications related to financial health, providing structured pathways for practitioners seeking in-depth expertise while establishing quality standards for practice (Financial Therapy Association , 2020). These certifications can help build workforce capacity while signaling commitment to evidence-based approaches.

Supervision models also play a crucial role in supporting practice integration. Clinical supervision approaches that explicitly address financial health can help practitioners navigate the complexities of incorporating financial dimensions into their existing practice frame works. Supervisors can model appropriate boundary-setting around financial interventions while supporting supervisees in developing competencies for recognizing, assessing, and addressing financial concerns within their scope of practice.

Service delivery models require substantial adaptation to effectively integrate financial health considerations. Single-provider approaches may need to evolve toward collaborative care models that leverage diverse professional expertise while maintaining coordination and continuity. These models might involve financial social workers, therapists, counselors, planners, and healthcare providers working together within integrated teams or through structured referral networks (Mancini, 2021). Technology platforms that facilitate communication and care coordination across disciplines can support these collaborative approaches while ensuring that clients experience seamless, rather than fragmented, service delivery.

Assessment approaches need refinement to capture financial health dimensions without overwhelming existing workflows or exceeding professional competencies. Needed are brief screening tools that identify financial concerns requiring further attention that can be integrated into standard intake procedures across helping professions (de Souza et al., 2017). These tools should flag both objective financial circumstances (such as ability to meet basic needs or handle emergencies) and subjective experiences (such as financial stress or efficacy) that may warrant intervention. Training practitioners to conduct these assessments competently and sensitively requires attention to cultural factors, trauma-informed approaches, and appropriate follow-up based on findings.

Intervention adaptation represents another crucial area for development. Existing evidence-based practices may require modification to address financial dimensions appropriately. For example, more widespread uptake of cognitive-behavioral financial therapy approaches could incorporate modules addressing financial anxiety or money-related cognitive distortions (Nabeshima & Klontz, 2015), while case management models might expand to include financial goal-setting and resource navigation. These adaptations should be guided by research evidence and developed through systematic processes that ensure fidelity to core intervention principles while effectively addressing financial concerns.

Reviewing and revising organizational policies to support financial health can remove barriers to implementation and create enabling conditions for success. This might involve examining intake and assessment procedures, documentation requirements, service eligibility criteria, and referral relationships to ensure they accommodate financial health integration. Modifying data collection and management systems to capture financial health indicators enables tracking of outcomes and continuous improvement, creating feedback loops that support ongoing refinement of integration efforts. Furthermore, creative approaches may be needed, such as reallocating existing resources, seeking external funding for pilot initiatives, or developing strategic partnerships that leverage resources across organizations.

10.5 Conclusion

The emergence of financial health as a distinct domain of behavioral health represents more than simply adding another component to existing frameworks. It signals a fundamental shift toward recognizing the interconnected nature of human well-being and the need for integrated approaches that address multiple domains simultaneously. The financial challenges clients face are not just about money—they are about dignity, relationships, hope, and the fundamental human need for security and choice. Understanding these connections is essential for providing effective service and compassionate care.

As helping professionals across disciplines begin to integrate financial health considerations into their practice, several principles should guide this evolution. First, financial health integration should enhance rather than replace existing evidence-based practices, building on established therapeutic relationships and intervention frameworks. Second, practitioners should work within their scope of practice while developing collaborative relationships that ensure clients receive comprehensive care across financial and other behavioral health domains. Third, cultural humility and recognition of diverse financial values and practices must inform all aspects of assessment and intervention. Fourth, attention to structural and systemic factors that influence financial outcomes should complement individual-level interventions.

The path forward requires sustained commitment from multiple stakeholders. Educational institutions must prepare future practitioners with foundational knowledge of financial health while professional associations develop standards and continuing education opportunities for current practitioners. Researchers must continue building the evidence base while attending to methodological innovations that capture the complexity of financial health phenomena. Policymakers must consider the behavioral health implications of financial policies while healthcare and social service systems adapt to integrate financial considerations into comprehensive care approaches.

Perhaps most importantly, this work requires ongoing attention to equity and social justice. Financial health disparities reflect broader patterns of structural inequality that cannot be addressed solely through individual interventions. Effective approaches must combine efforts to strengthen individual financial efficacy with policy and systemic changes that create more equitable opportunities for financial well-being. By addressing financial health as both a personal and collective challenge, helping professionals can contribute to broader social change while improving outcomes for the individuals and families they serve.

The integration of financial concerns into behavioral health practice represents an opportunity to better serve clients facing the complex, interconnected challenges that characterize modern life. By recognizing financial health as a legitimate behavioral health domain worthy of attention, practitioners can move beyond simple recognition of "financial stress" toward sophisticated, evidence-based approaches that address the full spectrum of human experience. This transformation requires time, resources, and commitment, but the potential benefits—for both clients and professionals—justify the investment.

References

American Psychiatric Association. (2020). *Stress in America 2020: A national mental health crisis.*

Anvari-Clark, J. (2022). Incorporating financial well-being into behavioral health social work education. *Journal of Teaching in Social Work, 42*(5), 520–537. https://doi.org/10.1080/08841233.2022.2120160

Anvari-Clark, J., & Rose, T. (2023). Financial behavioral health and investment risk willingness: Implications for the racial wealth gap. *International Journal of Environmental Research and Public Health, 20*(10), 5835. https://doi.org/10.3390/ijerph20105835

Archuleta, K. L., Dale, A., & Spann, S. M. (2013). College students and financial distress: Exploring debt, financial satisfaction, and financial anxiety. *Journal of Financial Counseling and Planning, 24*(2), 50–62. https://eric.ed.gov/?id=EJ1043230

Asebedo, S. D., & Wilmarth, M. J. (2017). Does how we feel about financial strain matter for mental health? *Journal of Financial Therapy, 8*(1), 62–80. https://doi.org/10.4148/1944-9771.1130

Åslund, C., Larm, P., Starrin, B., & Nilsson, K. W. (2014). The buffering effect of tangible social support on financial stress: Influence on psychological well-being and psychosomatic symptoms in a large sample of the adult general population. *International Journal for Equity in Health, 13*(1), 85. https://doi.org/10.1186/s12939-014-0085-3

Asset Building Clinic. (2020). *Financial First Responder Certificate Training. ABC.* Retrieved March 7, 2024, from https://www.assetbuildingclinic.org/training

Baker, S. R., & Kueng, L. (2021). *Household financial transaction data* (Working Paper No. 29027). National Bureau of Economic Research. https://www.nber.org/system/files/working_papers/w29027/w29027.pdf

Berman, K., & Gorlin, M. (2018, March 5). Hourly employees need reliable schedules: Can behavioral science help companies deliver? *Behavioral Scientist.* Retrieved May 11, 2020, from https://behavioralscientist.org/hourly-employees-need-reliable-schedules-can-behavioral-science-help-companies-deliver/

Birkenmaier, J., Kim, Y., & Maynard, B. (2021a). Financial outcomes of interventions designed to improve retirement savings: A systematic review. *Journal of Gerontological Social Work, 64*(3), 238–256. https://doi.org/10.1080/01634372.2020.1865496

Birkenmaier, J., Kim, Y., & Maynard, B. (2022a). Financial outcomes of interventions designed to improve financial capability through individual development accounts: A systematic review. *Journal of Evidence-Based Social Work, 19*(4), 408–439. https://doi.org/10.1080/26408066.2022.2059427

Birkenmaier, J., Kim, Y., & Maynard, B. (2023). Financial outcomes of interventions to improve financial capability through children's development accounts: A systematic review. *Journal of the Society for Social Work and Research, 14*(2), 523–552. https://doi.org/10.1086/716103

Birkenmaier, J., Lane, L. B., Callahan, C., & Hageman, S. A. (2021b). Teaching note-course models for increased competency for practice integrated with financial capability and asset building. *Journal of Social Work Education, 57*(3), 604–611. https://doi.org/10.1080/10437797.2020.1714522

Birkenmaier, J., Maynard, B., & Kim, Y. (2022b). Interventions designed to improve financial capability: A systematic review. *Research on Social Work Practice, 32*(6), 651–677. https://doi.org/10.1177/10497315221080127

Callahan, C., Jacobson Frey, J., Imboden, R., & Hatcher, S. (2022). A financial social work certificate program for community and family practitioners. *Families in Society, 103*(1), 78–85. https://doi.org/10.1177/10443894211061098

Cassidy, R., Singh, N. S., Schiratti, P.-R., Semwanga, A., Binyaruka, P., Sachingongu, N., et al. (2019). Mathematical modelling for health systems research: A systematic review of system dynamics and agent-based models. *BMC Health Services Research, 19*(1), 845. https://doi.org/10.1186/s12913-019-4627-7

Collins, S. E., Clifasefi, S. L., Stanton, J., Straits, K. J. E., Espinosa, P. R., Andrasik, M. P., et al. (2018). Community-based participatory research (CBPR): Towards equitable involvement of community in psychology research. *The American Psychologist, 73*(7), 884–898. https://doi.org/10.1037/amp0000167

Consumer Financial Protection Bureau. (2017). *CFPB Financial well-being scale: Scale development technical report.* https://www.consumerfinance.gov/data-research/research-reports/financial-well-being-scale/

de Souza, J. A., Yap, B. J., Wroblewski, K., Blinder, V., Araújo, F. S., Hlubocky, F. J., et al. (2017). Measuring financial toxicity as a clinically relevant patient-reported outcome: The validation of the COmprehensive score for financial toxicity (COST). *Cancer, 123*(3), 476–484. https://doi.org/10.1002/cncr.30369

Despard, M., & Roll, S. (2024). Job loss and financial distress during COVID-19: The protective role of emergency savings. *Journal of Financial Counseling & Planning, 35*(2), 157–172. https://doi.org/10.1891/JFCP-2022-0048

Dew, J. (2007). Two sides of the same coin? The differing roles of assets and consumer debt in marriage. *Journal of Family and Economic Issues, 28*(1), 89–104. https://doi.org/10.1007/s10834-006-9051-6

Ekman, E., & Coleman, S. (2012). Social work in the campaign against predatory consumer financing: An interview with Shawna reeves. *Journal of Progressive Human Services, 23*(1), 55–75. https://doi.org/10.1080/10428232.2012.623976

Financial Therapy Association. (2020). *Become a certified financial therapist (TM).* Retrieved August 6, 2020, from https://www.financialtherapyassociation.org/certification

Frydman, C., & Camerer, C. F. (2016). The psychology and neuroscience of financial decision making. *Trends in Cognitive Sciences, 20*(9), 661–675. https://doi.org/10.1016/j.tics.2016.07.003

Gaffney, A. W., Himmelstein, D. U., McCormick, D., & Woolhandler, S. (2020). Health and social precarity among Americans receiving unemployment benefits during the COVID-19 outbreak. *Journal of General Internal Medicine, 35*(11), 3416–3419. https://doi.org/10.1007/s11606-020-06207-0

Gudmunson, C. G., & Danes, S. M. (2011). Family financial socialization: Theory and critical review. *Journal of Family and Economic Issues, 32*(4), 644–667. https://doi.org/10.1007/s10834-011-9275-y

Hamilton, L., Choplin, V., & Paputseanos, T. (2024). From scarcity to security: Participant well-being in the first 2 years of a basic income pilot. *Analyses of Social Issues and Public Policy, 24*(1), 44–72. https://doi.org/10.1111/asap.12370

Heo, W., Cho, S. H., & Lee, P. (2020). APR financial stress scale: Development and validation of a multidimensional measurement. *Journal of Financial Therapy, 11*(1). https://doi.org/10.4148/1944-9771.1216

Hoge, G. L., Stylianou, A. M., Hetling, A., & Postmus, J. L. (2020). Developing and validating the scale of economic self-efficacy. *Journal of Interpersonal Violence, 35*(15–16), 3011–3033. https://doi.org/10.1177/0886260517706761

Huang, J., Sherraden, M., Johnson, L., Birkenmaier, J., Loke, V., & Hageman, S. (2021). Preparing social work faculty to teach financial capability: Where we stand. *Journal of Social Work Education, 57*(4), 688–706. https://doi.org/10.1080/10437797.2020.1714524

Jeanfreau, M., Noguchi, K., Mong, M. D., & Stadthagen, H. (2018). Financial infidelity in couple relationships. *Journal of Financial Therapy, 9*(1), 2. https://doi.org/10.4148/1944-9771.1159

Long, K. M., McDermott, F., & Meadows, G. N. (2018). Being pragmatic about healthcare complexity: Our experiences applying complexity theory and pragmatism to health services research. *BMC Medicine, 16*(1), 94. https://doi.org/10.1186/s12916-018-1087-6

Lown, J. M. (2011). 2011 outstanding AFCPE® conference paper: Development and validation of a financial self-efficacy scale. *Journal of Financial Counseling and Planning, 22*(2), 11.

Lusardi, A., Schneider, D. J., & Tufano, P. (2011). *Financially fragile households: Evidence and implications*. Working Paper,. National Bureau of Economic Research. https://doi.org/10.3386/w17072

Mancini, M. A. (2021). *Integrated behavioral health practice*. Springer International Publishing. https://doi.org/10.1007/978-3-030-59659-0

McKnight, A., & Rucci, M. (2020). *The financial resilience of households: 22 country study with new estimates, breakdowns by household characteristics and a review of policy options* (No. CASE/219). London, UK: Centre for Analysis of Social Exclusion–London School of Economics. Accessed June 21, 2023, from https://sticerd.lse.ac.uk/dps/case/cp/casepaper219.pdf

Meuris, J., & Leana, C. (2017a). The price of financial precarity: Organizational costs of employees' financial concerns. *Organization Science, 29*. https://doi.org/10.1287/orsc.2017.1187

Meuris, J., & Leana, C. R. (2017b). The price of financial precarity: Personal finance as a barrier to work performance. *Academy of Management Proceedings, 2017*(1), 12992. https://doi.org/10.5465/AMBPP.2017.323

Morduch, J., & Schneider, R. (2017). *The financial diaries*. Princeton University Press.

Nabeshima, G., & Klontz, B. T. (2015). Cognitive-behavioral financial therapy. In B. T. Klontz, S. L. Britt, & K. L. Archuleta (Eds.), *Financial therapy: Theory, research, and practice* (pp. 143–160). Springer.

Netemeyer, R. G., Warmath, D., Fernandes, D., & Lynch, J. G. (2018a). How am I doing? Perceived financial well-being, its potential antecedents, and its relation to overall well-being. *Journal of Consumer Research, 45*(1), 68–89. https://doi.org/10.1093/jcr/ucx109

Netemeyer, R. G., Warmath, D., Fernandes, D., & Lynch, J. G. (2018b). Perceived financial well-being scale. From: How am I doing? Perceived financial well-being, its potential antecedents, and its relation to overall well-being. *Journal of Consumer Research, 45*(1), 68–89. https://doi.org/10.1093/jcr/ucx109. https://sjdm.org/dmidi/Perceived_Financial_Well_Being_Scale.html

O'Neil, C. (2017). *Weapons of math destruction*. Crown | Penguin Random House. Accessed June 12, 2025, from https://www.penguinrandomhouse.com/books/241363/weapons-of-math-destruction-by-cathy-oneil/

Park, S. S., Wiemers, E. E., & Seltzer, J. A. (2019). The family safety net of Black and White multigenerational families. *Population and Development Review, 45*(2), 351–378. https://doi.org/10.1111/padr.12233

Prabhakar, R. (2021). *Sidecar savings* (No. CBP 9410). House of Commons Library. Retrieved June 12, 2025, from https://oro.open.ac.uk/81260/1/CBP%209410.pdf.

Richardson, T., Elliott, P., & Roberts, R. (2013). The relationship between personal unsecured debt and mental and physical health: A systematic review and meta-analysis. *Clinical Psychology Review, 33*(8), 1148–1162. https://doi.org/10.1016/j.cpr.2013.08.009

Sánchez-Román, S., Chavarri-Guerra, Y., Vargas-Huicochea, I., Alvarez del Río, A., Bernal Pérez, P., Morales Alfaro, A., et al. (2022). Financial toxicity among older Mexican adults with cancer and their families: A mixed-methods study. *JCO Global Oncology, 8*, e2100324. https://doi.org/10.1200/GO.21.00324

Shiffman, S., & Hufford, M. (2008). Ecological momentary assessment. *Applied Clinical Trials, 10*.

Shippee, T. P., Wilkinson, L. R., & Ferraro, K. F. (2012). Accumulated financial strain and women's health over three decades. *The Journals of Gerontology Series B: Psychological Sciences and Social Sciences, 67*(5), 585–594. https://doi.org/10.1093/geronb/gbs056

Stavins, J. (2020). Unprepared for financial shocks: Emergency savings and credit card debt. *Contemporary Economic Policy, n/a*(n/a). https://doi.org/10.1111/coep.12477

Swensen, I. D., & Urban, C. (2023). *Literature review on the effect of physical and mental health on financial well-being* (Vol. 198). Institute of Labor Economics (IZA). https://hdl.handle.net/10419/278411

Thaler, R. H., & Sunstein, C. R. (2008). *Nudge: Improving decisions about health, wealth, and happiness* (p. 293). Yale University Press.

Theise, N. (2023). *Notes on complexity: A scientific theory of connection, consciousness, and being*. Spiegel & Grau. Retrieved January 21, 2025.

Turner, J. R., & Baker, R. M. (2019). Complexity theory: An overview with potential applications for the social sciences. *Systems, 7*(1), 4. https://doi.org/10.3390/systems7010004

Warmath, D., Chen, P.-J., Grable, J., & Kwak, E. J. (2021). Soft landings: Extending the cushion hypothesis to financial well-being in collectivistic cultures. *Journal of Consumer Affairs, 55*(4), 1563–1590. https://doi.org/10.1111/joca.12408

Werner, A., & Lim, M. (2016). The ethics of the living wage: A review and research agenda. *Journal of Business Ethics, 137*(3), 433–447. https://doi.org/10.1007/s10551-015-2562-z

West, S., & Castro, A. (2023). Impact of guaranteed income on health, finances, and agency: Findings from the Stockton randomized controlled trial. *Journal of Urban Health, 100*(2), 227–244. https://doi.org/10.1007/s11524-023-00723-0

Willson, A. E., Shuey, K. M., & Elder, G. H., Jr. (2007). Cumulative advantage processes as mechanisms of inequality in life course health. *American Journal of Sociology, 112*(6), 1886–1924. https://doi.org/10.1086/512712

Zafar, S. Y. (2016). Financial toxicity of cancer care: It's time to intervene. *Journal of the National Cancer Institute, 108*(5), djv370. https://doi.org/10.1093/jnci/djv370

Index

J. Anvari-Clark, *Financial and Behavioral Health for Helping Professionals*,
https://doi.org/10.1007/978-3-032-02632-3

GPSR Compliance
The European Union's (EU) General Product Safety Regulation (GPSR) is a set of rules that requires consumer products to be safe and our obligations to ensure this.

If you have any concerns about our products, you can contact us on

ProductSafety@springernature.com

In case Publisher is established outside the EU, the EU authorized representative is:

Springer Nature Customer Service Center GmbH
Europaplatz 3
69115 Heidelberg, Germany

www.ingramcontent.com/pod-product-compliance
Lightning Source LLC
Chambersburg PA
CBHW062210171125
35560CB00004BA/254
* 9 7 8 3 0 3 2 0 2 6 3 1 6 *